SPORTS
PEACEBUILDING
AND ETHICS

Peace & Policy, Volume 18

SPORTS
PEACEBUILDING
AND ETHICS

LINDA M. JOHNSTON

EDITOR

Transaction Publishers
New Brunswick (U.S.A.) and London (U.K.)

Copyright © 2014 by Transaction Publishers, New Brunswick, New Jersey.

This book is printed on acid-free paper that meets the American National Standard for Permanence of Paper for Printed Library Materials.

Library of Congress Catalog Number: 2013042876
ISBN: 978-1-4128-5388-0
Printed in the United States of America

Library of Congress Cataloging-in-Publication Data

Sports, peacebuilding and ethics / Linda M. Johnston, editor.
     pages cm. — (Peace & policy ; volume 18)
  Includes bibliographical references.
  ISBN 978-1-4128-5388-0
  1. Sports—Moral and ethical aspects. 2. Social ethics. 3. Peace-building.
I. Johnston, Linda M.
  GV706.3.S69 2014
  174.9796—dc23

                                                    2013042876

Contents

Sports and Peacebuilding

Acknowledgments

I am grateful to the Toda Institute for their help with this publication. I am also amazed at how just one conversation can lead to such a fruitful collaboration. Olivier Urbain and I were sitting over coffee talking about the need to document the role that sports and ethics are playing in current day peacebuilding efforts. After our initial discussion at the 2010 International Peace Research Association (IPRA) Conference in Sydney, Australia, I contacted a few colleagues who I knew were conducting research in this area. They connected me to others, and the project for this book was set in motion. The authors were eager to come together for a dialogue about the project, and especially to be in contact with scholars all over the world who shared their interest in this topic.

I am very grateful to Olivier for his personal enthusiasm for this project and his assistance at every step of the way. The Toda Institute provided a framework for the publication, contacted expert peer reviewers, and found a publisher. They continued their assistance with the final editing of the manuscript. It was a pleasure to work with Olivier and members of the Toda team.

Linda M. Johnston
Kennesaw State University

Introduction: Sports and Peacebuilding: Issues and Solutions

Linda M. Johnston

Recently, there has been an increased interest in the study of sports as it relates to peacebuilding and ethics. Not only are the number of sports and peace programs increasing, but there is also an increased desire by both the funders of the programs and the academic community to look at these programs through an analytical and detailed lens. Why should someone interested in peacebuilding activities include sports as an integral part of the peace process? What are the programs achieving; how are they being implemented; how are they measuring success; what are the challenges; what sports are being included; who is interested in funding the programs; what problems have the programs encountered; who is involved in the programs; what is the background of the people involved; and what values and methods are being incorporated? In this special edition dedicated to the study of sports, peacebuilding, and ethics, we have decided to step back from solely promoting such programs in order to examine some of the questions and challenges posed above. We have attempted in this volume to explore the subject of sports, peacebuilding, and ethics as a polygon, and then turn it several ways, examine it from several different angles and various directions. We have not taken this approach in order to critique the programs, but rather to respond to some of the concerns raised by the programs themselves, the funders, the professionals in the peace field, and the participants. The programs have been in existence long enough now, for those in the field to be aware of the potential for

1

success, the particulars that need to be in place for that success to occur, and some of the continuing challenges the programs face. Many of these programs were designed to deal with issues of post-conflict aggression and violence. Many have accomplished their mission of bringing people together after a conflict. And yet, accepting all the successes they have achieved, there are still issues which need to be addressed, especially if these programs want to continue to receive funding and increase in size and scope. In this volume, we intend to look carefully at some of those issues which have arisen, discuss why they have become concerns, and look at some possible ways to deal with the concerns.

The first chapter by Claudia Stura and myself, discusses the role of sports in peacebuilding. In this study, we interviewed fourteen sports program managers working in the field on programs related to sports and peace. We asked questions about their target populations, how long their projects had been going on, when they had started their projects in terms of the conflict, how they recruited and trained their coaches, which organizations they worked in collaboration with, how they were financed, formal and informal partnerships, skill sets they taught in the programs, internal and external factors which influenced their projects, how they evaluated their success, and their thoughts on the potential for sports to be an integral part of peacebuilding. We looked at programs in Jordan, Sri Lanka, Morocco, Turkey, Croatia, Armenia, Northern Ireland, Uganda, Dubai, Benin, Cypress, Lebanon, Poland, France, Ethiopia, Iraq, Bosnia-Herzegovina, Palestine, and Israel. Some programs used soccer, basketball, volleyball, cricket, rugby, Gaelic football, or martial arts; others used several in combination or mixed with other games. We concluded with a section on the role sports can play in reducing violence and contributing to a peacebuilding process, especially in creating a safe space for education and allowing the participants to learn new skills to facilitate change.

The next section of the volume focuses on various aspects of culture and how those aspects relate to sports programs. In the first of the three chapters related to sports, Kirk Smith looks at the role of the coach in creating a culture of peace, integrity, and honor. He looks at the impact that a sports leader has on the culture of his/her team or program, and how this culture can fit into a peacebuilding process. Smith uses Schein's leader-centered, three-level cultural model as a theoretical framework to examine the case of a very public football figure in a well-publicized case. He focuses in on the level of basic taken-for-granted, underlying assumptions that determine behavior, perception, thought, and feeling in sports. Smith uses news stories to show the Schein's model's usefulness in a sports setting within a large, public institution of higher education. The author analyzed fourteen news stories that were chosen by their titles to likely contain evidence of artifacts, values, and/or statements that hinted at underlying assumptions. While it has long been accepted that coaches have a significant impact on the persona, team cohesion, communication, and motivation of their team, relatively little has been written about the coach's impact on the culture. Coaches have the capacity to instill sportsmanship and the value of teamwork. They can apply the rules in a visible manner to set the tone for the team, for the game, for the sport, and therefore, contribute to the peacebuilding process. In the second chapter in this series on culture and sports, Ji-Ho Kim looks at conflict and identification of immigrants with professional sports teams. He discusses the cultural elasticity of immigrants of a minority group toward sports consumption in the United States, a contemporary multicultural society, and considers the creation of in-groups and out-groups, the outcome of which can have great impact on the dynamics of sports especially when dealing with post-conflict sports and peacebuilding activities. We have very little research to know what happens when you bring different groups of people together to play on a team in a peaceful culture and even less information on what happens when those groups have been in conflict with each other. We know even less about how peacebuilding processes can market their sports teams to groups of people post-conflict. Kim offers reasons why minority immigrants may follow a particular professional sports team, as well as offers suggestions for implications for sports practitioners and those who market games in the sports industry. He looks at these issues through the lens of the different cultural and social values of sports across cultures. Kim concludes with thoughts about how team identification has been considered one of the most crucial tasks of sports marketers and many studies showed significance of team identification as a predictor of sport's consumer behaviors. The third chapter of this set on culture and sports is by Sarah Hillyer. Hillyer focuses on a particular sport and cross-cultural building project for women's sports in Iran. This project was designed for the purpose of creating cross-cultural understanding through the use of sports for peacebuilding and the role sports can play in fostering cross-cultural understanding. The goals of this project were to evaluate girls' and women's sports programs in schools, clubs, and federations; to identify strategies to improve girls' and women's sports participation in an Islamic context; and to promote dialogue and friendly relations between Iranian and American women through sports-based educational exchanges and competitions. Hillyer uses autoethnography to illustrate the use of women's sports for bringing about dialogue and understanding between cultures. This chapter demonstrates the potential use of women's sports to foster peaceful and friendly relations, as well as provides a counter narrative to the current understanding of women's sports in Iran. Through her interviews with sports participants, Hillyer discovers the impact that cross-cultural sports can have on the participants and role that women play in shaping the way their children think about sports and peace.

The next set of three chapters looks at the role of sports in various contexts: in trauma relief programs in Rwanda; the role of universities in sport, development, and peace; and the role of sports in the demilitarization of child soldiers. In the first of these chapters, Niina Toroi examines how teaching yoga to victims of trauma can benefit the women living with HIV/AIDS and who are also survivors of the genocide, rape as a weapon of war, as well as domestic violence. She looks at how the physical movement of yoga can have positive results post-conflict and thereby broadens our thinking about which sports and physical activities can be used in the peacebuilding process. She also tries to understand if yoga has positive effects on the violent behavior among the men. Toroi discusses how the most vulnerable segments of society often suffer multiple traumas especially through sexual exploitation and lack of physical security. These traumas can have long-lasting effects, long after the cycle of violence has ended. She points out that unhealed trauma can lead to turning one's trauma energy in on oneself (acting in), as well as turning trauma energy out on others (acting out). Besides the inward scars of conflict and war, there are also many outward scars such as HIV/AIDS, loss of limbs, and unwanted children born as a result of rape. Post-conflict unemployment and poverty can lead to further feelings of fear and powerlessness, creating frustration and anger among the population. The program Toroi examines, Project Air, is using yoga to help individuals in Rwanda to overcome these devastating effects of the genocide, genocidal rape, and sexual violence. In conclusion, Toroi explores the psychological, physical, and social benefits of using yoga in a holistic program of trauma relief efforts. Yoga can help strengthen the body as well as calm the mind. The second in the set of chapters on sports in various contexts, is Kim Fletcher and Peter St. Pierre's chapter on using sports programs as part of a peacebuilding process for demobilization efforts with child soldiers. Fletcher and St. Pierre examine the use of sports for programs aimed at disarmament, demobilization, and reintegration of the child soldiers back into civilian life. They discuss the difficulties and challenges associated with both adults and children as they make the adjustment from leading to an ex-combatant existence. Children, in particular, lack the prior experience, training, and maturity to make the transition easily. The authors argue that a community must be recreated through sports, where the children can now belong, especially since they are often not welcome in their former villages. A family must be recreated that now provides the youth with food, shelter, and protection. At the same time, the sports community can be used to dismantle the old hierarchy in the minds of the program participants. The authors discuss the long history of sports being used for character building, development of social traits, and social change, both at the individual and particularly at the team level. While sports have been thought of as to have social and psychological benefits for the participants, the research shows that sport in and of itself is not all positive. Indeed, sports have been used to augment and promote violence and aggression. The authors go on to say, however, that sports can be used as a method of getting participants involved so as to achieve other ends. The third chapter in this section is by Marion Keim and talks about the role universities could and should play in promoting sports, development, and peace. Keim discusses how faculties at universities can engage in research and teaching which promote community engagement and build capacity in the communities they serve. She gives the example of the University of the Western Cape and its success in establishing the first Interdisciplinary Center for Sport Science and Development (ICESSD) in 2009. Coming out of a period of segregated education during the apartheid era, the University of the Western Cape was in a unique position to establish these town/gown relationships. Because sports have played an important and powerful role in South African history and society, sporting institutions could now play a strong role in the shaping of the new state. South Africa has come a long way, with having the Rugby World Cup in 1995 and the Soccer World Cup in 2010, and later South Africa was elected the Chair for Peace and Sport for the UN International Working Group (IWG) in 2011 in Geneva. The unique mission of universities, the author states, has been the pursuit of truth, carrying with it a commitment to objectivity and an openness to diverse values, interpretations, ethics, worldviews, and frames of reference, as well as in the case of the University of the Western Cape, a commitment to conflict resolution and peacebuilding. The discourse that occurs within the university creates a space for students to learn from their academic work, as well as from experiential education and practice. Through conferences, seminars, and scholarship, the University promotes dialogue around conflict resolution, peacebuilding, and social transformation.

The last three chapters in this special edition cover topics of interest related to sports and peacebuilding not addressed in the prior sections, yet vital to an understanding of what makes sports and peace programs successful or not. The first of this series is the chapter by M. Lee Brooks and Michael Shapiro. In this chapter, Brooks and Shapiro explore the marketing strategies of professional sports corporations of the four major sports in the United States and how these strategies are designed to protect their product. They tackle some of the tougher questions in sports: what happens when sports teams live by the idea of winning at any cost and what does fairness in sports really mean? Are good conduct and professional demeanor really the goal of sports? One of the criticisms of using sports to build peace is that sports are by nature competitive. In defining and articulating clearly established rules, coaches can avoid and prevent unnecessary conflict and promote peace. The authors look at the special protections due to their very public nature extended to the leagues and the players which other corporations do not have access to. The human resources side of the business is by far the largest investment of the sports corporation. The players who gain celebrity and hero status are the public face and have to represent the organization to the public; they are the product the corporation is marketing. Does the gladiatorial way of doing sports promote this hero status? These players become the role models younger players look up to. In light of this and in response to it, each league enters into collective bargaining agreements that govern and bind both parties to acceptable levels of conduct in the marketplace. The sports organizations have an image to protect if they are going to sell their product to the consumer, which in turn, affects the support of the fans, the marketing of merchandize, the comfort the public has with sports, and attendance at sporting events. Failure to address a negative event can cause a loss of reputation which can have long-lasting ramifications for the organization and, in fact, its viability in the marketplace. Because the cost of a public crisis can be so high, sports organizations institute collective bargaining agreements, contracts, and disciplinary procedures. Sports are an entertainment-based industry and because people revere their athletes, care must be taken to promote a positive image. The second chapter in this last series is looking at the critical issue of team cohesion, especially as it relates to the difference between task and relationship conflict. This chapter, by Claudia Stura, also deals with public image and the pressure on college teams to perform well. She specifically looks at factors that influence conflict and the influence of leadership on team cohesion. For this research, she interviewed both coaches and players and used both interview methods and direct observation. Not surprisingly, trust was named as the most important factor in team cohesion, followed by such things as holding each other accountable and having team rituals. She concludes with discussing the role of the coach and the coach's style in facilitating cohesion. If one can build cohesion on a team through good coaching and the promotion of values such as trust, then can sports be seen as a microcosm of society where the lessons we learn from sports teams might be applicable to a larger setting? The last chapter in this set is by "Doc" Holliday. Holliday explores the building of values, tenants, and traits in both structured and non-structured sports. He focuses specifically in the involvement of young males in sports activities and the challenges that young men face in terms of being defined by physical characteristics such as being tough, strong, athletic, and intimidating. Holliday talks about how participants in sporting activities learn the importance of working together as a team unit, and how to recover from both individual and group adversity, as well as how to lose with grace. He explores all of the lessons young males can learn from sports: hard work, the power to dream, the importance of a healthy body and mind, the value of fun, instant and long-term gratification, the need for friendship, the opportunity to feel values, the importance of a sense of belonging, independence and interdependence, discipline, responsibility, fairness, and respect. He points out that even in the intense competition of the Olympic Games, that brotherhood is fostered in the end. Holliday concludes with a discussion about the roles adults play in securing a safe and secure space for young men to practice their sport, acquire new knowledge and skills, and create the building blocks for adulthood.

This volume is a first step in examining some of the issues faced by programs aimed at sports and peacebuilding. It also examines some of the ongoing ethical dilemmas faced by the programs and ways in which the programs have dealt with those dilemmas. The successful programs seem to already have worked through some of the issues of funding; alliances with other programs and entities; proper training of coaches and other staff; which sports are most conducive to the peace process; which knowledge, skills, and abilities need to be included; how to best market the programs to their communities; and how to succeed at working across various cultures. Historically, these programs are still in their infancy, but they have already accomplished a great deal, especially for the youth in their communities. Their staff are dedicated to the process and many programs have proven that they can exist over time, even with sporadic funding lines. They each adjust to the realities of their own situation, working through the complex dilemmas in their respective communities.

Sports and peacebuilding activities have clearly made their mark on peace processes. As we in the peace field continue to gain experience with these programs and can see the benefits they provide to a peacebuilding process, working through any issues which arise will become easier in light of the overall success. The legitimate concerns first raised about using sports for peace: sports being competitive, sports being violent, sports being focused on winning, etc., have all been dealt with by the programs in a very creative manner. In the past few years, we have learned to mix teams from formerly opposing sides, to make the competition about doing our best rather than beating the opponent, to screen potential coaches and the value of training our coaches to understand the values of peacebuilding prior to working with young people, to hold up values such as honesty and integrity important to sports as being paramount to the game, and we have also learned to market our programs to communities in such a way that it invites the entire community to be part of the peacebuilding process.

There are still unanswered questions regarding sports and peacebuilding. Can sports be used to promote justice, as a form of reconciliation, to build compassion for the other, or to reduce violence in the whole society? These are still areas which need future research.

The Role of Sports in Peacebuilding

Claudia Stura and Linda M. Johnston

Introduction

What started with the initiative of former Olympic athletes in 1995 with "giving something back" is an established movement today. "Sport and development" has increased tremendously in the past years and is still growing. Between 2006 and 2010, the International Olympic Committee (IOC) invested about USD 200 million in development projects, and more than 166 organizations worldwide are involved in development through sport projects today.

Today, sports are used as a tool for reconciliation in regions of conflict. The belief in sport as a reconciliation tool has powerful supporters. Nelson Mandela said: "Sport has the power to unite people in a way little else can. It can create hope where there was once only despair. It breaks down racial barriers, and it laughs in the face of discrimination" (according to HMSO, in Armstrong and Vest 2013a, 2013b, 2013c, 1). "Sport for Peace" contributes to the realization of the United Nations Millennium Development goals (Kidd 2008). Former United Nations Secretary General Kofi Annan (2003) stressed: "Sport has the global ability to go beyond cultural differences and can facilitate social change in the world." His statement in a press release followed the United Nations resolution in 2003 (Darnell 2010, 55), which emphasized the role of sports in achieving the goals.

Many sport programs have been evaluated separately, but not as part of the "big picture." In this exploratory study, we looked at patterns, common themes, similar experiences, and perceptions in regard to the possibilities and limits of sport as a contributor to reconciliation in unstable socio-political situations. In addition to that, we examined how sport projects could be utilized as an integral part of a peacebuilding process. Hence, this study examined the following research question: How can and does sport play a role in building peace?

Many of the goals of conflict resolution are included in and reinforced with well thought out sports activities. In the well-designed programs, the participants learn skills such as cooperation, communication, and sharing, as well as get the opportunity to view reconciliation and negotiation processes first hand. They are able to break down stereotypes through these experiential learning activities. The role of experiential learning for learning conflict resolution processes is reinforced through these activities (see, e.g., Hettler and Johnston 2009).

Today, many sporting programs have also been established to encourage reconciliation after conflict, such as in Rwanda, Sierra Leone, Sudan, Liberia, Bosnia-Herzegovina, Sri Lanka, and Northern Ireland. These grassroots interventions seem to show that sport can make a modest contribution to wider efforts to promote conflict resolution and peaceful coexistence. How does sport play a role in peacebuilding? As a review of the literature has shown, many sports programs have been evaluated separately, but not as part of the "big picture." Thus, we aimed to find patterns, common themes, similar experiences, and perceptions in regard to the role that sports can play in building peace. We studied the possibilities and limits of sports as a contributor to reconciliation in unstable socio-political situations. In addition to that, we examined how sports projects may be an integral part of a holistic peacebuilding strategy.

The State of Sports and Peace Research

Sports projects to promote peace have been conducted all over the world. In the Balkans, children of parents who waged war against each other now set foot in enemy territory and play soccer together (Armstrong and Vest 2013a, 2013b, 2013c). In Srebrenica, children came together for a multiethnic sporting event for the first time after the end of the civil war and the massacre in 1995. Some organizations have established sporting programs to encourage reconciliation after conflict, for example, UNICEF in Rwanda, World Vision in Sierra Leone, and Right to Play in Sudan, Liberia, as well as in Rwanda (Armstrong and Vest 2013a, 2013b, 2013c). "Football for Peace" in Israel is another grassroots intervention using sport as a modest contribution to wider efforts to promote conflict resolution and peaceful coexistence.

Many scholars stress that efforts should be made at the grassroots level. For example, Sugden (2006) stressed, "In doing so, not only mainly the chances of achieving peace would be enhanced, but also the day to day existence of those laboring in the shadow of conflict might also be improved" (221). As in the case of the Israeli-Palestine Conflict, coexistence is the way forward if a lasting peace is to be achieved (Said 2000). He continued, "We cannot coexist as two communities of detached and uncommunicatingly separate suffering (…) the only way of rising beyond the endless back-and-forth violence and dehumanization is to admit the universality and integrity of the other's experience and to begin to plan a common life together" (208).

Scholars reported that sports can serve useful roles in peacebuilding and peacekeeping. In Northern Ireland, for example, where sports were once a theatre for the expression of cross-community animosity, sports are formally recognized as a key element in the peace process today (Sugden and Wallis 2007, 3). In South Africa, sports are regarded by many people as a means to promote nation building (Keim 2003). In a Bosnian Muslim village, the recreation of the football club was an important step in the rebuilding, reconstruction, and reconciliation of the community and their neighbors (Armstrong and Vest 2013a, 2013b, 2013c).

Sports offer a setting where conflicting groups are able to rehumanize their vision of each other through engaging in a neutral sports-based intervention (Tokarski 2009, 195). "It has the capacity to address the whole issue of reconciliation," as the South African Minister of Sport once said (Keim 2003, 184). Moreover, the German Sport Confederation declared that "Sport contributes towards the integration of different sectors and marginalized groups" (Keim 2003, 183).

Sports projects can contribute to positive peace (Right to Play 2008). One of the advantages often mentioned is that sports projects can help in building and sustaining long-term commitments and relationships in the face of ongoing uncertainty (Black 2010) as well as break down prejudice and barriers between people (Hakim 2005), reduce fear and anger (Interviewee 10), and encourage acceptance of the other (Seytanoglu and Lesta 2010). Even though these projects stand outside of the normal institutions of the state, it is nonetheless vital in securing consensus and control. It is peacebuilding "from below"—peacebuilding at the grassroots level, as Tokarski (2009, 195) stressed. Eichberg and Levinsen (2009) called it "peace by doing," because it is not a conflict management tool that has the conflicting parties sit around a table talking about their conflict. Rather, it is a tool that creates a space where people act and play together

(348). Moreover, it creates a setting where players, coaches, parents, and administrators are required to leave their political views and ideological positions outside.

"Peacebuilding from below" seems to be especially suitable in cases of protracted social conflict, such as in Northern Ireland. In those cases, formal peace agreements have mostly been put in place. Conflicts fizzle out and drop below the threshold, but are prone to break out again (Ramsbotham, Woodhouse, and Miall 2011). Furthermore, sports projects may be part of multitrack diplomacy to consider particular issues, such as distributive justice, that cannot always be addressed by diplomacy at the official state level. These programs may be able to bring a variety of people on different levels to a table to change the relationships between different parties into partnerships or even friendships (Davies and Kaufman 2003).

As the idea of sports as being a universal social good is somewhat naive, it is required that political positions are not expressed in and around the sports projects (Sugden and Wallis 2007, 19). In this way, members learn to value and appreciate social diversity in the sport setting as an apolitical circumstance of its own (Tokarski 2009).

Sports are not a panacea for most social conflicts, as Schnitzler, Stephenson, Zanotti, and Stivachtis (2011) stressed. The scholars pointed out that sports are not a substitute for developing social norms and values that support mutual tolerance and shared commitment to nonviolent conflict management. Sports are neither good nor bad, and are rather a social construct, of which the roles and functions depend largely on what we make of it, as the Sport for Development and Peace International Working Group (2008) stated.

There are examples where sports have been used to divide a society. Reiche (2011) reported in his study of Lebanon that sport is used to divide the society and not unite it. In a country with eighteen state-recognized religious sects having a strong sectarian identity, the professional sports sector not only reflects sectarianism in Lebanon, "It is also contributing the most to manifest it" (274): "Almost all professional sports clubs have clear sectarian and political affiliations" (263). Armstrong and Vest (2013a, 2013b, 2013c) supports this problem with his study of soccer in Bosnia. Arguing that sport offers occasions where you can choose your identity, he found that it has the potential to create a "with us or against us" culture and/or a winner-loser culture, either of which has the potential to "undermine the peace-building process" (4).

Scholars also reported some limitations to sports projects, such as technical problems in project implementation regarding resourcing and sustainability (Armstrong 2007). Giulianotti and others cited in this text described how projects may reinforce imperialistic and neocolonial relationships (2011).

However, if carefully designed, sports can make a valuable contribution to conflict reconciliation (Sugden and Wallis 2007, 18) and can be focused on having fun as well as be used to "break the ice" between conflicting groups. Taking into account the complexity of conflicts, it has been debated how sport can and how it should make a contribution to reconciliation in unstable socio-political situations (Tokarski 2009). Sports programs must carefully navigate the waters, so as not to interfere with, but rather to support, the work of other groups in achieving lasting peace.

As Schnitzler, Stephenson, Zanotti, and Stivachtis (2011) argued, this field provides robust potential for interdisciplinary research. Many sport programs have been evaluated separately, but not as part of the "big picture." Hence, we studied patterns, common themes, similar experiences, and perceptions in regard to the possibilities and limits of sport as a contributor to reconciliation in unstable socio-political situations. In addition to that, we examined how sport projects may be an integral part of a holistic peacebuilding strategy. Hence, this study examined the following research question: How does sport play a role in building peace? As this study was of an exploratory nature, no hypotheses were formulated and tested.

Research Methodology

Galtung (1996) distinguished peace between negative and positive peace. In this study, the term peace is understood in accordance to his definitions. Negative peace generally refers to the time after the violence has ended. Instead, positive peace refers to the actions taken to build a sense of community after a conflict has ended. Some projects are carried out during positive peace, which refers to the eradication of indirect, structural, and cultural violence (2). In addition, positive peace refers to the replacement of violence by social justice and the presence of many states of mind and society, such as harmony and equity (Webel 2007, 6).

For this research, we chose to interview project managers who directly run sports and peace-related programs postconflict. The projects analyzed in this study refer to formalized programs using sports as a main vehicle to promote the end of the conflict, defuse tension, bring rival communities together, maintain a nonviolent system of dealing with conflict and promote coexistence between conflicting groups and positive peace (Tokarski 2009). In this study, we did not attempt to reach child soldiers, for example, who had been involved in the fighting themselves. For this research, we focused on programs where the families of the participants may have been involved in the conflict or that the conflict was occurring or had occurred nearby.

For the project managers we spoke to, most had begun their projects immediately after the cessation of the conflict. A couple of interviewees mentioned that the conflict had erupted again during the course of their program, but they chose not to discontinue the program once they made sure the participants would not be in any danger. Another mentioned that they have to be aware of and deal with the political realities of their situation everyday.

The data was collected over a period of three months, from September to December 2011. We made a list of potential interviewees via a website search of projects which involved sports and peacebuilding activities. We also searched the Internet for publically available reports on sports and peace programs. Initial contacts with the interviewees for the project were made by phone or email. We chose in-depth interviews via Skype as the main research method. We conducted semi-structured interviews with a list of interview questions. Findings from former studies were considered for developing the guide. After the literature review, we drew up a list of questions based on the gaps in the studies. Questions included information about their target populations, how long their projects had been going, when they had started their projects in terms of the conflict, how they recruited and trained their coaches, which organizations they work in collaboration with, how they are financed, formal and informal partnerships, skill sets they teach in the programs, internal and external factors which influence their projects, how they evaluate their success, and their thoughts on the potential for sports to be an integral part of peacebuilding. In addition, we included document analysis in our re-search. The documents consist of working papers the study participants had provided us with, in our examination of prior research on how sports play a role in building peace.

The Choice of Participants

For this in-depth research, nonprobability sampling was chosen. In contrast to the many projects using sports to promote development, the analysis of this study focused only on projects that used sports to build peace. To gain insights into the interviewees' experiences and perceptions as they work at the grassroots level, we chose local project managers as informants. We contacted project managers of twenty-five projects, located all over the world. We specifically sought out those individuals who actually were "on the ground" managing projects. The fourteen project managers, eight men, and six women, who responded, were interviewed for our study. Their projects take place in Jordan, Sri Lanka, Morocco, Turkey, Croatia, Armenia, Northern Ireland, Uganda, Dubai, Benin, Cypress, Lebanon, Poland, France, Ethiopia, Iraq, Bosnia-Herzegovina, Palestine, and Israel. Some of the interviewees had been running these projects for many years, and even were involving their own children in the future or current running of the projects.

Results

For the analysis of the study, we used the deductive approach of content and narrative analysis, because certain aspects indicating the role of sports in peacebuilding have been examined in former studies of single sport programs. In addition, we used the inductive approach to explore aspects that have not emerged from former studies, but may be important.

The Frameworks

The interviewees reported the usage of different kinds of sports. Some use soccer, basketball, volleyball, cricket, rugby, Gaelic football, or martial arts, others use several in combination or mixed with small games. While many sports programs use soccer, some interviewees argued that soccer is not as suitable, because it is often highly politicized.

The participant population for most of the projects are children. Some interviewees added that it is more difficult to work with adults. Most of the interviewees stressed that it is important to start working with children at a young age. Hence, the children are mainly six or eleven years old when they become participants and fourteen or eighteen when they leave the projects. Some of them even offer projects for young adults aged twenty-one and over. Some of the projects particularly chose coaches from their former youth participants. Others offered a mentoring program for teens who had been through the programs as youths. Some stressed the importance of offering projects in particular for girls as well as working with children with disabilities. When it would be best to start the sports programs was answered very differently. While some sports programs take place or began during or immediately after the cessation of violence associated with the conflict, others started in the absence of war or the threat of war. One interviewee stressed that it may be important to have been there during the conflict to get credibility from the participants.

"We could say that we know what you are talking about. It is dangerous but important" (Interviewee 1). Interviewee 2 stated, if the conflict is still going on, the project may offer a platform of change for the locals.

Regarding the duration of the programs, most interviewees stressed the importance of long-term projects. "If you are interested in community building, you have to be there for a long time, it is about being an integral part of the community" (Interviewee 1). And another interviewee stressed that "People need a long time to change their mind-set, but many donors do not consider this" (Interviewee 3). This problem was reported from many study participants; donors often do not fund long-term projects. This resulted in the consequence that some projects have been insufficiently monitored and evaluated to gauge the effectiveness of the programs.

Surprisingly, less than half of the organizers reported that they get funded by national governmental organizations. If so, they mentioned their ministries of education, youth, and/or sport. Only some reported on local partners. Interviewee 2 stressed the importance of a local partner organization that is open to new developments and that wants to learn themselves; to grow themselves. Nevertheless, most get their funding from UN organizations, such as UNICEF and UNESCO, as well as from foreign development institutions or embassies, institutions of the European Union, sports retail companies, and private and public foundations.

Many stressed the potential working with local people offers. One stated: "The organizations that were working in the field during the conflict left in the 100s when the violence stopped since funding was only available for them as long as the conflict was ongoing" (Interviewee 1). Hence, it is important to work with locals since they may continue working without getting paid. Some interviewees even stressed that it is important that the locals work voluntarily from the beginning; that way they can assure they do not stop working when the funding goes away. "When there is not much money at stake, you get the genuine volunteers who are not keen of the money and you get people who are there anyway" (Interviewee 1).

In his working paper, Levinsen (2011) pointed out that to ensure reconciliation at all levels, all involved volunteers have to represent all the previous parties of the conflict and, if possible, different societal levels. However, choosing local people as coaches also offers the opportunity that they are most familiar with the participants' cultures and backgrounds. It may also provide an exercise in meeting participants, where they are and letting the things develop in their own conditions and circumstances

(Levinsen 2011). But working with locals, especially local coaches, was also emphasized in regard to the credibility of the projects. That way, the projects are not perceived as hegemonic.

Almost all of the interviewees stressed the importance of a careful selection and intense training of the coaches. Often the coaches have been with the projects since the beginning, or they are former participants. The duration of their trainings differs from several days to even one year. Ongoing training for coaches was a vital part of several of the programs. Many interviewees emphasized the importance of the coaches learning to be moderators, role models, and community relations facilitators. Some stressed the use of training the same coaches every season to build a high level of expertise; others emphasized the training of different coaches as an advantage to broaden the number of coaches. Still others mentioned utilizing former participants as future coaches.

Potentials and Limits of Sports and How They Are Used and Handled

Regarding the potential of sports in peacebuilding, all study participants explained that by its nature, sports, and especially team sports, helps develop certain skills. Aside from promoting acceptance, respect, cooperation, and fair play, the project organizers stressed that they aim to teach their participants to be curious, be open minded, and to develop listening skills. Another major value all interviewees reported was teaching how to build trust. Many emphasized also the role of the locals in this regard. Locals often already knew each other or at least lived near each other. If a problem arose, they could easily reach each other and talk it out.

All study participants reported that they also teach social skills, such as social awareness and openness, as well as certain communication skills. Most of the interviewees reported the use of the sports projects as a vehicle to educate, change perceptions, and develop future leaders. They also teach the children how to nonviolently deal with conflict by using special conflict resolution tools. "They learn to become able to disagree but having a strong enough relationship that is doesn't emerge into conflict. When they go off the field they are still friends" (Interviewee 4).

The organizers bring the children together to break down their stereotypes, learn to see each other as a person, accept people who are different, and in the end to develop relationships among them. "When you bring children to play together, one day they can also live together. So, we are giving them the skills to look at the other not as their enemy, but as their playmates, as their friend" (Interviewee 5).

To ensure that the participants learn, the coaches often reflect on the activities and connect them with questions, such as when they play cooperation-type games. Others explained that they integrate the reflection part into the games directly, for example, when a foul happens. Then they stop the game and raise the issue of how that can be resolved instead of kicking each other. Still others wait until after the game to discuss anything, but then incorporate what happened during the game into further discussion away from the field. Another example that was mentioned was the importance of teaching different ways a person can be seen:

> If you see someone as an object, you can use or ignore them or you can see them as an obstacle. We transfer that to the court, how does that make you feel in the court that someone treats you as an obstacle, ways to help the kids thinking outside of their mindset (Interviewee 5).

The organizers emphasized that they teach theory which is reinforced by the sports practice. Most of the interviewees stressed the experiential learning approach for acquiring and internalizing the prospective values, attitudes, perceptions, and skills. The children reflect on what they experience during the games and how they may apply it in the future (Interviewee 9).

To ensure that the participants get in touch and communicate with each other, they pair the kids up and always mix the teams differently. All interviewees stressed the importance of using coaches from both sides of any conflict on each team; therefore all coaches are mixed in the same way the players are. In some projects the participants take over leadership tasks, where they can apply what they have learned. Some interviewees reported that they have separate sessions, and those where they get together once a month and do sports as well as other cultural activities. To create a safe space and to enable the participants to "break the ice" (Interviewee 13), they wear uniforms to make all the players look the same.

Another aspect that was mentioned by many interviewees is to ensure that the sport does not have a competitive character. As in the case of martial arts, the coaches teach the participants that it is not about winning but about testing and improving your abilities. The opponent is called a partner, "Who helps you improve yourself, the one you bow to" (Interviewee 10), rather than an opponent or enemy. Other interviewees who mainly use team sports in their projects stressed the necessity to change the sizes and the compositions of the teams frequently, to make sure all conflicting parties are part of each team, and to include games/exercises with small teams. Moreover, they also reported the use of exercises and games that require a strong cooperation among single participants or even teams.

Others referred to the so-called "peace games," where the practice is used to create cooperation. One interviewee pointed out the method of changing the rules of the games by letting the children set them up by themselves, purposely changing the rules of the game so that they are less competitive, and including a mediator instead of a referee in the games.

"Sport is a unifying language, you don't need a language for," as one of the interviewees stressed (Interviewee 9). Other interviewees reported that they have coaches or coordinators who speak several languages; others said that they make sure that at least one of the coaches on each team speaks the language of each of the participants, or they make use of interpreters. Others stressed that sport is seen as third culture, that the participants adapt to and where they put their own culture aside. The language of sports can be understood by the players as being separate and different from whatever they speak off the field.

The interviewees also stated that sport as a culture offers many factors for promoting peace. Especially the "can-do" attitude, its potential to break down ignorance and fear, and its usage as a mediator were reported as positive aspects. Furthermore, "team sport offers great opportunities to mix participants which never came across before . . . we don't allow a church versus a mosque," as one of the study participants pointed out (Interviewee 1). "The kids have to collaborate in order to become a team" (Interviewee 5).

Sports may promote a change in perceptions not only at the micro-level, but also at the macro-level: the children are the change agents and may help to create systemic changes. "It is hard for the kids to fight in the conflict zone when they have played together on the pitch before," as one interviewee (Interviewee 1) stressed.

All interviewees emphasized the importance of using sports apolitically; their projects are politic-free zones. "It may create a safe space when carefully used . . . it is still possible to reach the population with sport projects even when the political situation gets worse" (Interviewee 8). Interviewee 12 stressed that they rather emphasize the social aspects than playing soccer to engage children to participate. Some reported that if they promoted the peace aspect of the projects, the parents did not want their children to participate in the projects. Hence, they stressed the importance of not putting the emphasis on peacebuilding, but on the educational aspects of the sport. In this regard, Interviewee 7 described different topics as incentive, such as crime prevention. Other interviewees reported that meeting academic requirements may be an important factor to gain participants.

The sports projects may also be used for networking. Many interviewees stated that they may be linked to other clubs in the region, to other social or cultural activities or the international community. Some projects were sending participants to international tournaments or camps in other countries. Others stressed that they may be used to stay in touch via social media. However, all interviewees stressed that it should and cannot be the only component in peacebuilding. "Sport is not a supplement, it is just an addition" (Interviewee 3). Furthermore, if the basic living conditions such as food and drinking water are not met, sports programs are not effective. Interviewees also emphasized that sports may also be used to create hatred. It is a political decision. Levinsen (2011, working paper), however, referring to his experience with their projects Open Fun Football Schools, reports that:

> When we claim to challenge the existing stories, it does however not imply that we want to change people's perception of what happens, . . . rather we want to give new stories a chance to become dominating in people's lives, stories that tell of trust, hope and of a future in which positions involve inclusiveness rather than oppositions (2–3).

In the perspective of the holistic peacebuilding strategies, the sports projects may only play certain roles, as the interviewees stressed. One interviewee stated that "We each got a role to play in the peace building process" (Interviewee 1). Just as many interviewees pointed out that their projects address all kinds of social issues that governments, UN organizations, or the World Health Organization (WHO) fail to meet, because they do not have the resources or the know-how. Most interviewees state that they do mix ethnic and social backgrounds, gender, and abilities. As one stressed, "You automatically break down barriers" (Interviewee 1).

Bringing children together in such a systematic way opens up certain opportunities, such as for constructive dialogue between children and having them become change agents. As one interviewee pointed out: "We cannot change politics, but we can open opportunities to meet someone, this is the key . . . to engage in open dialogues, make the children active citizens" (Interviewee 5). A study participant stressed that working at the grassroots level is a good and safe entry point to support dialogue. Even when peacebuilding may not be most attractive to people, they may still send their kids to educational programs, because they are interested in getting good education for their kids, as Interviewee 2 stressed. One interviewee pointed out that when the leaders of the conflicting communities see efforts bringing out positive messages, that this helps the peace process:

> I feel, when politicians and the media see that there is something positive coming out of interactions, it creates optimism. That is very important for the peace process: trying to find peace in order to help the future of this country; and the future of this country is youth (Interviewee 5).

Emphasized limitations were external factors that influence the sports projects. The on-going conflict, the media, the parents, and the schools were mainly mentioned. One interview stated: "[A limit is the] . . . political rhetoric which constantly reminds of war" (Interviewee 13). Another interviewee stressed:

> We are working against the established, against communities saying "we are the victims and the others are the perpetrators," the media, history books, the schools, sometimes the whole political situation (Interviewee 9).

A different interviewee reported: "You keep fighting something that is sometimes fighting back. It is sometimes like taking one step forward and one step back" (Interviewee 3).

Discussion of the Findings

Several important themes became evident in this study and we will discuss each separately: the value of team sports, sports as a vehicle for peace education, the values imparted by the sports programs, the trust building process, the value of initiating friendships, rehumanization of the other, the apolitical nature of sports, and the involvement of local people and resources in the events.

Most interviewees stated that they use team sports in their projects. This conforms to Henley and Colliard's (2005) finding, that team sport can help to foster teamwork and team spirit, and can even (re)build social cohesion. Keim (2003) stressed that instead of individual sports, team sports can more effectively develop intercultural friendships. Teamwork skills are important in peacebuilding: a lasting positive peace requires the promotion of forms of common identification toward achieving collective goals, as Galtung (2000) pointed out.

As our interviews stressed the importance of the experiential learning approach, former studies reported from its application as a powerful vehicle in peace education. One of its many strengths, as Dewey (1900) supports the interviewees' experiences, is its approach of fostering directed, active learning (Hettler and Johnston 2009). Bar-Tal (2002) supported this argument with his findings. He stressed experimental learning as key method for the acquisition of values, attitudes, perceptions, and skills and emphasized that internalization is mainly acquired by practice. Learners explore and evaluate their roles as members of a community and the development of healthy social skills (Hettler and Johnston 2009).

Acceptance, respect, and cooperation were mainly reported by all interviewees as values that they aim promote with their programs. Furthermore, they emphasized the ability to deal with conflicts nonviolently as a teaching objective. These findings seem to conform to Bar-Tal's (2002) statement that the learning climate should include conditions reflecting objectives of peace education, such as tolerance, cooperation, peaceful conflict resolution, and respect.

The aim of trust building was also highlighted by all interviewees. This finding supports Lederach and Jenner's (2002) argument, emphasizing trust building as another core component of building positive peace. It seems to be a process to which sports programs seem to be ideally suited. Training exercises involve or may be modified to trust-based activities, and as in team-sports in general, it is a requirement of success that the participants in the training sessions trust their teammates (Lea-Howarth 2006).

Using sports to build friendships among the participants with different ethnic backgrounds also seems to be a key element in all projects. This finding is supported by Sugden and Wallis' (2007) study results. They reported that facilitating contact between people in a natural way promotes building friendships and the desire for and the commitment to peaceful coexistence among the participants (Sugden and Wallis 2007). This phenomenon may be explained with the contact hypothesis. The leading theory advocating for reducing intergroup conflict was developed for diverse ethnicities and cultural groups (Pettigrew 2008). Its primary argument is that contact typically diminishes intergroup prejudice and reduces intergroup threat and anxiety (Pettigrew and Tropp 2006). The sports arena certainly can be one area where the opportunity for continued contact can occur. The theory's potential mechanisms are a behavior-driven attitude change: people rather form a positive attitude toward out-group members after being involved in a cooperative learning task with them and generating affective ties (Pettigrew 2008). Sports-related games can be seen as positive cooperative learning opportunities. In his research among Catholics and Protestants suffering personally from sectarian violence in Northern Ireland, Hewstone (2003) even monitored that intergroup friendship can engender forgiveness and trust. The reported equal status of the sports program participants and their motivation to reach a goal that requires cooperative interdependence, meet the conditions of the contact hypothesis (Allport 1954) as much as the distinctive characteristic of sport: the interaction takes place rather on a personal than on a formal level (Amichai-Hamburger and McKenna 2006).

The focus on seeing another person as person and not as an object, refers to Tokarski's (2009) point that sports offer a setting where conflicting groups are able to "rehumanize their vision of each other through engaging in a neutral sport based intervention" (195). Furthermore, being a "third culture," as Interviewee 3 stressed, sport has the potential to act as an informal forum that may help in conflict reconciliation. It can enhance forgetting people as "themselves" and open up to each other.

The apolitical approach of all studied projects conforms to Sugden and Wallis' (2007) statement. They remark that organizers stress their sport sessions as a political-free-zone, where the political discourse that surrounds the conflict has no place (16). But the interviewees also stated it as a challenge and hereby seem to confirm Black's (2010) statement; "No serious sport studies scholar would any longer defend the 'myth of autonomy'—the idea that sport is apolitical, 'above' or autonomous from politics" (125). Armstrong and Vest (2013a, 2013b, 2013c) found that sport is even used to confirm difference, such as in Bosnia-Herzegovina. Hence, Schnitzler, Stephenson, Zanotti, and Stivachtis (2011) even argued that literature clearly suggests program planners should proceed with caution, mindful of the potential for sports to augment even greater conflict.

Another theme that stood out in the responses of the participants was the role of the locals in the sports programs. Well-trained local coaches seem to be a main factor for successful, sustainable projects. Interviewees talked extensively about the value of putting a lot of time and energy into the training of coaches and the value of ethnically mixed coaches on each team. They do not only seem to depend so much on funding, but also may be crucial from the perception of the communities, because they help to foster trust among the participants and give the projects credibility. Many projects that are funded and organized by Western institutions may not be perceived as imperialistic and neocolonial as Giulianoti (2011) and others cited in this work stressed. They may help to develop the certain kind of contextualized understanding of the communities in which the projects take place, which may be hard to achieve otherwise, as Black (2010) reported.

Remarkably, most interviewees did not specifically refer to the role of the parents of the children that participate in the projects. To focus on including them may be helpful—or even crucial—on two levels. On the micro-level, the participating children may need their parents to understand that their new experiences, learned understandings, and social skills are valuable, worthy to be implemented in daily life and further developing. Furthermore, aside from other locals who are involved in the projects the parents may also connect the micro-level with the macro-level, because of their ability to facilitate change on the level of politics and media. Both "players" were cited by most interviewees as the biggest limiting factors for peacebuilding and reconciliation.

However, engaging citizens as participants and coaches seems to support Galtung's (2000) point of including as many people as possible. Participation and observation teach what the scholar emphasized as the awareness of the positive or negative influences and the impact behavior can have on others. On the other hand, it also has to be considered, that some locals, who are actively involved, may use the programs only to have fun and not put their experiences into the bigger picture of peacebuilding, as Lea-Howarth (2006) argued. Or, as she further stressed, the people involved may be the people who actually want to reconcile, and not those who would resist reconciliation efforts.

In this regard, the projects studied focus on conflict resolution and peacebuilding strategies at a subsystem level of contribution. By using this approach, a wider system change can be made. The sports programs may be seen in accordance to Tokarski (2009, 195) as a means of building cross-community relations at a grassroots level and may contribute to social change in multiethnic societies. Black (2010) emphasized the challenge of connecting "top-down" and "bottom-up" strategies and possibilities. They may not be sufficient on their own to generate sustainable and broadly based improvement in development conditions. Bar-Tal's (2002) statement about peace education supports this argument: as long as peace education without a wider social campaign is disconnected from social reality, the participants may feel that it is irrelevant to their life experience (Bar-Tal 2002). On a grassroots level, sports projects can help to facilitate peace processes, but they cannot be a sole factor. Hence, sports programs are not able to represent a substitute for other processes in need of peacebuilding.

Conclusion and Recommendations for Future Research

As this exploratory study has demonstrated, sports have developed a role in reconciling formerly antagonistic groups. Its popularity may help bringing conflicting groups together and its big potential for modification offers its application for promoting reconciliation and positive peace in unique contexts. As a necessary precondition, all interviewees stressed a very detailed and careful planning and execution to be successful: to rephrase and reframe sports away from its heavy reference to competition to a playful means, to promote certain values, such as tolerance, respect, and trust and furthermore, to use it as a safe space to teach the understanding of the value and the need for peacebuilding, and to further develop certain skills to facilitate change.

Our study was limited by choosing only interviews of project managers and document analysis as research methods. Even though the interviewees have extensive working experience and expertise, direct observations and interviews with sport program participants may have been a good complementary research method to further ensure validity. Hence, future studies may also consider on-site observations and interviews with participants in time intervals to get a full picture of the role of sports in building peace.

Even though sports cannot substitute other factors and only play one role in the peacebuilding process, it may have three main advantages in comparison to other means. First, it may play an important role in developing the awareness of the positive or negative influences and the impact behavior can have on others. Second, it is not mostly limited to a certain number of participants that can get actively engaged. And last, because of its popularity, sports may be an excellent tool to build sustainable peace continuously, since peacebuilding is a process which has no end, as Galtung stressed (1996). These advantages need to be explored in more depth in order to understand their contribution to the total endeavor.

References

Allport, Gordon W. 1954. *The Nature of Prejudice*. Cambridge, MA: Addison-Wesley.

Amichai-Hamburger, Yair K., and Katelyn McKenna. 2006. "The Contact Hypothesis Reconsidered: Interacting via the Internet." *Journal of Computer-Mediated Communication* 11, no. 3: 1–19.

Armstrong, Gary. 2007. "The Global Footballer and the Local War-Zone: George Weah and Transnational Networks in Liberia, West Africa." *Global Networks* 7: 230–47.

Armstrong, G. and E. Vest. 2013a. "Consuming Bodies: Bridges of Desire: Football and Conflict in Mostar, Bosnia." In *Playfields: Power, Practise and Passion in Sport*, ed. M. Vaczi. Reno, NV: Basque Studies.

Armstrong, G. and E. Vest. 2013b. "Reflections on Football in Post-Conflict Bosnia, Herzegovina." In *Sport, Peace and Development*, ed. K. Gilbert and W. Bennett. Champaign, IL: Common Ground.

Armstrong, G. and E. Vest. 2013c. "Mirror to the State: The Politicisation of Football in Bosnia-Herzegovina." *Journal of the International Centre for Sports Security* 1, no. 1: 44–52.

Bar-Tal, Daniel. 2002. "The Elusive Nature of Peace Education." In *Peace Education: The Concept, Principles and Practices Around the World*, ed. Gavriel Salomon and Baruch Nevo, 27–36. Hillsdale, NJ: Lawrence Erlbaum.

Black, David. 2010. "The Ambiguities of Development: Implications for Development through Sport." *Sport in Society* 13, no. 1: 121–29.

Darnell, Simon. 2010. "Power, Politics and 'Sport for Development and Peace': Investigating the Utility of Sport for International Development." *Sociology of Sport Journal* 27: 54–75.

Davies, John, and Edy Kaufman. 2003. *Second Track/Citizens' Diplomacy: Concepts and Techniques for Conflict Transformation*. New York, NY: Rowman & Littlefield.

Dewey, John. 1900. *School and Society*. Whitefish, MT: Kessinger Publishing, LLC.

Eichberg, Henning, and Anders Levinsen. 2009. "Inter-Ethnic Football in the Balkans: Reconciliation and Diversity." *Sport, Ethics and Philosophy* 3, no. 3: 346–59.

Galtung, Johan. 1996. *Peace by Peaceful Means*. Thousand Oaks, CA: Sage.

———. 2000. *Searching for Peace*. London: Pluto Press.

Giulianotti, Richard. 2011. "Sport, Transnational Peacemaking, and Global Civil Society: Exploring the Reflective Discourses of 'Sport, Development, and Peace' Project Officials." *Journal of Sport and Social Issues* 35, no. 1: 50–71.

Hakim, D. 2005. "Budo's Potential for Peace Breaking Down Barriers in the Israeli/ Palestinian Conflict." In *Budo Persepctives*, chap. 21. Aukland, New Zealand: Kend World Publications, Ltd.

Henley, R., and C. Colliard. 2005. "Overcoming Trauma through Sport." Second Magglingen Conference Sport and Development, December 4–6.

Hettler, Shannon, and Linda M. Johnston. 2009. "Living Peace: An Exploration of Experiential Peace Education, Conflict Resolution, and Violence Prevention Programs for Youth." *Journal of Peace Education* 6, no. 1: 101–18.

Hewstone, Miles. 2003. "Intergroup Contact Panacea for Prejudice?" *Psychologist* 16, no. 7: 352–55.

Keim, Marion. 2003. *Nation Building at Play*. Oxford: Meyer and Meyer.

Kidd, Bruce. 2008. "A New Social Movement: Sport for Development and Peace." *Sport in Society* 11, no. 4: 370–80.

Lea-Howarth, Jonathan. 2006. "Sport and Conflict: Is Football an Appropriate Tool to Utilise in Conflict Resolution, Reconciliation or Reconstruction?" Contemporary War and Peace Studies. MA diss., Masters diss., University of Sussex.

Lederach, John Paul, and Janice Moomaw Jenner. 2002. *A Handbook of International Peacebuilding: Into the Eye of the Storm*. San Francisco, CA: Jossey-Bass.

Levinsen, A. 2011. *The Landscape We Work In*. Working paper.

Pettigrew, Thomas F. 2008. "Future Directions for Intergroup Contact Theory and Research." *International Journal of Intercultural Relations* 32, no. 3: 187–99.

Pettigrew, Thomas F., and Linda R. Tropp. 2006. "A Meta-Analytic Test of Intergroup Contact Theory." *Journal of Personal and Social Psychology* 90, no. 5: 751–91.

Ramsbotham, Oliver, Tom Woodhouse, and Hugh Miall. 2011. *Contemporary Conflict Resolution*. Malden, MA: Polity Press.

Reiche, Danyel. 2011. "War Minus the Shooting? The Politics of Sport in Lebanon as a Unique Case in Comparative Politics." *Third World Quaterly* 32, no. 2: 261–77.

Right to Play. 2008. "Sport for the Development and Peace International Working Group: Harnessing the Power of Sport for Development and Peace: Recommendations to Governments." http://www.un.org/wcm/webdav/site/sport/shared/sport/pdfs/SDP%20 IWG/Final%20SDP%20IWG%20Report.pdf (accessed September 19, 2012).

Said, Edward W. 2000. *The End of the Peace Process: Oslo and After*. New York, NY: Random House.

Schnitzer, M., M. Stephenson, L. Zanotti, and Y. Stivachtis. 2013. "Theorizing the Role of Sport for Development and Peacebuilding." *Sport in Society* 16, no. 5: 595–610.

Seytanoglu, Idil and Stalo Lesta, Stalo (January 2010). "Evaluation Report: PeacePlayers International – Cyprus" (January 2010), 11. Unpublished.

Sugden, John. 2006. "Teaching and Playing Sport for Conflict Resolution and Co-Existence in Israel." *International Review for the Sociology of Sport* 41, no. 2: 221–40.

Sugden, John, and James Wallis. 2007. *Football for Peace? The Challenges of Using Sport for Co-Existence in Israel*. Oxford: Meyer and Meyer.

Tokarski, Walter. 2009. "Conflict Resolution through Sport Intervention in Multi-Ethnic Societies." *Sport Tourism* 16: 193–200.

Webel, Charles. 2007. "Introduction: Toward a Philosophy and Metapsychology of Peace." In *Handbook of Peace and Conflict Studies*, ed. Charles Webel and Johan Galtung, 3–13. Abingdon: Routledge.The Role of Sports in Peacebuilding

The Role of Sports Coaches in Creating Culture: A Dysfunctional Case

Kirk Smith

Introduction

Athletic coaches can have a significant impact on the persona, or culture, of their team (Schroeder 2010). At all levels—university, club, and league—coaches can, and do, build cultures that reflect their personalities and values. However, compared to the organizational culture perspective, there is little in the sports management literature about culture. According to Schroeder (2010), most of the literature about coaches relates to leadership, team cohesion, communication, and motivation (Chelladurai 2005; Duda and Balaguer 2007; LaVoi 2007; Widmeyer, Brawley, and Carron 2002). Colyer (2000) explored the cultural dimensions and competing values of sports organizations in Australia and found that competing values can create tensions between subcultures within the same organization. In exploring the positive and negative aspects of university athletics in the United States, Beyer and Hannah (2000, 105) show that "athletics function as cultural forms that carry cultural meanings and argue that many of the meanings carried by athletics reflect cultural ideologies of the wider society." Beyer and Hannah's work was carried out with the understanding that reforms were needed in the culture of intercollegiate athletics: reforms to curb violence, cheating, sex discrimination, sexual misconduct, alcohol, and drug abuse. The implications of their analysis suggest, "that the cultural significance and positive functions of university athletics represent formidable barriers to reform" (Beyer and Hannah 2000, 105). The positive influence perceived by society of university athletics would seem to outweigh the outcry for cultural reform (Splitt 2007). Ethical and legal lapses at universities are not confined to athletics, however. Kelley and Chang (2007) studied ethical lapses in athletics, research, and administration at universities and developed a typology based upon the types, levels of seriousness, and originating location. Once occurring, these incidents "cause problems of declining credibility and deteriorating trust in universities" (Kelley and Chang 2007, 402).

Considerably, more literature on culture is available in the domain of business organizations (Denison, Haaland, and Goelzer 2004; Kotter and Heskett 1992; Schein 2010; Smart and St. John 1996; Xenikou and Simosi 2006). Probably, no one has studied organizational culture and its relationship to leadership more than Edgar Schein. According to Schein (2010), leaders in all organizational contexts have the greatest influence on culture and coaches should be no exception (Schroeder 2010). Schein (1992) states, "Neither leadership nor culture can be understood by itself. In fact, one could argue that the only thing of real importance that leaders do is to create and . . . change cultures" (5). Their status and the close relationships coaches develop with their players afford them a considerable amount of influence to be able to create and change cultures (Schroeder 2010). The purpose of this chapter is to show, through the lens of a systemic model, how the role of coaches in culture creation can generate unintended consequences of violence from a seemingly peaceful and idyllic public veneer.

Theoretical Framework

Perhaps, the most important contribution to the organizational culture epistemology is Schein's (1992) three levels of culture model or framework. Schein's (2010) organizational culture model identifies three levels of culture: artifacts, espoused beliefs and values, and basic underlying assumptions that interact with each other. Artifacts are the visible things that you can see and touch such as the architecture of the buildings and what is hanging on the wall. Espoused values are what the group perceives a leader wants or what some anthropologists call "dominant value orientations." Underlying assumptions can be thought of as the part of the iceberg below the surface of the water (i.e., not seen) and these assumptions have the greatest impact on the organization's behavior, including decision making. They represent "the implicit assumptions that actually guide behavior, that tell group members how to perceive, think about, and feel about things" (Schein 2010, 149). They are similar to what Argyris and Schon (1996) called "theories in use."

This chapter uses Schein's three-level model as a theoretical framework with which to analyze and explain a culture that received a lot of news coverage in late 2011 and early 2012—Pennsylvania State University (PSU). The limitations of this conceptual chapter include the fact that the author never was physically on the PSU campus nor talked directly with anyone associated with the case. The information was gleaned from news stories, written and broadcast, and PSU websites. The author made assumptions about the veracity of the news reports. The author also made assumptions about what some comments made by PSU officials meant from the perspective of Schein's third level of culture—basic underlying assumptions. No generalizations are meant to be made from this work, only to show how a theoretical model with systemic interrelationships can help explain what happened at PSU and how and why something like that could happen at an institution and football program so highly thought of and revered. The basic research question is, can Schein's three-level cultural model help to explain the dichotomy of the PSU football program culture of being held up as an example of integrity and honor and at the same time allow such a tragic and violent pattern of wrongdoing to occur?

Other violent incidents involving coaches have occurred in the United States and around the world. Sports violence related to coaches nurturing a culture that condones, or at the very least, looks the other way at violence have been reported in Tasmania, Australia, New Zealand, and the United States (Ja 2011; McConnell 1997; Stockdale 2006). These stories have a common thread of violence based upon a culture of "unwritten rules of conduct." In one instance in Tasmania, an Australian rules football coach was accused of being a hypocrite because he publicly stated that Tasmanian junior coaches should be screened to keep out thugs, then shortly thereafter was dismissed from a game himself for striking an opposing player—clearly a case of espoused values not being aligned with underlying assumptions. No more disciplinary action was taken. In Australia, another Australian Rules football coach was suspended for three years for striking opposing players during a brawl on the field. In New Zealand, a sports psychologist blamed rugby and cricket coaches for allowing violent reprisals in games to become a part of tradition by encouraging the practice. In the United States, a very successful professional football team was recently sanctioned with long suspensions and heavy fines for its coaches for a scandal involving paying players if they injured targeted opposing star players during games.

The PSU story is one where the violent outcome and shattering consequences were based upon a culture that was a bit more subtle and nuanced, and surely more isolated and protected. It is an example of how all the artifacts and espoused values in the world are not as powerful as underlying assumptions.

Case Description

Joe Paterno was the head football coach for PSU's football team from 1966 through 2011. His 409 victories are the most by any coach in American collegiate football's most prestigious category—The National Collegiate Athletic Association (NCAA) Football Bowl Subdivision (FBS). He won two national championships, had seven undefeated seasons, and was voted into the College Football Hall of Fame (Maisel 2011). Despite his unsurpassed on-the-field success, he was just as well known for his outspoken passion for sportsmanship and penchant for the phrase "success with honor" (Maisel 2011). The NCAA never sanctioned his football team during his tenure in an era when few can claim the same record. To many he was synonymous with class and integrity. He projected an almost boyish innocence. It all began to unravel in early November of 2011.

A longtime assistant coach at PSU, Jerry Sandusky, who many thought would be the heir apparent to Paterno, suddenly retired from his job at PSU in 1999 to allegedly devote more time to his charitable foundation for troubled boys, The Second Mile. It came to light in 2011 that Sandusky had been investigated in 2002 (and possibly even earlier) for improper sexual contact with young boys while on the premises of the PSU football facility. There were also allegations that the child abuse involved up to ten more boys and had been going on for fifteen years. Upon his retirement, he had been granted Professor Emeritus status and had an office, parking space, and access to many university facilities.

In 2002, an assistant coach for Paterno allegedly witnessed a sexual encounter between Sandusky and a young boy in the PSU locker room showers. The next day, the assistant coach told Paterno what he witnessed. Exactly what he said is still speculative and part of the ongoing investigation but apparently it was detailed enough for Paterno to notify his boss, the PSU athletic director. This is all that Paterno was compelled to do according to university policy. The details of what happened to the information at this point are still under investigation but the police were not notified. Despite the seriousness of what was described to Paterno, he did not follow up with his superiors when nothing further happened.

An official of the Pennsylvania State Police and the PSU Trustees later deemed Paterno met his legal but not moral obligations. During this time the US news media was flooded with reports of the scandal. Over the next two weeks, Paterno, the athletic director, and the university president were dismissed from their jobs, and a university senior vice-president resigned. Sandusky was arrested and is currently pending trial for child molestation charges. How could one of the most admired figures in college sports have his life come crashing down on him so unceremoniously? The details of the story were kept to a minimum in this chapter because, at the time of writing, the investigation is still ongoing. It is hoped that there are enough details to communicate the gravity of the story and its devastating consequences. Sadly, Joe Paterno died within three months of the story breaking.

The PSU Culture and Schein's Framework

Although not involved in the allegations against Sandusky, Paterno's fall from grace can possibly be traced back to the culture—or subculture— he built over his forty-six-year career. The first level of Schein's cultural model is the level of artifacts. They were easy to find and more numerous because they were visible by observation in the media, written, and broadcast. The second level, espoused beliefs and values were a little more difficult to uncover but were still gleaned and interpolated from the enormous media attention and historical observations by the author. Uncovering the underlying basic assumptions within the culture of PSU's football program was the most difficult but accounts of PSU employees and others close to the institution made the job easier. The author analyzed fourteen news stories that were chosen by their titles to likely contain evidence of artifacts, values, and/or statements that hinted at underlying assumptions at PSU.

According to Schein (2010), the superficial layer of culture is the level of artifacts. These are "phenomena that you can see, hear, and feel when you encounter a new group with an unfamiliar culture" (77). Observed behavior is included in artifacts but is difficult to interpret or decipher. The news stories contained the following list of cultural artifacts:

- The university library containing Mr. Paterno's name (he donated millions of dollars to the school).
- The PSU Sports Hall of Fame Museum (there is no academic Hall of Fame).
- A football stadium that seats over 100,000 fans.

- A statue of Joe Paterno just outside the football stadium.
- A scholarship fund started by Joe Paterno.
- Special retirement benefits for coaches.

The power of a leader in creating a culture is embodied in the level of espoused beliefs and values. Schein (2010, 10) asserts that, "All group learning ultimately reflects someone's original beliefs and values, his or her sense of what ought to be, as distinct from what is." They can come from ideals, goals, aspirations, ideologies, and rationalizations. Over time as these beliefs and values are reinforced, the group tends to propose and do what they perceive the leader wants. This can create a divergence in what is and what is perceived especially if the results of problem solving and other actions are positive, or they work. Following is a list of espoused beliefs and values at PSU gleaned from quotes by people affiliated with the university:

- Always do the ethical thing.
- Always be open and transparent.
- Keep a balance between academics and athletics.
- Success with honor.
- Embody the highest standards of personal conduct coupled with academic excellence.

The third level of basic underlying assumptions includes "unconscious, taken-for-granted beliefs, and values that determine behavior, perception, thought, and feeling" (Schein 2010, 78). These assumptions can rise to the surface through facilitation, reflection, or during a particularly traumatic time. This level is the essence of what drives organizational culture but is the most difficult to uncover. Most of the entries below come directly from opinions of people at PSU or extrapolated from those opinions. This method is similar to what Schein (2010) would suggest but in a remote mode instead of face-to-face meetings or direct observations. As mentioned above, this is one of the limitations of this chapter, but the author had the benefit of hindsight, plenty of press coverage, and investigative documents released by law enforcement officials. The list of basic underlying assumptions is below:

- Academic concerns are overshadowed by sports.
- Athletics have gotten out of hand.
- Paterno can challenge the authority of the administration and Trustees and get away with it.
- Paterno was the most powerful person at the university.
- We are very isolated from the world.

- The football program handles all of their discipline problems internally instead of the campus disciplinary process for students and university or municipal law enforcement.
- We are cloaked in secrecy (PSU is exempt from the state's open records law).
- There may have been too much concentration of power in one person (Paterno).
- Paterno was above the rules.
- If I, as an employee, report something undermining the football program I may lose my job.
- Look the other way if it will embarrass the football program.

Why did all of this come out after the tragedy? Underlying assumptions are always the most difficult to decipher. In assessing a culture to uncover its basic underlying assumptions, individual and group interviews by skilled facilitators are the best techniques (Schein 2010). But that requires a conscious effort to assess. There was no effort, which we are aware of, to study the culture at PSU. Absent a conscious effort to discover the assumptions, a major scandal may have been the only way for them to surface. Any culture would be the same way because of the unconscious, unmentionable, and nondebatable nature of basic underlying assumptions.

Conclusion

This chapter attempted to determine whether Schein's (2010) three-level cultural model could help explain the extreme dichotomy at PSU. It is leader-centered and was well suited to be used as a theoretical framework with which to contextualize the events at PSU. The public face of the football program and the university was that of integrity and honor but the reality of the disaster suggests something much less than that. The artifacts show what the public sees and are monuments to a spurious ideal built up by decades of memes in a sheltered, geographically isolated environment. The espoused beliefs and values are ideals that seemed congruent with the artifacts in this almost idyllic college setting. It is when you get to the basic underlying assumptions that the iceberg reveals its true size and danger. This example is consistent with what Schein (2010) has found in large corporations in his decades-long career as a scholar of culture and leadership. His model is robust enough to cross over to other organizational domains such as sports and even institutions of higher education. Schein also speaks of subcultures within a larger overall organizational culture. Subcultures can develop by profession, department, geography, etc. In the case of PSU, a subculture within the larger university culture—the football team—over time was strong enough to affect the larger culture. Schein (2010) actually mentions universities as an example of organizations with subcultures with different and sometimes competing needs that need to be balanced:

- The needs of the students.
- The needs of the faculty.
- The needs of the administration.
- The needs of the community.

Somehow the needs of the subcultures at PSU got out of balance. It is easy to do. According to Schein (2010), there are cultural boundaries between subcultures that, when crossed, can create serious communication problems because of the sometimes conflicting values and assumptions of the various subcultures that create filters that are barriers to effective communication. This distorts and can even subvert what different subcultures want and they can work at cross-purposes with each other. Ultimately, leadership has to align subcultures to the organization's shared organizational goals. If one subculture becomes dominant, this domination can be seen as the explanation of success or failure. One could conclude that the face of the university and the dominant subculture at PSU was the football team and that its culture was seen as the reason for the overall success of the university.

The author is in no way claiming that Joe Paterno purposely tried to deceive people. He, by all accounts of his supporters, did not, but the lack of transparency and denial inherent in the basic underlying assumptions helped lead to a tragic situation for him and others at PSU and unfortunately even more tragic consequences for the alleged victims of child abuse.

How could this happen? In the case of PSU we can look to several factors. First, the leader was powerful and dynamic and had a "squeaky-clean" reputation. Second, the football program was very successful, bringing in a lot of revenue and goodwill. Third, PSU was insulated from major news media markets. Finally, it was working. Happy Valley, as PSU is euphemistically called, was considered an idyllic institution where athletics and academics were perceived as flourishing together in a classic American university setting.

According to Schein (2010), his organizational culture model applies to all organizational types: business, nonprofit, government, and even mentions football teams as an example of a leadership-defined culture based upon the time spent under the same coach. All cultures are vulnerable to becoming dysfunctional and creating a similar level of tragedy. For each of the organizational categories, it could be financial, ethical, moral, or other. This is a sad story of the power that lies in the role of coaches in creating an environment of peace and harmony or one that can become a slippery slope to awful violence.

Cultures of sports teams have not been studied as much as business organizations. Further research is warranted to study the specific dynamics and drivers of culture. Schein's three levels are structural. Development of typologies of cultural content specific to sports teams is one area to be explored. Another is, who besides coaches are instrumental in creating and changing culture: owners, player leaders, front office staff, and communities?

References

Argyris, Chris, and Donald Schon. 1996. *Organizational Learning II*. Reading, MA: Addison-Wesley.

Beyer, Janice, and David Hannah. 2000. "The Cultural Significance of Athletics in US Higher Education." *Journal of Sport Management* 14: 105–32.

Chelladurai, P. 2005. *Managing Organizations for Sport and Physical Activity*. 2nd ed. Scottsdale, AZ: Holcomb Hathaway Publishers.

Colyer, Sue. 2000. "Organizational Culture in Selected Western Australian Sport Organizations." *Journal of Sport Management* 14: 321–41.

Denison, Daniel, Stephanie Haaland, and Paulo Goelzer. 2004. "Corporate Culture and Organizational Effectiveness: Is Asia Different from the Rest of the World?" *Organizational Dynamics* 33: 98–109.

Duda, Joan, and Isabel Balaguer. 2007. "Coach-Created Motivational Climate." In *Social Psychology in Sport*, ed. Sophia Jowette and David Lavalee, 117–30. Champaign, IL: Human Kinetics.

Ja, C. 2011. "AFL: Roos 'Wrong': AFL Boss Andrew Demetriou." *AAP Australian Sports Wire*, May 25.

Kelley, Patricia, and Pepe Chang. 2007. "A Typology of University Ethical Lapse: Types, Levels of Seriousness, and Originating Location." *The Journal of Higher Education* 78, no. 4: 402–29.

Kotter, John, and James Heskett. 1992. *Corporate Culture and Performance*. New York: The Free Press.

LaVoi, Nicole. 2007. "Interpersonal Communications and Conflict in the Coach-Athlete Relationship." In *Social Psychology in Sport*, ed. Sophia Jowette and David Lavalee, 29–40. Champaign, IL: Human Kinetics.

Maisel, Ivan. 2011. "Joe Paterno's Penn State Legacy." ESPN. http://espn.go.com/college-football/story/_/id/7212678/penn-state-nittany-lions-coach-joe-paterno-legacy (accessed February 2, 2012).

McConnell, L. 1997. "Tradition and Hype Blamed for Violence." *Dominion Post*, March 19.

Schein, Edgar. 1992. *Organizational Culture and Leadership*. 2nd ed. San Francisco, CA: John Wiley & Sons.

———. 2010. *Organizational Culture and Leadership*. 4th ed. San Francisco, CA: John Wiley & Sons.

Schroeder, Peter. 2010. "Changing Team Culture: The Perspectives of Ten Successful Head Coaches." *Journal of Sport Behavior* 32, no. 4: 63–88.

Smart, John, and Edward St. John. 1996. "Organizational Culture and Effectiveness in Higher Education: A Test of the 'Culture Type' and 'Strong Culture' Hypotheses." *Educational Evaluation and Policy Analysis* 18: 219–41.

Splitt, Frank. 2007. "Sports in America 2007: Facing Up to Global Realities." The Drake Group. http://thedrakegroup.org/splittessays (accessed February 2, 2012).

Stockdale, D. 2006. "Wade a Hypocrite, Says Footy Boss." *The Mercury*, September 12.

Widmeyer, Neil, Lawrence Brawley, and Albert Carron. 2002. "Group Dynamics in Sport." In *Advances in Sport Psychology*. 2nd ed., ed. T. Horn, 285–308. Champaign, IL: Human Kinetics.

Xenikou, Athena, and Maris Simosi. 2006. "Organizational Culture and Transformation Leadership as Predictors of Business Unit Performance." *Journal of Managerial Psychology* 21: 566–79.

Conflict and Identification of Asian Immigrants with Professional Sports Teams in the United States: Cultural Elasticity of American Sports

Ji-Ho Kim

Conflict and Identification of Asian Immigrants with Professional Sports Teams in the United States

Sports have been known as a means to help immigrants adapt into a host society. In particular, when considering the cultural value of sports in the United States (US), sports would be seen as something immigrants have to understand to learn American culture. According to previous studies (Kim 2010; Kim and Love 2010; Kim, DeSensi, and Koo 2009; Stodolsak and Alexandirs 2004), immigrants utilize sports as a tool both to learn American culture and to retain ethnic identities. The US Census (2012) showed that there are about forty million immigrants from numerous and divergent cultures in the US and more than 96 percent of immigrant populations are concentrated in major cities in the US, such as New York, Chicago, Washington DC, Atlanta, Los Angeles, San Francisco, and Seattle. This means that we are interacting with people from different cultures. Furthermore, along with a long immigration history in the US, it would not be surprising to find immigrant communities in major cities, such as Chinatown in San Francisco, Koreatown in Los Angeles, and numerous Hispanic communities. When considering different cultural backgrounds of immigrants in the US, it would be crucial to understand different attitudes and cultural distance among immigrants toward sports in America. In other words, it would be hard to understand why Korean and Japanese immigrants follow major league baseball (MLB) even though most of Asian immigrants do not follow MLB, such as Chinese and Indian immigrants. Interestingly, although China, Korea, and Japan are geographically close and also these ethnic groups are sharing many similar cultures, baseball has a totally different status in China compared to Korea and Japan. Therefore, this chapter attempts to illustrate how the Korean immigrant group, one of the largest Asian ethnic populations in the US, utilizes sports as an adaptation tool into the host society, especially through its experiences with baseball games. Furthermore, the author provides managerial implications toward Korean immigrant MLB consumers at the end of this chapter.

Even though there has been a growing interest in ethnic minority markets due to their growing size, purchasing power, and geographic concentration (Jamal and Chapman 2000), little attention has been paid to ethnic minority markets in the sport industry. This chapter focuses on understanding immigrants' experiences in sports as an ethnic minority in the US where arguably sport is considered the most representative culture when considering excessive media coverage allocated to sport and the gigantic scale of the sport industry (Coakley 2009). Plunkett Research estimated the 2011 sport industry size in the US at about $422 billion. The following concept and theories are utilized as a lens to expand our understanding of how immigrants view and experience sports in the US: (a) cultural elasticity, (b) acculturation theory, and (c) social identity theory.

Cultural Elasticity of Immigrant Sport Consumers on American Sports

Economists define the elasticity of supply as "the percentage change in quantity that results from a given percentage change in price" (Leeds and Allmen 2010, 23). Meanwhile, the elasticity of demand is defined as "the percentage change in quantity demanded for a given percentage change in price" (23). These definitions were utilized to explain sport experiences of immigrants in the US. In this chapter, the cultural elasticity of immigrant sport consumers is defined as the extent of immigrants' reaction or acceptance of the American sports culture based on cultural distance related to sport and preacculturation of immigrants. Cultural difference has been considered a significant factor influencing consumers' decision making (Briley, Morris, and Simonson 2000). In addition, viewing Asian immigrants as a homogeneous consumer group is a misconception when considering their different cultures and values (Kaufman-Scarborough 2000). The reaction of immigrants toward American sports is dependent upon the sports culture of their origins and cultural/social value of sports in the local area where immigrants live. In the US, there are about thirty-nine million immigrants from numerous countries and these countries may have either similarities or unique differences in relation to American sports culture. In addition, immigrants' attitude toward American sports culture could vary depending on their cultural distance and preacculturation with American culture before their migration. As is well known, developed technology accelerated globalization, and these days people can easily access and learn about foreign cultures via various media outlets, such as the Internet, TV shows, and social network services. In this regard, recent immigrants may come to the US with a better understanding of the American culture compared to immigrants who came before the 1990s. For instance, MLB became a popular sporting event in South Korea after the first Korean major leaguer had a successful season with the Los Angeles Dodgers in 1996. The emergence of MLB with Korean MLB players as a rival league to the Korean professional baseball league in Korea is considered a significant reason for the decline in the Korean baseball league's attendance between 1995 and 2000 (Lee 2006). In this regard, for Korean immigrants who immigrated to the US after 1996, MLB is not new. Rather, MLB is a form of US-based entertainment that they are used to in Korea through supporting Korean MLB players. From this perspective, Korean immigrants are considered an immigrant group with high-cultural elasticity toward MLB. On the other hand, baseball would be a new sport to Chinese immigrants. Although China is only few hours away from Korea and Japan, cultural values and the position of baseball in its sport culture are very different. In line with this perspective, meanings and attitudes Chinese immigrants have toward baseball would be different from Korean, Japanese, and Taiwanese immigrants in the US. However, in the case of basketball, China has dominated basketball in Asia, and Yao Ming, a Chinese National Basketball Association's (NBA) star player, enhanced the popularity of basketball even greater. At the same, NBA became the most popular sporting event in China with Chinese star players in NBA, such as Yao Ming and Yi Jianlian. Currently, China is the largest NBA market outside the US and it draws an average of thirty million viewers per week and about half of the NBA's international revenue is from China. Approximately, three hundred million people in China play

basketball and the NBA marketing value in China is estimated at roughly
$2.3 billion (Gottlieb 2011). In this regard, recent Chinese immigrants in
the US may have a much less cultural distance toward NBA compared to
MLB. In this case, we can see the different cultural elasticity of Chinese
immigrants toward NBA and MLB.

In brief, American sports are perceived in different ways by immigrant sports consumers and the variance in perception is dependent on
the status of the sports teams, the sporting events, and the nature of the
immigrants' original sports culture. In other words, even though it is
widely accepted that sports have been used as an adaptation means for
immigrants (Coakley 2009), we need to be aware that cultural elasticity
of immigrant sports consumers toward American sporting events can be
a significant moderator on immigrants' experiences in sports.

Acculturation Theory

Acculturation theory has been widely used to explain not only the
adaptation patterns of immigrants (Berry 1997; Berry 1980; Phinney
1992; Zea, Asner-Self, Birman, and Buki 2003), but also recreational
participation (Lee and Funk 2010) and team identification of immigrants
with sport teams (Kim 2010). This theory explains how immigrants have
developed in one cultural context and managed to adapt to new contexts
resulting from migration (Berry 1997). In acculturation theory, acculturation is defined as "the general processes and outcomes (both cultural and
psychological) of intercultural contact" (8). Berry (1980) proposed four
types of acculturation strategies: integration, assimilation, separation,
and marginalization. These four strategies are the results of immigrants'
efforts to adapt to new cultural contexts and the extensiveness of relationships to new and old societies. The positive attitude toward both new
and original societies yields integration. Assimilation is the process by
which immigrants relinquish their culture and accept a new culture; they
become a part of a new society. Segregation occurs when immigrants do
not accept a new culture, but retain their original culture. And, marginalization is caused when immigrants lose their relationship to both their
original and a new culture. Based on the review of the previous immigration studies, Berry (1997) proposed factors that have significant influence
of immigrants' acculturation as moderators on the adaptation process
in the host society. The factors are categorized as prior to acculturation
and during acculturation. The following are considered factors prior to
acculturation: age, gender, education, preacculturation, socioeconomic

status, migration motivation and expectation, cultural distance between the host society and their original culture, and immigrants' personality. Factors that have significant influence on acculturation include length of residence, acculturation strategies (attitudes and behaviors), social support from host society, and social attitudes (prejudice and discrimination from the host society members). In addition, these four different adaptation patterns show bi- or multidimensional adaptation strategies of immigrants entering into the new society. Previous studies showed that Korean immigrants seek to learn the new culture, and at the same time they tend to keep their culture of origin and social ties in the ethnic community (Kim, Lim, and DeSensi 2007; Hurh and Kim 1984; Hurh and Kim 1990; Lee, Sobal, and Frongillo 2003; Stodolska and Alexandris 2004). In consumer research, acculturation has been considered as a significant predictor of immigrant consumer behaviors (Jamal and Chapman 2000; Penaloza 1994). Penaloza (1994) defined consumer acculturation as "the general process of movement and adaptation to the consumer cultural environment in one country by persons from another country" (33). The following are considered significant factors influencing the consumer acculturation: (a) individual differences (i.e., age, language skills, work status, rural/urban residence, social class, and gender), (b) environment surrounding immigrants, and (c) marketing toward immigrants. These factors are similar with the identified moderators in acculturation theory (Berry 1980).

Social Identity Theory

Social identity theory (Tajfel 1982) provides researchers a paradigmatic lens to understand immigrant sport consumer behaviors, and this theory has been utilized as a theoretical framework for team identification in previous studies (Kwon, Trail, and James 2007). Social identity is defined as "the part of the individual's self-concept which derives from their knowledge of their membership in a social group together with the value and emotional significance attached to that membership" (Tajfel 1982, 2). Social identity motivations include self-enhancement/positive distinctiveness and uncertainty reduction. These motivations are considered to lead groups to strive to be both better than and distinct from other groups (Hogg, Sherman, Dierselhuis, Maitner, and Modffitt 2007). Self-enhancement and positive distinctiveness are considered significant motives an individual needs in order to have self-esteem and positive social identity (Sedikides and Strube 1997). With uncertainty reduction, people would like to reduce subjective uncertainty about their social world and their place within their social world. Thus people would like to know "who they are and how to behave and who others are and how they might behave" (Hogg, Sherman, Dierselhuis, Maitner, and Modffitt 2007, 136). In line with this perspective in social identity theory, immigrants in the US may identify themselves as Americans, not immigrants, and this helps them to reduce subjective uncertainty about who they are in the US and to understand expected behaviors as members of the American society, not immigrants. In brief, identifying themselves as a member of a group (social categorization) is particularly effective to reduce uncertainty because "it furnishes group prototypes that describe how people (including self) will and ought to behave and interact with one another" (Hogg, Sherman, Dierselhuis, Maitner, and Modffitt 2007, 136). When considering a symbolic image of major professional sport teams in the US, following representative sport teams in immigrants' local areas would be considered an effort to enter into a mainstream of the host society and to reduce uncertainty about who they are in the US.

Understanding Asian Immigrant MLB Consumer Behavior

Asian Americans count for about 5 percent (13.1 million) of the total American population and more than 95 percent are concentrated in large metropolitan cities in the US, such as New York, Los Angeles, Chicago, Atlanta, and San Francisco (US Census Bureau 2010). These cities are where a number of America's major professional sports teams are located. However, as Kaufman-Scarborough (2000) argued, considering Asian Americans as a group is a misconception. In particular, given the different cultural and social value of sports across different countries, generalizing Asian immigrant sports consumers who are from over thirty Asian ethnic groups in the US would be a misunderstanding. Immigrants from China, India, Vietnam, Philippines, Korea, and Japan account for about 90 percent of Asian immigrants in the US and baseball is only popular in Korea and Japan. With the exception of a few studies, there has been very limited attention paid to Asian immigrant sport consumer behaviors (Kim 2010; Kim, DeSensi, and Koo 2009; Stodolska and Alexandris 2004).

Baseball is the most popular sport in South Korea, Japan, and Taiwan and MLB games became popular in these countries after the arrival of Asian players from these countries. The number of Asian MLB players gradually increased after Nomo Hideo and Chan-Ho Park's successful debut in 1996. In this regard, MLB may not be considered a new culture to Asian immigrants who have watched MLB in their countries before coming to the US. However, except several countries including the US, Canada, and a number of Latino countries, baseball is not popular at all, and baseball was excluded as an official event in the Olympics following the 2008 Beijing Olympics. Only sixteen countries participated in the 2009 World Baseball Classic and with the exception of a few countries, such as America, Japan, Korea, Dominican Republic, Cuba, and Puerto Rico, most teams did not prove to competitive. Therefore, immigrants' reactions and attitude toward American sports could vary depending on cultural positioning and value of baseball in immigrants' origins. At the same time, the status of baseball in their host cities and communities in the US would be another significant factor as the cultural value and popularity of baseball vary geographically. For instance, baseball in Boston and Tennessee would be viewed differently by immigrants in these respective regions.

MLB Revenues from Foreign Countries

Revenues of MLB from international markets have dramatically in-creased since obtaining Asian players, especially from Japan and Korea. The majority of this revenue is from broadcasting right fees. Since the first Korean MLB player, Chan-Ho Park, came to the US in 1995, broad-casting rights fees from Korea have increased more than 1,100 percent from 1995 to 2007. In addition, the broadcasting rights fees from Japan dramatically increased more than 300 percent from 1999 to 2005 and this correlated with the increasing number of Japanese players in MLB (Kim and Jeon 2008). Furthermore, when Chan-Ho Park, a Korean pitcher, was scheduled to play as a starter, there were an additional five thousand people in attendances per game during the 1997 to 2001 seasons. Further, the estimated revenues from Korea and Japan accounted for about 75 percent of MLB's total revenue from its international markets (Kim and Jeon 2008).

Motivation and Team Identification of Korean Immigrant MLB Consumers

Even though there has been considerable attention given to investigat-ing how Asian immigrants use sports as an adaptation means into their host society through participating in sports, little attention, with the exception of a few studies (Kim, DeSensi, and Koo 2009; Kim and Love 2010) has been focused on the motivation of Asian immigrant sport consumers to attend sporting events in the US.

Kim and his colleagues (2009) presented a sociocultural motivation scale of Korean immigrant MLB consumers based on acculturation theory (Berry 1980) and findings of a previous qualitative research exploring meanings of sports to Korean students in the US. The presence of Korean MLB players was shown as the most significant reason to watch MLB games and this is consistent with previous studies (Allen, Drane, Byon, and Mohn 2010; Min and Kim 2009) that Korean immigrants use sports by supporting athletes from the same country to retain their ethnic identity. In addition, both learning American culture and creating social interactions with members of the host society were considerable reasons to attend and to watch MLB games as an ethnic minority in the US. In addition, Kim and Love (2010) compared the sociocultural motivation scale of Korean immigrant MLB consumer and the motivation scale for sport consumption (MSSC) developed by Trail and James (2001) by confirmatory factor analysis (CFA). The MSSC was developed based on data obtained from American sport consumers. The results of the comparison showed that Kim and Love's scale provided a good model fit with data, however, MSSC did not provide an acceptable model fit. The findings of this study showed that Korean immigrant MLB consumers have unique reasons to attend MLB games featuring Korean players. As the researchers expected, sport is utilized as a means to adapt into the host society, while at the same time, sport is used as a means to retain immigrants' ethnic identity.

Team Identification of Korean Immigrants with MLB Teams

Developing team identification has been considered one of the most crucial tasks of sport marketers and many studies showed significance of team identification as a predictor of sport consumer behaviors, such as ticket purchase decisions (Wakefield and Wann 2006), team loyalty during a poor performance period, impulse buying (Kwon and Armstrong 2002), and satisfaction with attending a sporting event (Fink, Trail, and Anderson 2002; Matsuoka, Chelladurai, and Harada 2003). Team identification and satisfaction with game experiences showed significant influences on intention to attend future games (Matsuoka, Chelladurai, and Harada 2003).

With the exception of the studies by Kim and his colleagues, there was no previous attempt to explain team identification of Asian immigrants with professional sports teams in the US. Kim (2010) investigated team identification of Korean immigrants with their local MLB team and MLB teams with Korean players by utilizing mixed-method research approach. Acculturation theory (1980), social identity theory (Tajfel 1982), and sport involvement (Shank and Beasley 1998) were employed to explain team identification among Korean immigrants and MLB teams. The findings of this quantitative research showed that acculturation levels of Korean immigrants and involvement in MLB were significant predictors explaining their team identification with the local MLB team. In particular, when considering a high acculturation level of Korean immigrants as a positive attitude toward their host society, this result could be considered similar with a previous study that "team identity may be caused by the symbolic power of sport teams to represent an associated group identity, such as university, work, gender, or nationality, among others" (Heere, James, Yoshida, and Scremin 2011, 606).

On the one hand, maintaining ethnic identity and cultural competence toward Korea were revealed as significant factors explaining Korean consumers' team identification with MLB teams showcasing Korean players. In addition, the presence of Korean players in MLB games was shown the most attractive factor encouraging Korean immigrants to watch MLB games and approximately 80 percent of the Korean immigrants participated in this study showed that having a Korean player is a significant factor increasing their preference toward a team. The findings of this study were similar to previous studies on consumer behaviors as acculturation was identified as a significant predictor on immigrant consumer behaviors (Penaloza 1994; Watchravesringkan 2011). In particular, Watchravesringkan argued, "Minorities may have attempted to be part of mainstream culture via an expression of certain belief of supporting and buying products made by mainstream culture" (2011, 388). In addition, consumer ethnocentrism was employed to explain immigrant consumer behaviors in many previous studies (Marcoux, Filiatrault, and Cheron 1997; Rose, Rose, and Shoham 2009). According to the concept of ethnocentrism (Campbell and McCandless 1951), ethnocentric individuals tend to be negative toward out-groups, meanwhile they tend to be positive toward in-groups. Previous research showed that consumers showing a high level of ethnocentricity revealed a negative preference toward imported products (Marcoux, Filiatrault, and Cheron 1997; Rose, Rose, and Shoham 2009).

In addition, Kim's qualitative research (2010) showed that previous residence before current residence, attitude toward new culture, and satisfaction with immigrant life in their current residence were significant moderators on the relationship between acculturation and team identification with the local MLB team. According to Gordon (1964), immigrants go though the cultural adaptation period at the early stage of their immigration. Kim's qualitative research showed interesting findings that even though immigrants with high level of acculturation and MLB involvement, some of them were not attached toward their local MLB teams if they claimed the current residence as their second or third residence, but still followed teams located in their first residence area. Furthermore, even some of the segregation adaptation pattern group showing a low level of acculturation revealed high interest in their local MLB team. In this case, the immigrants come to the US as fans of MLB from Korea and they tend to have positive attitudes toward accepting American culture, but they have stayed in the US for a relatively short time to learn American culture and to improve their English language skills. However, MLB was portrayed as a useful tool to learn American culture and to create social interaction opportunities with Americans by supporting their local MLB teams.

Suggestions for Future Study and Implications to Practitioners in the Sport Industry

Cultural elasticity of immigrant sport consumers toward American sporting events and teams would be a useful marketing tool to sport marketers in terms of finding an attractive niche markets among numerous ethnic immigrants in the US. For instance, even though there are more than thirty ethnic groups from Asia, only Asian immigrants from Korea, Japan, and Taiwan are considered consumer groups indicating high cultural elasticity toward MLB. This is attributed to the well-developed baseball culture in their original countries and presence of Asian MLB players. However, the term cultural elasticity is initially used in this chapter by the author to provide a paradigmatic lens. In order to be practically and accurately utilized as a marketing tool, extensive empirical follow-up studies analyzing cultural elasticity of immigrant sport consumers should be conducted. Acculturation theory (Berry 1980), social identity theory (1982), and the concept of consumer acculturation (Penaloza 1994) could provide a starting point for the theoretical framework.

Even though limited studies have been conducted, the discussed theories in the chapter and findings of empirical studies on Korean immigrant MLB consumers provide sport marketers with several implications for their marketing campaigns. First, marketing campaigns toward immigrant sport consumers have to be developed based on a comprehensive understanding of their sport cultures in immigrants' origins. In other words, sport marketers have to be aware of cultural elasticity of immigrant sport consumers toward sport products in the US, such as sporting events, goods, and sport lessons. Second, the presence of athletes from the same country was one of the most appearing factors encouraging Korean immigrants to watch and follow the sport teams to which Korean players belong. Therefore, highlighting the presence of Korean players in marketing campaigns would be effective to attract immigrants' attention toward the games. Third, when considering cultural adaptation generally occurred at the early period of immigration and the significance of the first residence in the host society on immigrant sport fans in developing team identification with American sport teams, public relation activities to communicate with immigrant communities would be an effective way to increase sport teams' brand awareness to recent immigrants. In addition, developing youth sport programs for immigrant families would be appropriate as a long-term strategy when considering the fast growing second-generation immigrant population in the US.

References

Allen, James T., Dan D. Drane, Kevin K. Byon, and Richard S. Mohn. 2010. "Sport as a Vehicle for Socialization and Maintenance of Cultural Identity: International Students Attending American Universities." *Sport Management Review* 13, no. 4: 421–34.

Berry, John W. 1980. "Acculturation as Varieties of Adaptation." In *Acculturation: Theory, Models and Some New Findings*, ed. Amando M. Padilla, 9–25. Boulder, CO: Westview Press for the American Association for the Advancement of Science.

———. 1997. "Immigration, Acculturation, and Adaptation." *Applied Psychology* 46, no. 1: 5–34.

Briley, Donnel A., Michael W. Morris, and Itamar Simonson. 2000. "Reasons as Carriers of Culture: Dynamic vs. Dispositional Models of Cultural Influence on Decision Making." *Journal of Consumer Research* 27, no. 2: 157–78.

Campbell, Donald T., and Boyd R. McCandless. 1951. "Ethnocentrism, Xenophobia and Personality." *Human Relations* 4, no. 2: 185–192.

Coakley, Jay J. 2009. *Sport in Society: Issues and Controversies*. Boston, MA: Irwin/McGraw-Hill.

Fink, Janet S., Galen T. Trail, and Dean F. Anderson. 2002. "An Examination of Team Identification: Which Motives are Most Salient to its Existence?" *International Sports Journal* 6, no. 2: 195–207.

Gordon, Milton M. 1964. *Assimilation in American Life: The Role of Race, Religion and National Origins*. USA: Oxford University Press.

Gottlieb, Benjamin. 2011. "Will Yao Ming's Departure Endanger the NBA in China?" *CNN*, July 12, 2011. http://business.blogs.cnn.com/2011/07/12/yao-ming-departure-could-devastate-nba-in-china/ (accessed March 8, 2012).

Heere, B., J. James, M. Yoshida, and G. Scremin. 2011. "The Effect of Associated Group Identities on Team Identity." *Journal of Sport Management* 25, no. 6: 606–21.

Hogg, Michael A., David K. Sherman, Joel Dierselhuis, Angela T. Maitner, and Graham Moffitt. 2007. "Uncertainty, Entitativity, and Group Identification." *Journal of Experimental Social Psychology* 43, no. 1: 135–42.

Hurh, Won Moo, and Kwang Chung Kim. 1984. "Adhesive Sociocultural Adaptation of Korean Immigrants in the US: An Alternative Strategy of Minority Adaptation." *International Migration Review* 18, no. 2: 188–216.

———. 1990. "Religious Participation of Korean Immigrants in the United States." *Journal for the Scientific Study of Religion* 29, no. 1: 19–34.

Jamal, Ahmad, and Malcolm Chapman. 2000. "Acculturation and Inter-Ethnic Consumer Perceptions: Can You Feel What We Feel?" *Journal of Marketing Management* 16, no. 4: 365–91.

Kaufman-Scarborough, Carol. 2000. "Asian-American Consumers as a Unique Market Segment: Fact or Fallacy?" *Journal of Consumer Marketing* 17, no. 3: 249–62.

Kim, Ji-Ho. 2010. "The Relationship between Adaptation Patterns of Recent Korean Immigrants and Team Identification with the Atlanta Braves Major League Baseball Team: A Mixed Methods Study." PhD diss., University of Tennessee.

Kim, Ji-Ho, and Adam Love. 2010. "Comparison of Motivation Scales in Understanding Korean Immigrant Major League Baseball Consumers: (a) the Sociological Motives of Korean Immigrant Major League Baseball Consumers and (b) the Motivation Scale for Sport Consumption." Paper presented at the annual conference for the North America Society for Sport Management Conference, Tampa, Florida, June 1–5, 2010.

Kim, Ji-Ho, Joy T. DeSensi, and Gi-Yong Koo. 2009. "The Development of a Scale for Sociological Motive of Korean Immigrant MLB Consumers." Paper presented at the annual conference of the North America Society for Sport Management, Columbia, South Carolina, May 27–30, 2009.

Kim, Ji-Ho, Seoungyub Lim, and Joy T. DeSensi. 2007. "The Meaning of Sport to Korean Students in the US." Paper presented at the annual conference of the North America Society for Sport Sociology, Pittsburgh, Pennsylvania, October 31–November 3, 2007.

Kim, Ji-Ho, and Yong-Bae Jeon. 2008. "The Economic Impact of Asian Players Major League Baseball, Focus on Los Angeles Dodgers and the Seattle Mariners." *Journal of Sport and Leisure Studies* 33, 172–82.

Kwon, Hyungil H., and Ketra L. Armstrong. 2002. "Factors Influencing Impulse Buying of Sport Team Licensed Merchandise." *Sport Marketing Quarterly* 11, no. 3: 151–63.

Kwon, H. H., G. Trail, and J. D. James. 2007. "The Mediating Role of Perceived Value: Team Identification and Purchase Intention of Team-Licensed Apparel." *Journal of Sport Management* 21, no. 4: 540–54.

Lee, Soo-Kyung, Jeffery Sobal, and Edward A. Frongillo. 2003. "Comparison of Models of Acculturation: The Case of Korean Americans." *Journal of Cross-Cultural Psychology* 34, no. 3: 282–96.

Lee, Young Hoon. 2006. "The Decline of Attendance in the Korean Professional Baseball League: The Major League Effects." *Journal of Sports Economics* 7, no. 2: 187–200.

Lee, Young-Sook, and Daniel C Funk. 2011. "Recreational Sport Participation and Migrants' Acculturation." *Managing Leisure* 16, no. 2: 1–16.

Leeds, Michael, and Peter Von Allmen. 2010. *The Economics of Sports*. Boston, MA: Prentice Hall.

Matsuoka, Hirotaka, Packianathan Chelladurai, and Munehiko Harada. 2003. "Direct and Interaction Effects of Team Identification and Satisfaction on Intention to Attend Games." *Sport Marketing Quarterly* 12, no. 4: 244–53.

Marcoux, Jean-Sebastien, Pierre Filiatrault, and Emmanuel Cheron. 1997. "The Attitudes Underlying Preferences of Young Urban Educated Polish Consumers towards Products Made in Western Countries." *Journal of International Consumer Marketing* 9, no. 4: 5–29.

Min, Pyong Gap, and Young Oak Kim. 2009. "Ethnic and Sub-Ethnic Attachments among Chinese, Korean, and Indian Immigrants in New York City." *Ethnic and Racial Studies* 32, no. 5: 758–80.

Penaloza, Lisa. 1994. "Atravesando Fronteras/Border Crossings: A Critical Ethnographic Exploration of the Consumer Acculturation of Mexican Immigrants." *Journal of Consumer Research* 21, no. 1: 32–54.

Phinney, Jean S. 1992. "The Multigroup Ethnic Identity Measure a New Scale for Use with Diverse Groups." *Journal of Adolescent Research* 7, no. 2: 156–76.

Plunkett Research. 2011. "The Scale of the 2011 Sport Industry in the US." http://www. plunkettresearch.com/sports-recreation-leisure-market-research/industry-statistics (accessed April 8, 2012).

Rose, Mei, Gregory M. Rose, and Aviv Shoham. 2009. "The Impact of Consumer Animosity on Attitudes towards Foreign Goods: A Study of Jewish and Arab Israelis." *Journal of Consumer Marketing* 26, no. 5: 330–39.

Sedikides, Constantine, and Michael J. Strube. 1997. "Self-Evaluation: To Thine Own Self Be Good, to Thine Own Self Be Sure, to Thine Own Self Be True, and to Thine Own Self Be Better." *Advances in Experimental Social Psychology* 29: 209–69.

Shank, Matthew D., and Fred M. Beasley. 1998. "Fan or Fanatic: Refining a Measure of Sports Involvement." *Journal of Sport Behavior* 21: 435.

Stodolska, Monika, and Konstantinos Alexandris. 2004. "The Role of Recreational Sport in the Adaptation of First Generation Immigrants in the United States." *Journal of Leisure Research* 36, no. 3: 379–413.

Tajfel, Henri. 1982. "Social Psychology of Intergroup Relations." *Annual Review of Psychology* 33, no. 1: 1–39.

Trail, G. and J. James. 2001. "The Motivation Scale for Sport Consumption: Assessment of the Scale's Psychometric Properties." *Journal of Sport Behaviour* 24, no. 1: 108–127.

US Census Bureau. 2010. "Asian Population." http://2010.census.gov/2010census/data/ (accessed November 8, 2011).

Wakefield, Kirk L., and Daniel L. Wann. 2006. "An Examination of Dysfunctional Sport Fans: Method of Classification and Relationships with Problem Behaviors." *Journal of Leisure Research* 38.

Walseth, Kristin, and Kari Fasting. 2004. "Sport as a Means of Integrating Minority Women." *Sport in Society* 7, no. 1: 109–29.

Watchravesringkan, Kittichai Tu. 2011. "Exploring Antecedents and Consequences of Consumer Ethnocentrism: Evidence from Asian Immigrants in the US." *International Journal of Consumer Studies* 35, no. 4: 383–90.

Zea, Maria Cecilia, Kimberly K. Asner-Self, Dina Birman, and Lydia P. Buki. 2003. "The Abbreviated Multidimensional Acculturation Scale: Empirical Validation with Two Latino/Latina Samples." *Cultural Diversity and Ethnic Minority Psychology* 9, no. 2: 107.

Coaching Women's Softball in Iran: The Tale of One American's Journey toward Peace and Understanding through Sports

Sarah J. Hillyer

> *Can I say something directly to the women from your country? I want to send them all a message of peace and tell them that despite our differences, despite the differences in our societies and the ways that we live, we can be great friends. I wish that we keep on having these sports competitions and that one day we go there [America] to play softball and that more women's sports teams come here. We will be very glad to host them and to continue this very important dialogue.*
>
> *—Iranian female softball player, age 27*

Introduction

In February 2000, I traveled to the Islamic Republic of Iran per the invitation of Faezeh Hashemi, President of the Islamic Federation of Women's Sports (IFWS). The purpose of the invitation was threefold: (1) to evaluate women's sports programs in schools, clubs, and federations; (2) to identify strategies to improve women's sports participation in an Islamic context; and (3) to promote dialogue and friendly relations (solidarity) between Iranian and American women through sports-based educational exchanges and friendly competitions.

I confess that I harbored serious doubts about achieving success on all three fronts. Truthfully, I was informed *only* by my own ignorant stereotypes. My imagination of Iran was stifled by haunting images of black shrouds, angry mobs, blindfolded Marines, and burning American flags. I was only eight years old during the American Hostage Crisis, but the black and white television images of the 444-day standoff remained etched in my memory. Regarding Iranian women, I filtered my perceptions through dominant Western media images consumed over a lifetime. What I expected to find in Iran was a backward approach to women's sports—nothing more than a token system completely void of any real or meaningful activity. I also assumed that I would face anti-American hostility, especially as a single, Christian woman traveling alone.

Since 2000, I have traveled to Iran ten times as a sports consultant and coach for Global Sports Partners (GSP). In October 2001, I attended *The Third Muslim Women's Games* as a goodwill ambassador. One year later, I returned to Tehran with a women's basketball team to play in the *Iran-USA Solidarity Cup Friendship Tournament*. Our team was comprised of former NCAA athlete-volunteers and became the first American women's team to compete in Iran since the 1979 Islamic Revolution. In December 2002,[1] I agreed to introduce women's fast pitch softball in three cities: Tehran, Isfahan, and Mashad, per the request and invitation of the Iran Softball Federation (ISF).[2] The following year, I presented a paper titled, "Sport and Religion: A Reciprocal Relationship," at the 2003 *International Council of Health, Physical Education, Recreation, and Dance (ICHPERD) Middle-East Conference* held at the National Olympic Academy in Tehran. In 2005, I represented the United States of America in *The Fourth Islamic Women's Games* as a coach and manager for Sarah Kureshi, an American-Muslim runner. Ms. Kureshi participated as the first and only American-Muslim woman to compete in Iran since 1979. Two years later, the ISF and GSP organized Iran's first-ever international women's softball tournament. The friendly games were held in Tehran's Azadi Sports Complex and included teams from Tehran, Mashad, Bushehr, and an American team made up of former high school and college player-volunteers. In May 2008, I spent one month training players, coaches, and umpires for Iran's inaugural National and Junior National Softball teams. Sadly, I have not returned since the 2009 Iran presidential elections.

Purpose

The purposes for writing this autoethnographic chapter are deeply embedded within a series of life-changing personal experiences as an

American softball coach working with Iranian sportswomen between February 2000 and August 2008. More specifically, the purposes of this chapter are: (1) to confront my previously held stereotypes and reveal my personal transformation toward a new understanding of peace; (2) to provide an alternative narrative that extends sociological understanding; (3) to demonstrate the ways sport works to promote peace; and (4) to offer new ways of knowing and telling through autoethnographic research. This chapter highlights events surrounding the 2007 *Iran-USA Friendship Games*, a friendly softball competition organized by the Iran Softball Federation and Global Sports Partners. The *Games* marked the first and only international competition for Iran's first generation of softball players.

Methods

Autoethnography as defined by Ellis and Bochner, is "an autobiographical genre of writing and research that displays multiple layers of consciousness, connecting the personal to the cultural . . . Autoethnographers vary in their emphasis on the research process (graphy), on culture (ethnos), and on self (auto)" (Ellis and Bochner 2000, 739–40). In autoethnography, the author can no longer claim a detached or neutral position of authority; instead, the author's voice is foregrounded, exposing the author's "naked" thoughts and forcing the author to take responsibility for the way others are framed (Ellis 2004). Autoethnographers, writing within a branch of narrative inquiry (Ellis and Bochner 2000), believe in the power of story and that humans learn through stories lived and told (Ellis 2004). As the writer of an autoethnography, I must tell a story that invites the reader to feel my dilemmas, to think *with* my story rather than *about* it (Ellis 2000). I must write in such a way that the reader can make personal connections to the stories and relate to the narratives emotionally, intellectually, morally, and esthetically (Richardson 2000a). In order to create this two-way engagement with the reader, I must seek transparency and verisimilitude in my writing. As Richardson stated, autoethnographies are:

> Highly personalized, revealing texts in which authors tell stories about their own lived experiences, relating the personal to the cultural. The power of these narratives depends upon their rhetorical staging as "true stories," stories about events that really happened to the writer. In telling the story, the writer calls upon fiction-writing techniques as dramatic recall, strong imagery, fleshed-out characters, unusual phrasings, puns, subtexts, allusions, the flashback, the flash-forward, tone shifts, synecdoche, dialogue, and interior monologue (Richardson 2000a, 11).

As the author of this text, I hope that my writing style will allow the reader to remain actively engaged and make connections to the text that otherwise may not have been possible using other modes of expression.

Expectations: The Reader-Writer Relationship

Just as the writer of an autoethnography is no longer granted permission to "commentate" from the broadcaster's booth, neither is the reader allowed to "spectate" from the bleachers. In autoethnography, the writer and reader have responsibilities—both are expected to actively participate in constructing the meaning of the text. As the author, it is my duty to "capture the imagination of the reader and offer something meaningful about the world [I] have experienced" (Ellis 2000). I will resist the temptation to over-simplify, generalize, or over-theorize sport as a tool for peacebuilding or the sporting context for females in Iran (Bochner 2001). As Bochner suggested, autoethnographers must "think of the life being expressed not merely as data to be analyzed and categorized but as a story to be represented and engaged . . . we shouldn't prematurely brush aside the particulars to get to the general" (Bochner 2001, 132). To be clear, I am not claiming to speak on behalf of *all* Americans, women, or athletes who have ever traveled to Iran since 1979, nor am I declaring to speak on behalf of *all* Iranian sportswomen. Rather, I am maintaining that this autoethnographic text is partial, local, and historically situated (Richardson 2000b), and simply represents my interpretations of the *2007 Iran-USA Friendship Games*.

2007 Iran-USA Friendship Games

Play Ball! Day One

I delivered the pitch and Sarvenaz, a player for Tehran's Red Team, took a hard swing. She made contact and the ball flew high into the air, drifting toward foul territory between the catcher, third-basewoman, and me—the pitcher. Instinctively, we all moved toward the ball and at the last minute, I decided I had the best angle and chance for a diving catch. I waved my arms in the air and yelled at the top of my lungs several times, "I got it, I got it!" Then, I planted my right foot and lunged past the foul line. With my arms and legs completely outstretched, the ball tipped the end of my glove and . . . fell to the ground. "FOUL BALL," the umpire yelled. I immediately grabbed my right knee. Rainey, our team's third-basewoman, knelt down beside me.

Rainey: What happened? I thought you had it?
Sarah: Me too, my bad—but I think I *really* hurt my knee . . .
Rainey: Oh no, are you serious? Did you hear anything pop?
Sarah: I'm not sure—I think so. All I remember is my entire body going forward, but my knee buckled and went in the opposite direction.
The president of the Iran Softball Federation and his assistant walked over from the makeshift press box under the pine trees to check on me.
Ms. Arastoo (assistant to president): Sarah, my dear, honey—are you ok?
Sarah: Thanks Arastoo, I'm not sure. I think I hurt my knee.
Ms. Arastoo: Is there anything you need? We can arrange anything for you, dear.
Sarah: Is it possible to get a bag of ice?
Ms. Arastoo: Yes—I will send for someone right now.
Mr. Zardooz (ISF president): Sarah, are you ok? Do you think it is necessary to see a doctor? We have many qualified sports doctors in Iran. I can begin to make arrangements for you to get your knee examined by a specialist right away.
Sarah: Unfortunately yes—I think I will need to see a doctor. Thank you.
Mr. Zardooz: Please excuse me; I will make some phone calls now and arrange your appointment.
Rainey: Let's move you over to the tent so you can get out of the sun. Water?
Sarah: Yeah, that would be great.
Several players from Tehran's team came over to help me to the large white tent on the third base side of the field. I took a seat in a dark green plastic chair and propped my leg up in front of me on a bench.

The game continued—I put ice on my knee and spent the rest of the time talking to players from the two teams waiting to play in the next game. We discussed strategies, positions, and situations happening throughout the contest. After the game was over, Mr. Zardooz and a few Iranian friends loaded me in the mini-van and took me to see the orthopedic specialist. After the physical exam and MRI results, the doctor called me early the next day at our downtown Tehran hotel to inform me of the news:

"I'm sorry Ms. Sarah, but as I suspected,
you have torn your ACL."

The news made me sick—I was beyond disappointed . . . and a little bit scared. I had managed to avoid knee injuries for an entire collegiate basketball career. *Why now???* I drifted back into a hazy, half-conscious sleep shortly after the team left the hotel to go sightseeing and shopping around the city with our hosts.

Flashback to September 11, 2001

I was riding a stationary bike in my living room when it happened. I watched the second airplane hit the tower in real time. Then my phone rang . . .

Hello.
   Are you watching the news?
Yes, I can't believe this is happening!
   Oh my God. What is this world coming to?
I don't know. I don't know.
   The Pentagon! They just hit the Pentagon too. Please stay inside today.
   I will call you later. I need to call your dad.

Shortly after news filtered in that Osama bin Laden claimed responsibility for the attacks, my phone rang constantly and my inbox filled up with messages:

You're not still going to Iran next month, are you?

If you go, you're crazy and reckless. You shouldn't do that to your family. Not now.

Please don't go again—it's not a good time to be an American in the Middle East!

If you love your grandfather, you won't go back ever again. He'll pay you to stay here.

Can't you postpone your trip until everything settles down?

I felt torn. I felt selfish. I felt confused. I felt strangely curious. It seemed risky (but somehow worth it). On one hand, I felt obligated to honor the wishes of my family and friends. On the other hand, I grappled with an unexplainable urge to overcome *my own fears* about the uncertainty of the world's condition . . . and doing so in the name of supporting the *Third Muslim Women's Games* made it all the more compelling.

I often wonder . . . if I had *not* boarded the plane in October 2001, would I have been invited the next year to introduce women's softball in Iran? I will never know the answer—but I cannot help imagining sometimes that my decision to support the *Muslim Women's Games* on the heels of 9/11 somehow "proved" to my Iranian colleagues that I no longer feared them—instead, I was beginning to trust them; I no longer doubted them—instead I was starting to support them; and I no longer judged them—instead I was believing in their vision to grow women's sports according to their own cultural and religious interpretations.

Play Ball! Day Two

I woke up again when the team returned to the hotel. They came back with lots of shopping bags—an obviously successful shopping excursion for Persian souvenirs and gifts.

Sarah: Did you guys have fun?

Rainey: Amazing. I really cannot believe we are here. It is so much to take in and process. No matter how many times I pinch myself—I still cannot believe it. All the stories you have told us came to life. It is almost like traveling in a time machine—I feel like we have been transported 30 years back in time. The buildings, the cars, the pollution, the atmosphere . . .

Sarah: What time are we leaving for the field? Did you guys already eat lunch?

Rainey: No, we didn't eat yet—we should head downstairs now to meet everyone at the restaurant. You feel up to going today?

Sarah: Absolutely, I am going. I definitely do not want to miss any of it! Besides, since I am not playing I have a lot more time for interviews. Maybe I can actually finish collecting data while we're here.

Rainey: Well, that is one way to make the best of tearing your ACL!

After eating a late lunch (delicious chicken and saffron rice) with our hosts, we loaded up the minibus with our equipment and headed back to Azadi Stadium. On the way, Alison asked me if I knew much about multi sports complex where we were playing our games. I was happy to share a brief history lesson.

"Freedom" Stadium

The Azadi Complex was erected on the western outskirts of Tehran to host the 1974 Asian Championships, the last grand-scale international sporting event hosted in Iran (Amirtash 2005). *"Freedom"* Stadium, the English translation of the word *Azadi*, bears the scars and neglect of the 1979 Islamic Revolution that sought to eradicate all forms of sport.[3] Azadi also reaped the consequences of a long and devastating eight-year war with Iraq (Amirtash 2005). The war left few resources, time, or manpower to maintain the once impressive multi sports complex.

Azadi felt like home to me—I had been training softball players there every year since 2002, even though there are no softball (or baseball) fields on the property. Sometimes women are not even allowed inside Azadi's gates. After the 1979 Islamic Revolution, all sporting venues and events are strictly segregated by gender. For example, Azadi is home to one of the largest football (soccer) stadiums in the world, seating over 108,000 fans. Women are strictly forbidden from the stadium and from watching men play soccer (in shorts). The women's softball teams, however, *have* negotiated the exclusive use of Field Number Four (F#4). F#4 is a poorly maintained practice football (soccer) field situated on the remote back side of the Complex. The deepest corner of the field, farthest away from the gravel driveway, serves as home plate. On the first and third base sides of the field, a few pine trees provide shade from the hot summer sun for the players, umpires, and fans. My favorite part of training or playing at Azadi is an image I hold very dear—Mr. Hassan grooming the field. Mr. Hassan is an older, white-haired gentleman who always arrives at the field on time with two one-gallon cans of white paint, a 2″ paintbrush, a roll of string, and a sweaty, folded piece of paper with the dimensions of a softball field tucked in his back pocket. Mr. Hassan has worked as the chief of the Azadi Sports Complex field maintenance crew since the 1970s. Always smiling, he meticulously paints the field for the women's teams before every competition—complete with a batter's box, base lines, and an outfield "fence."

Game Time

After both teams warmed up for the first game of the afternoon, I set up my video camera, voice recorder, and back-up microphones. I quickly turned my attention from feeling sorry for myself to taking full advantage of the timely opportunity to interview players, coaches, managers, and tournament organizers. By this time, I had already logged more than forty hours of qualitative interviews over the past two years. Now, I was eager to capture thoughts about the first-ever international competition (albeit a friendly competition) for the first generation of women's softball players in Iran. I was also interested in learning more about the ways players have interpreted their experiences as women playing softball since the sports' inception in 2002.

Conversations on Camera

Maryam was the first to volunteer for an interview—nothing about that surprised me. Maryam is strong; physically she is stocky and solid with muscle. She has a strong, loud voice that demands respect—perfect for a catcher. She is an athlete with *presence*. She is humble, yet confident. She is a leader and considers herself the best catcher in Iran. She works hard everyday—she is always the first one to the field for training—she runs laps on her own to improve her conditioning, always before everyone else arrives. She stays after every practice to work on blocking balls in the dirt, framing pitches, taking extra batting practice, and helping younger Iranian players understand the game and improve their skills. As a university coach in the United States, I would *love* to have Maryam on my team—better yet, I'd *love* to have a whole team of Maryams!

Maryam: In the name of Allah, I am Maryam from Mashad, which is in the northeast of Iran near Turkmenistan and Afghanistan. My city is most famous for her beautiful Islamic shrines. Millions of pilgrims travel to my city every year. We are a devout community and take our faith very seriously. I am 27 years old and ever since I was a little girl I really liked baseball. I watched it on satellite television with my father and brothers and I dreamed of learning how to play. I was very glad when I heard that softball has become a new sport for women in Iran. I think softball is a beautiful game that's both fun and entertaining.

Sarah: What is it about softball that is "beautiful, fun, and entertaining" for you?

Maryam: There are so many reasons I believe softball is a beautiful game. If it is okay, I would like to mention three aspects that come to mind right away.

• Number one: Playing softball makes me feel strong and free.
• Number two: Playing softball improves my relationships.
• Number three: Playing softball gives me the feeling and hope that the world can be a better place for our children, our grandchildren, and even this generation.

Sarah: Do you mind sharing some examples of what you mean?

Maryam: Of course not, but please let me know if I talk too much, because I have so much to say.

Perhaps I should tell a story about the first time my father came to watch me play softball.

As you know, I have been an athlete my whole life. I was a "busy and naughty" child as my mother used to say—always full of energy and into everything I could try. I really loved playing sports with my brothers. When I started school, my favorite class was physical education. My father was a very good football player and my mother was a swimming and gymnastics champion.

I started playing organized sports in school at a very young age. I played handball, football, and basketball. I loved them all very much but unfortunately my father and brothers never had the chance to see me play. We respect our religious leaders very much and obey all of the Islamic laws designed to protect the woman, so please do not misunderstand me. Because we [women and girls] play most sports without hijab, men are not allowed to watch and we should not take any photographs of the competitions because we are unprotected. We have a saying in Iran that is really more than just a proverb: "Hijab is not a limitation, but a protection."

Then softball came to Iran. We developed and adapted the sport according to our Islamic traditions, which opened a lot of doors for women who wanted try a new thing. We play outdoors, which is another beautiful part of the game, and our uniforms are modest and appropriate. Catchers like me, we even made a new hijab that fits tightly enough to wear underneath the catcher's mask—when we have to take off our mask during a play, we do not need to worry about our hijab coming off too.

Now, about the first time my father saw me play softball. I will never forget how proud I was to put on all of the equipment in front of him—shin guards, chest protector, facemask, and my catcher's glove. I think the equipment is part of what makes me feel so strong. I feel like a superhero—I feel capable of doing anything in that moment. I played a great game. I hit the ball well and I played very solid defense and our team won! After the game my father was so proud of me. I could see it in his eyes too. He said he couldn't believe how strong I was and he also mentioned that I was a great leader.

I am not sure anyone outside of this situation can understand what it means to share something so special and important with your father. My whole life I felt like something was missing. I knew my father loved me, but until softball became a part of me—he could never *really* understand me. I think now, after *seeing* me play, he not only understands me better, but he also respects me as an athlete. That is one of the greatest feelings for me.

Sarah: I love that story, Maryam! Thank you for sharing it again. Would you mind expanding on some of the ways softball gives you a feeling of hope?

Maryam: As I have told you many times before, I think there ought to be more of these exchanges going around because in order to change their [American women's] minds about us and to see the positive aspects of women's sports in Iran, someone has to do what you are doing. You have to come to Iran and see us for yourself and if you cannot come for yourself, someone needs to tell you or show you the true story. There is nothing to be done, we can only show others that the impression they have of us is wrong. And also, I want to add, having sports without politics is one major way to get friendships in the future between our countries. It's a big way to start friendships and communication.

For example, this friendly tournament, I really like this. I like it when women from around the world can connect through a shared interest like softball and communicate about everything including hijab, religion, and even politics. The foreign media often portrays Iranian women as oppressed because of our hijab; this is not true.

I want to thank your team for coming here with the Islamic hijab and that you played in the same kind of Islamic dress that we wear. It was excellent! We really enjoyed that your team accepted to wear this covering. It is great that, although you are not used to wearing hijab the way we are from childhood, you could still respect our customs and play with the veil. I say this because in the previous years, they [Western people] thought that hijab is a limitation—and that you cannot be a good athlete and still observe the Islamic dress code. But now you have experienced for yourself that you could wear hijab and play freely and with good quality. We appreciate this gesture. I believe talking about things like sports, politics, religion, and Islamic beliefs in hijab, as well as learning about one another's cultures, bring us closer.

Before we started playing softball together, we never really had a chance to meet or speak to an American woman inside our own country. We certainly never had the chance to play sports together and this helps us to understand and to move closer to peace between our people—mainly because we are making new relationships and forming new friendships. We have the chance to see and experience the similarities we share as athletes and as people. The differences seem trivial once we start learning more about one another.

Can I say something now to the *women* from your country who will see this interview?

[*Maryam looked directly into the camera*]

Thank you, yes, I want to send you all a message of peace and tell you that despite our differences, despite the differences in our societies and the ways that we live, we *can be* great friends. I wish that we keep having these sports competitions and that in the future we go there [to America] and play, and that more teams come here more often. We will be very glad to host you and continue this very important dialogue. Thank you.

One week after I returned home from Iran, my father sent me an email:

From: Hillyer, Doc
Sent: August 17, 2007 3:06pm
To: SJH
Subject: You guys are in the news

Hey Sis,
How is your knee feeling? I am praying for a speedy recovery. Let mom and I know if you need us to come down—sometimes ice cream makes ACL injuries feel

better—I'm always here if you need me. Have you seen this most recent blog post about your trip to Iran?

http://thespiritofman.blogspot.com/2007/08/friendship.html
Let me know what you think about it.
Love you,
Dad

THE SPIRIT OF MAN
HISTORY, LIBERTY, DESTINY

TUESDAY, AUGUST 7, 2007

Friendship?

Photo : Javad Moghimi   FARS NEWS

US Women's Softball team is in Tehran and their presence is all over the regime's news media as what I probably can call "Propaganda Campaign."

What does "Friendship" mean when Iranian regime is hell bent on killing American soldiers in Iraq? Well, you may say this is inter-people stuff but, hello!!!! Anything of this sort has the official stamp of the theocratic regime of Iran.

Moreover, look these Americans are wearing hijab . . . Wink! Wink!

More Photos

Post by "Blogger" at 9:28pm

7 COMMENTS:

8/07/2007 10:53 PM

Commenter 1 said . . . In the era of propaganda, these types of Friendships are the most desirable for the "public." On one hand, the regime in Iran calls the US, the Great Satan, and on the other, the American Sisters have been enjoying their stay in Iran, the country which was declared as one of the Axes of Evil.

So, a couple of year ago, we saw that Hollywood "discovered Iran." Then it was Mr. Sean Penn's visit of the country and his "penning his journal" in a Friday's prayer (Namaz-e Joomeh), and now we have the Sisters in Iran. I wonder when the president of the US is scheduled to have his state dinner in Jamah?

8/07/2007 11:17 PM

Commenter 2 said . . . Dear Blogger: Thanks for this educational post. I just realized that I don't know what is going on within the political world. Does it sound like the Government of the United States of America is making a deal with this fascist regime, or am I day-dreaming for some unknown reason?

8/08/2007 12:11 AM

Commenter 3 said . . . It is a mixed message playing nice to great satan's people—a great distraction to the realities that Iran is exporting it's Islamic revolution at an increasing rate, holding off IAEA's requests for transparency and building weapons like mad.

8/08/2007 12:52 AM

Blogger said . . . It's highly unlikely that US government has a hand in such creepy moves. It's a democratic and transparent government and they wouldn't hide their intentions. But it is the naive westerners who bought into the hands of mullahs and their likes and become a tool in the mullahs' propaganda campaign. But, the Iranian women team can't hold any, and I say any, match with any foreign team unless it is approved by the ministry of intelligence or islamic [sic] guidance of the regime. That's why I am furious at such things. Americans must know better but it seems that they don't.

8/13/2007 11:42 AM

Commenter 4 said . . . Americans can be so naive sometimes and down right danger-ous when they do this stuff! Drives me crazy! Sean Penn just visited Chavez as well. More propaganda.

8/13/2007 2:03 PM

Anonymous Commenter 5 said . . . What if this softball stuff results in the populace learning more about the Americans and our values? What if it helps create a hunger for the freedoms we enjoy, that they do not? What if it plays a role in the growth of a movement that fosters a change in the Iranian regime? What if they supply enough women's softball bats to arm a feminist revolution?

8/14/2007 12:39 PM

Commenter 6 said . . . God Bless Adhmenijad.

From: SJH
Sent: August 17, 2007 9:17pm
To: Hillyer, Doc
Subject: You guys are in the news

Dad,

Wow!!! I don't even know where to begin!!! How can people talk this way? They don't know *anything* about *anything related to our work in Iran! Nothing!* I can't even wrap my head around the words they used, "Propaganda Campaign, inter-people 'stuff,' wearing hijab—wink, wink, creepy moves, naïve westerners, tools in the mullahs' propaganda campaign, Americans must know better, so naïve, downright dangerous, drives me crazy, Sean Penn (really?)."

I feel violated—personally and collectively. It is completely unfair that ignorant and harmful judgments can flow so freely from the lips of completely uninformed people. Could we turn the lens back on Mr. Blogger and Mr. and Mrs. Commenters? My questions to them are: Who is spreading propaganda? Who is creepy? Who is naïve? Who must know better? Who is downright dangerous? Who drives people crazy? (Who is Sean Penn? Just kidding—but really, somehow we are the Sean Penn anti-American flavor of the week? If they only knew us . . .).

That's my best effort to respond right now. I'm on my way to rehab and I'm sure more thoughts will come to my mind after I have some time to process this. More later . . .

Love you too,
Sis

Shortly after I hit the send button, I headed to the training room for rehab. While struggling through a fifth set of leg lifts, my own thoughts hit me like a ton of bricks! I struggled to admit to myself that Mr. Blogger and Mr. and Mrs. Commenters were *really no different than me*—I detested their words, their ignorant assumptions, their uninformed stereotypes, and their audacity to speak so carelessly about a group of people they knew nothing about. Ashamed and humbled, I remembered my own thoughts nearly eight years ago:

I confess that I harbored serious doubts about achieving success on all three fronts. I was informed only by my own ignorant stereotypes. My imagination of Iran was stifled by haunting images of black shrouds, angry mobs, blindfolded Marines, and burning American flags. I was only 8 years old during the American Hostage Crisis, but the black and white television images of the 444-day standoff remained etched in my memory. And regarding Iranian women, I filtered my perceptions through dominant Western media images consumed over a lifetime (Stonebanks 2008). What I expected to find in Iran was a backward approach to women's sports—nothing more than a token system completely void of any real or meaningful activity. I also assumed I would face anti-American hostility, especially as a single, Christian woman traveling alone.

A Journey of the Imagination

I distinctly remember the time when my imagination of Iran could only be described as "stifled." I lived within a vacuum of extremes that led to unethical representations of *all* Iranian women (Stonebanks 2008). I situated my life as an American, woman, and athlete in a distinct and dualistic category dialogically opposed to all women living in Iran. As athletes (and humans), Iranian women were "oppressed" because of the

1979 Islamic Revolution. On the other hand, I was "liberated" because of Title IX, the educational amendment passed in 1972. Iran called America the "Great Satan" and America labeled Iran an "Axis of Evil." America is the "sponsor of moral corruption" and Iran is the "sponsor of global terrorism." These dominant and dualistic narratives only serve to destroy what the imagination can hope for.

Relationships. Action. Risk. Paradoxical Curiosity. John Paul Lederach refers to these collective disciplines as the "Moral Imagination" and what makes peacebuilding possible (Lederach 2005). Conceptually speaking, softball provided the unique space and served as the creative action that allowed us to imagine the possibility for a new understanding of peace. Sports also gave us the opportunity to construct alternative narratives based on relationships, action, risk, and paradoxical curiosity. Stonebanks similarly refers to these narratives as the counternarrative. "The counternarrative is used to empower and repair group and individual damaged identities that have derived from the dominant group constructs of identities of certain people through their socially shared narratives or master narratives" (Stonebanks 2008, 294–95).

Through softball, we came into genuine relationship with one another. Through sharing this experience we grew in our understanding of respect, fairness, cooperation, dignity, and vulnerability. We depended on one another. I relied on the players to care for me. I needed them for language, food, transportation, and every other task related to daily living in a country that carefully managed my movements. I completely depended on them for my well-being and survival. As their coach, the players depended on me to teach them the game, the rules, the strategies, and the techniques. Prior to 2002, there was no record of women playing softball in the history of the Persian culture. We started with a chalkboard, a translator, plastic balls and bats (donated by coaches in America), and a small group of university women determined to try something new. We co-constructed the meaning and practice of softball in the context of their environment. In many cases, there were no Persian words or concepts to translate the rules, language, and strategies of the game. We developed our own softball language and negotiated our own space at Azadi to train and play together.

Sometimes this was risky. The women who played softball and the Iran Softball Federation were gently pushing the boundaries of what was deemed acceptable behavior for Muslim women in Iran. We played outdoors and even though we donned the appropriate Islamic attire, we were still taking part in physical activities that challenged gender norms.

Risks were constant, not unlike any constructive act that seeks to promote change. I grew to love and appreciate the women who demonstrated courage in the face of the unknown. Their commitment to improving conditions and opportunities for women to play sports and their ability to imagine better relations between Iranian and American sportswomen continues to inspire me.

Extra-Inning Thought

I thought more about the Spirit of Man BlogSpot and specifically about the statement:

"The naïve westerners who bought into the hands of the mullahs and their likes and become a tool in the mullah's propaganda campaign." I asked myself, "What were these people even talking about, what propaganda campaign?" Then it dawned on me—the banner! The vinyl banner we held in our photos that read:

Iran-USA 2007 Friendship Games
Tehran, Iran

The irony of the "propaganda campaign" accusation is that prior to our team boarding the airplane in Louisville, Kentucky, bound for Tehran, there was no such thing as the *"Iran-USA 2007 Friendship Games,"* not officially anyway. The Iran Softball Federation and Global Sports Partners had never discussed an *official name* for the friendly sports exchange—nor had there been any conversations about media coverage. We were just quietly continuing our collective efforts to grow women's softball in Iran. For us, this tournament was a celebration between the Iranian teams I had been training since 2002 and a team of American athletes who wanted to support their efforts.

But, thanks to my father who had just visited the flea market at the Louisville Fairgrounds—we decided to have a sign made for the *Games* exactly four hours before our flight departed.

Dad (while waiting with us at the airport): Hey Sarah, I was at the flea market yesterday and there was a guy at a booth making big vinyl signs on the spot. The price was really reasonable. Do you want me to run over there and have a sign made for the tournament next week?
Sarah: Sure, how much are they?
Dad: I think for the size you would need to hang up it would cost about $200. I'll be happy to pay for it.
Sarah: Awesome, thanks—what do you think the sign should say?
Dad: How about something like, *"Iran-USA 2007 Friendship Games, Tehran, Iran?"*
And that is the true story of the "Propaganda Machine."

Notes

1. Between 2002 and 2008, I spent at least one month every year introducing and training softball players, coaches, and umpires throughout Iran.
2. The official name is: "Iran Baseball, Softball, Cricket, and Rugby Federation," but for the sake of specificity, I will use the "Iran Softball Federation (ISF)."
3. The Shah of Iran, Mohammad Reza Pahlavi, viewed sports (for women and men) as an integral component of "modernizing" the State. The Islamists, however, viewed sports as nothing more than Western imperialism and a form of neglecting the real needs of the people (Sfeir 1985).

References

Amirtash, A. M. 2005. "Iran and the Asian Games: The Largest Sports Event in the Middle East." *Sport in Society* 8, no. 3: 449–67.

Bochner, Arthur P. 2001. "Narrative's Virtues." *Qualitative Inquiry* 7, no. 2: 131–57.

Ellis, Carolyn. 2000. "Creating Criteria: An Ethnographic Short Story." *Qualitative Inquiry* 6, no. 2: 273–77.

———. 2004. *The Ethnographic I: A Methodological Novel about Autoethnography.* Walnut Creek: AltaMira Press.

Ellis, Carolyn, and Art Bochner. 2000. "Autoethnography, Personal Narrative, Reflexivity: Researcher as Subject." In *The Handbook of Qualitative Research*, ed. N. K. Denzin and Y. S. Lincoln, 733–68. Thousand Oaks, CA: Sage.

Lederach, John Paul. 2005. *The Moral Imagination: The Art and Soul of Building Peace.* Oxford: Oxford University Press.

Richardson, Laurel. 2000a. "New Writing Practices in Qualitative Research." *Sociology of Sport Journal* 17, no. 1: 5–20.

———. 2000b. "Writing: A Method of Inquiry." In *The Handbook of Qualitative Research*, ed. N. K. Denzin and Y. S. Lincoln, 923–48. Thousand Oaks, CA: Sage.

Sfeir, L. 1985. "The Status of Muslim Women in Sport: Conflict between Cultural Tradition and Modernization." *International Review for the Sociology of Sport* 20, no. 4: 283–306.

Stonebanks, C. D. 2008. "An Islamic Perspective on Knowledge, Knowing, and Methodology." In *The Handbook of Critical and Indigenous Methodologies*, ed. N. K. Denzin, Y. S. Lincoln, and L. Tuhiwai, 293–321. Thousand Oaks, CA: Sage.

"Yoga Is Like Medicine": Yoga as a Form of Trauma Relief in Rwanda

Niina Toroi

Background

On April 6, 1994, the assassination of President Juvénal Habyarimana broke a tentative peace agreement signed the year before between the Tutsi rebel forces and Hutu-led government. From April to July 1994, the world witnessed genocide in Rwanda when the Hutu military, supported by the Hutu civilians mass slaughtered the Tutsi minority and moderate Hutu population. The genocide lasted for three months and claimed the lives of up to 800,000 people, 10 percent of the country's population at the time (Ashoka's Changemakers 2008, 2).

Women are among the most vulnerable groups during conflict for more than just violence, they face sexual exploitation and a lack of physical security. Rape and sexual violence are used as a systematic weapon of war. In Rwanda, it is estimated that between 250,000 and 500,000 women were raped during the genocide (United States Agency International Development 2007). The testimonies collected by Handrahan (2004) from the Rwandan genocide reveal how the bodies of Tutsi women became a battleground, a space where men took their revenge and marked their victory, an expansion of ethnic territory by the male conqueror. Rape affects not only its immediate victims, but also the men connected to the victims. It breaks ties between the victim and the rest of the society while helping to form bonds between the rapists (Shehreen 2010).

The genocide left Rwandese deeply traumatized. By the late 1990s, postgenocide Rwanda evolved into a society of collective traumas. In 1994, 24.8 percent of genocide survivors in Rwanda exhibited classic symptoms of posttraumatic stress disorder (PTSD); eight years later, a long-term study showed that this rate had not declined, indicating the lasting effect of trauma due to war and displacement (Ashoka's Changemakers 2008). According to Siegel (2006, xiii), "trauma has a huge impact on all aspects of our human civilization and individual lives. Yet, the reality of trauma is often overlooked in societal approaches to public policy, education, and the resources offered for the promotion of mental health." Trauma leaves unseen traces on everyone affected by the conflict, and unhealed trauma enables one to step out of the cycle of violence. Yoder (2005) explains how trauma and violence are integrally linked: violence often leads to trauma, and unhealed trauma in turn can lead to violence and further loss of security. Unhealed trauma can lead to turning one's trauma energy in on oneself (acting in) or turning trauma energy out on others (acting out). Contrary to the popular adage, time does not heal all the wounds and unhealed trauma can be passed from generation to generation in families, communities, and nations (Yoder 2005).

Besides the psychological effects, the genocide left permanent physical marks to the Rwandese. Most dramatically, the physical effects were experienced by one infected by HIV/AIDS. The mass rapes during 1994 contributed significantly to the spread of the HIV in Rwanda. According to UNAIDS (2008), HIV was transmitted to countless women through rape during the genocide. HIV is a health problem in Rwanda, where approximately 3.1 percent of the population is HIV+ and majority of those infected are women. HIV prevalence among men was 2.3 percent while HIV prevalence among women was 3.6 percent (UNAIDS 2008, 10). HIV/AIDS often doubles the trauma since finding out that one is infected can be tremendously traumatizing. Stigma or the fear of stigma can close the infected one outside the social surroundings and create discrimination.

Culture of Silence

In Rwanda, the victims of rape were not encouraged to come forth with the stories of the atrocities committed against them once the immediate aftermath of the war was over (Shehreen 2010). The culture of silence is strong in Rwanda and people find it difficult to share their stories, problems, or opinions with each other since during the genocide friends turned in friends, neighbors killed neighbors, and even the closest people could not be trusted. This fear of betrayal still echoes in Rwanda's society and makes group therapy, peer support, and story telling difficult. Patterson (2011) claims that social taboos mean that sexual violence remains a silent, unspeakable act. She continues by saying that to make matters even worse, communities often shun the survivors, leaving them alone to face HIV, pregnancy, injuries, and other consequences of sex attacks.

The need for addressing mental health issues sustainably is enormous, not only for the direct victims of the rape, but also addressing the psychological issues for the families and children. Women were not and are not the only ones dealing with trauma and psychological problems. Men as well were and still are in severe need for trauma counseling. Also men were affected by HIV/AIDS and face shame and stigma (Petersen-Coleman and Swaroop 2011). Men who carry the unspoken wounds of their past, are afraid of the stigma of HIV/AIDS, together with unemployment and poverty can easily lead to feelings of fear and powerlessness, creating frustration and anger. Unfortunately, the way many men channel their anger often comes out as violent behavior and their wives are the ones to deal with the consequences. Therefore, from the feminist point of view it is not only the women, who need to deal with their painful memories and need support to overcome domestic violence. In order to promote sustainability and create safe environments for the women, the men cannot be left out of the healing process.

Yoga as a Form of Trauma Relief

Yoga is a widely practiced and rapidly growing physical activity in the western world. Many would argue that yoga is not a sport. "On the physical level, yoga postures, called *asanas*, are designed to tone, strengthen, and align the body. These postures are performed to make the spine supple and healthy and to promote blood flow to all the organs, glands, and tissues, keeping all the bodily systems healthy. On the mental level, yoga uses breathing techniques (*pranayama*) to quiet, clarify, and discipline the mind" (*Farlex Medical Dictionary* 2012). Sport for Development and Peace International Working Group (SDP IWG 2007, 53) defines sport as: "Sport means all forms of physical activity which, through casual or organized participation, aim at expressing or improving physical fitness and mental well-being, forming relationships or obtaining results in competitions at all levels."

Im (2001) defines physical activity as bodily movement produced by skeletal muscles resulting in energy expenditure contrasting to exercise which is defined as a subset of physical activity that is planned, structured, and repetitive and has the improvement or maintenance of physical fitness as a final or intermediate objective.

Project Air is using yoga to help individuals in Rwanda to overcome the devastating effects of the genocide, genocidal rape, and sexual violence. Both ethnic groups are presented and therefore survivors and perpetuators are doing yoga side by side. All the participants are HIV/AIDS. Yoga participants have experienced severe trauma and many have symptoms of PTSD. The majority of the women were raped during the genocide. Many are victims of domestic violence and sexual violence. Poverty, illiteracy, and unemployment are high among the groups. In one of the groups the women are widows, the head of their households, and often their salary being the only source of money for the family. The stigma of HIV affects the whole family.

Many of the men have a history of violent behavior, often targeted at their wives and families. Many have problems with alcohol. Unemployment, the stigma of HIV, and poverty causes frustration and depression.

Project Air works together with a medical NGO called WE-ACTx. Together they are able to provide a holistic program for traumatized HIV+ individuals. Each participant receives HIV medication from WE-ACTx. Before each yoga class, the participants (except one group, independent sewing cooperative) receive trauma counseling. Group discussions are provided by WE-ACTx and facilitated by a Rwandese trauma counselor. The medical NGO also provides the transportation money for the participants. After the yoga class, the participants receive nutrition in order to regain the burned calories. For some, the snack provided by Project Air is the only meal during the day. They often do not get enough nutrition, which is essential for the HIV-medication to be effective.

Research is viewed from the feminist point of view and therefore it is trying to understand how yoga benefits the men, and ultimately affects the lives of the women. The research is a qualitative case study and it was part of master's thesis research project for the UN Mandated University for Peace, Costa Rica. The study focuses on the yoga perspective. However, the program is holistic. The counseling sessions, HIV-medication, nutrition, and transportation money cannot be left out of the analysis.

The data was collected over a period of five months, from July 2011 to November 2011 using in-depth interviews and group discussions. Two females, two males, and two counselors were interviewed using in-depth interviews. The group discussions were carried out for five different groups: four women's groups and one men's group (five to twenty-seven participants). The discussions were facilitated twice for the men's group. The following questions framed the research:

1. Is yoga (together with counseling sessions) an effective tool for trauma relief?
   - Can yoga be used as a tool to overcome the symptoms of PTSD?
   - What are the benefits of yoga on an individual basis? How do the participants experience the yoga practice?
2. How does yoga benefit the people living with HIV/AIDS?
   - Can yoga improve the quality of health and therefore increase the quality of life?
3. How does yoga and counseling benefit the perpetuators of domestic violence?
   - Can yoga positively influence violent behavior?

Results

Psychological Benefits

"Claudia" was fifteen years old during the genocide. Most of her family members were killed during 1994, including her husband. She was mass raped by the Interahamwe and kept as a sex slave for the Interahamwe members throughout the genocide. She was infected with HIV during that time. She remarried, but her husband left her when they found out that she was HIV+. She was left alone with one child. Claudia explained during the interview that until she started to do yoga (year 2007) she was very sick in her mind, like a mad person. She hated everyone and she hated her life. She said yoga changed her life:

> But when I do yoga I am very woman, I have a plan. I study. Trés, trés, bon!! Happy from yoga. Because yoga is like medicament . . . Everyday in the morning I do yoga, everyday I am very happy because I do yoga. Everything I like. You are eating . . . you eat yoga, I eat yoga, I drink yoga, I am yoga. . . my life.

One of the key points during Project Air's yoga class is to make the women and men laugh. When asked what is the best part of yoga or the most important thing during the class, most of women often answered that they are able to laugh. Many of the women thought that sport is only for little children, but now they find it very amusing and fun. Women at all ages can do physical activity, not just the kids, they had realized. Yoga makes them laugh and feel young again. They feel playful and energetic. They are able to laugh and just have fun, that's one of the reasons why they love yoga so much.

All the women's groups said that they enjoy *Savasana*, the final relaxation. They love the fact that they can just lie down and be quiet, and often that's the only time of the day when they can take a rest.

Many said that they have had psychological problems and yoga has helped to cope with those problems. One woman said that before she went from one place to another without really knowing what she was doing or why she was doing what she did. Now she feels she has a clear mind. Within many women depression and other psychological problems have diminished, added the group counselor. One mentioned that she used to be aggressive and angry, but now she has changed. She also said that whenever she feels mentally distracted she does yoga and that really helps her to feel better. One woman brought up that she feels a difference if she doesn't do yoga; she's more tired and her head does not function well.

Besides the traumatic experiences of the genocide, finding out that one is HIV+ can often be traumatizing:

> *You can loose your mind when the test shows that you are HIV positive. You have counselors to help you that you come back in the good mood . . . and there is yoga that can help you. When you are doing yoga practice you don't take time to think about your life. It takes time to focus what you are doing so that's best* (male participant).

In the beginning, it was not obvious either for the counselors or the participants how yoga could benefit one living with HIV. Now yoga has been used as one of the motivators, especially among the men, to join the counseling sessions: "Yoga completes the medication and counseling, together you will get the best benefits," explained one of the counselors. According to the men's trauma counselor, Rwandese men do not like to share their problems with others and often they would like to keep their problems within themselves. Rwandese men are expected to be strong both mentally and physically, which often means that they hide their HIV. The men often don't want to take their medication and they want to stay at home. This often leads to a drinking problem, mentioned the men's trauma counselor. The men also have symptoms of PTSD and many of them have been depressed. Yoga is called a therapeutic sport among the trauma counselors and the same name is used when they encourage the newly affected women or men to join the counseling and yoga groups. Especially, many men agree to come to counseling after hearing that there is the option of sport, mentioned the counselors.

Since yoga started the men always want to come to the practice and "*no one wants to miss the class,*" one man explained. This was not always the case since many of the men were often fighting with others and didn't come regularly for the counseling sessions. One mentioned that he has seen a change among his fellow participants and now the men have more skills to solve their problems without fighting.

When asked if the counselor for the men's group has seen the change in the men, she explained that moral change has happened. She told that there used to be a lot of problems to discuss, but now the counseling session can be shorter since the men don't have so many problems anymore. Earlier they had problems with anger management, problems with their families and they didn't know how to control themselves. One of the men admitted that he has changed after starting the program. He used to be violent and now he has changed. He is not violent anymore. One explained how counseling touches his heart and yoga helps to forget the problems that his heart is holding. One said that if he doesn't do yoga he is not able to feel good. Another one added that he likes the breathing part because it makes him feel good:

> Yes, there is a very big change in my behavior because I have started to practice yoga. I have realized and I feel like I have this change in my mind that it has also brought something . . . change in my behavior . . . because first of all I is feeling calm and . . . for instance yoga helps me to leave alcohol and some other drugs so when you leave that it also changes your behavior with other people and within yourself.

The men's trauma counselor believed that the possibility to share their experiences is psychologically beneficial for the men. Counseling teaches them also about moral and spiritual values. With sport, the men have a chance to forget their problems and just play. Sharing food and playing together are very good for them and they finish the session in a good atmosphere, added the counselor.

The women's counselor has noticed how counseling and yoga have helped the women to live with HIV. Earlier they thought that they would die soon. Now they have willingness to work and to make progress in their lives. They have even started a small cooperative and they are making different handicrafts. They are able to do it, because they are able to plan ahead and think about their future, said the counselor.

One of the counselors noted that she sees a big difference in those groups who do yoga compared to the ones who only get the counseling. The ones who don't do yoga leave counseling with a sad face, while the yoga participants are able to leave with a smile on their faces. "During yoga women don't have time to think about anything else. They don't have time to think about themselves, which is good since they have so many problems in their head."

According to the men's counselor, the men are doing much better now and she sees a difference between them and someone who is new in a group. She also mentioned that in the beginning the men were not nice at all, they were impolite and rude. But today, they are very different and they are able to move on in their lives.

The results of this study showed that yoga being apart of the holistic program has many benefits on an individual level such as: better sleep, feeling mentally more stable and calm, one can focus better, one is able to plan ahead, makes one laugh, allows one to relax, and helps one to forget problems. It showed that yoga helps one psychologically, which could help participant then to overcome symptoms of PTSD as well. The previous studies done about yoga supported (Bessel van der Kolk 2006; Brown and Gerbarg 2005a, 2005b) the idea that yoga could help one living with the symptoms of PTSD. The practice of yoga and strong body development through the physical exercise and the feeling comfortable in your own skin, can contribute substantially to help one to come into the here and now rather than staying stuck in the past (Bessel van der Kolk 2006).

The positive experiences of yoga motivate one to come to the counseling sessions regularly, so the long-term benefits to overcome trauma can therefore assumed to be helpful. The question of reducing symptoms of PTSD can also be considered the cause of the frequent participation in the program.

Physical Benefits

Throughout the group discussions and individual interviews, many of the participants mentioned that they feel young and energetic again. This could be part of the fact that many mention that they are able to sleep better. One woman explained how yoga helps her to feel good in your own skin, in your body, in your brain, and seeks the solutions to be calm.

The women's counselor has learned from the discussions that some of the women have less pain in their back and some have said that they are able to walk longer distances since they pay more attention on their breath while walking. Some find it motivating to do yoga since they want to get smaller bellies, explained the counselor.

During group discussion, two women mentioned that they think that yoga has helped them with osteoporosis. One had seen a doctor and explained that she does physical exercise called yoga, and the doctor had seen it to be helpful. Many in the groups said that their muscle pain or the pain in the body has decreased. Both women and men mentioned that they find the breathing exercises very effective. One woman said that if she's not able to sleep, she just listens her own breathing that helps her to go back to sleep.

The men's counselor remembered that before yoga started many of the men were very weak and she has seen the physical change in them. According to the counselor, they seem to look stronger and more energetic. She also pointed out that in the beginning most of the men had problems with breathing and it was even painful for them. The men had complained that they had pain around their chest when they breathed. The men themselves said that they feel physically stronger than before. Two said that the pains in their bodies have vanished. One explained that he was almost paralyzed and after starting to do yoga he feels great and he is even able to do all the exercises, which in the beginning was not possible for him. One had problems with his hands; they were cramping and very stiff. Now his hands feel much better and not so painful. One of the men used to go often to the chiropractic, but now he doesn't need to go anymore. An older man said that yoga has been good for his rheumatism. One male participant, who has been part of the men's group for two years and has been doing yoga for more than eight months, has seen a change in himself, but also in his fellow yoga participants:

> *For example those who had problems with their back or those who were not able to walk properly are now able to walk well. So for him, he sees a very, very big difference from what was happening before yoga and then what is now happening.*

One man remarked that he is smaller and more muscular than before and also people come up to him telling him that his body has changed and he looks strong. Another one mentioned that he has done other sports and after starting to do yoga he is able to play basketball or football longer than earlier.

When one feels strong and healthy in his/her own body, it has an affect on mind as well. Seeing the person from the holistic point of view, being healthy physiologically, mentally, and socially can be assumed to be helpful to overcome trauma. Besides the psychological benefits, yoga seemed to have many physical benefits. In this study, yoga made one stronger and more energetic, made one feel young, reduced muscle pain and pain in the body, breathing became more effective, one felt fit and healthier. A few mentioned that yoga has helped with osteoporosis, rheumatism, one didn't need chiropractic anymore, and one was almost paralyzed, but is able to move well now.

The fact that one felt physically stronger and mentally more stable helped one to believe that by taking care of one's own health holistically improves well-being, and therefore improves the quality of life. The counselors said that earlier the participants did not want to think about the future, since they believed that with the HIV they die soon. General well-being helped the participants to plan ahead and dream about the future.

Social Benefits

Gathering together as a group once a week proved to be important for most of the participants. HIV/AIDS is still a taboo in Rwanda and many HIV+ people face a stigma. Both women and men explained that counseling and yoga have helped them to accept that one is HIV+. One of the men said that whenever he goes to the WE-ACTx clinic to get the medicine and he sees the other HIV+ people lined up there, he feels sick. But it is different when he comes to the men's counseling/yoga group, he feels like part of the group and the feeling of sickness is absent. He mentioned that it is good to be together as a group: *"We share our lives in a group."* The groups have become an important source of support and the members have become friends. One man explained how he considers his fellow counseling participants to be his friends now.

One women's group works together (sewing cooperative), and they mentioned that yoga has really brought them together. One's history, background, age, or life conditions do not matter. They feel like they share something together since they practice yoga twice a week during the workday. They feel unity among the group. They are now one and they care each other. Before yoga started everyone only thought about oneself and didn't care about the others, but it has changed now. They have a same future and they want to work together to make it look better.

Also in the women's group, one brought up the fact that being part of the counseling and yoga group has helped her to accept being HIV+. Others nodded, and added that they are able to share their ideas, problems, and health issues (not only their own, but family health issues as well) and find solutions for their problems. They are able to discuss about similar issues and recognize that they are not alone with their problems.

One of the male participants felt that yoga has helped him to improve his relationships with others: *"After opening your mind it also helps you to improve your relationships with your neighbors, people you live together with a family or just everywhere that you come across others, everyone."*

Many of the participants said that they don't only practice yoga during the class, but also at home and often with their families. One said that since she has seen a change in herself, she wants to be a yoga teacher so she can help others in the community. The question of practicing yoga at home was not asked in the interviews and most often the participants brought up the issue spontaneously. A few times the answer came up when they were asked if and how yoga and counseling have improved their relationships with others. One of the men explained that his wife, who is also HIV+ and doesn't have a chance to go to the support group, has started to do yoga home since she has seen how yoga has changed him: *"My wife, she always tries to do or to repeat some exercises that she has learned from me and so . . . she always wants to do it because she has seen the change in me."*

According to the men's counselor, practicing together as a family is helpful and the men have said that it changed a lot of the atmosphere at home. One of the men said during the group discussion that he is able to be well with his family since he feels good in his head, and yoga helps him to feel good. Many of the women mentioned that it is easy to do yoga with the children at home.

Counselors pointed out that eating together after the practice had a social meaning: "It is extraordinary to eat weekly together as a group. The Rwandese share their meals usually only during celebrations, so for the yoga participants it is a party or celebration every week when they share their milk and bread with others."

This study proves that the opportunity to come together as group and practice yoga together can be effective for mental well-being and rebuilding trust with others. The counseling sessions, as well as the time before and after the yoga practice, offered a safe place to share memories, opinions and feelings, discuss problems, and share joy. One was able to extend social network beyond family and create new relationships. Providing a specified space for women's and girl's sports activities, not only has practical aspects but also has a symbolic character, since public spaces and physical activities are often provided to males. Women were able to share, get support, advice, and get aid during the counseling session for questions such as domestic violence and sexual violence. A holistic program with yoga binds vulnerable people together and teaches one's rights. Program also made participants realize that they have someone to listen to them.

Being part of a support group has helped the men to understand their violent behavior and to find solutions to overcome aggressive behavior.

A few men admitted that they are no longer violent. Also the counselors supported this view. The men's counselor explained that she has seen the change in the men, not only physically but also mentally as well. She sees a change in their moral values and believes that it is learned through talking, sharing, and getting advice from the other men. The counselor believed that the men are able to address their violent behavior and frustration in the practice of yoga. Also the men are teaching yoga to their wives and children. This has helped to change the atmosphere at home, and brought the family members closer. It also showed that when one feels mentally more stable it helps her/him to interact better with others.

Social togetherness seemed to be important aspect to become familiar and to accept one's life with HIV/AIDS. Participants were able to discuss with HIV without the fear of being stigmatized. Seeing other infected individuals helped women and men overcome difficulties related to HIV.

Conclusion and Recommendations

This study shows how a holistic program may benefit one living with trauma. Yoga as part of the holistic program can be used as a trauma relief. However, the findings are based on a small number of people interviewed ($n = 6$), and five groups, which consisted of five to twenty-seven participants. More studies need to be done before yoga can be fully be recognized and recommended as a tool for trauma relief. There are several limitations of the study that the readers should be aware of. The research did not have focus groups that could have been compared with the groups who get counseling and yoga. Most of the participants did not speak English or French, they only communicated in Kinyarwanda. Counselors spoke French so during the classes they were able to help with the instructions if needed. All the yoga classes were taught in Kinyarwanda, which limited my ability to give precise instructions. One of the limitations for both the group discussions, and the interviews, was the translation process. The individual interviews were conducted either in English or in French, for one I had an interpreter helping with the interviews. For the group interviews, counselors translated from French to Kinyarwanda. The process of translation always affects the message delivered.

Many of the participants did not know how to read and write. Therefore, written questionnaires were inappropriate. The vulnerability of these marginalized people casts a shadow over the research and makes it very challenging in terms of not risking anyone's identity or creating more stigma around these people. Therefore, the questions had to be mindfully chosen so the research would not unfold the traumatic experiences, creating more harm than good.

Extra awareness and carefulness needed to be taken under consideration when I mentioned any of the comments made by the counselors. They have created a safe place for the participants to share any of their feelings or problems, and they are deeply trusted and respected. Any information coming from the counselors that might reveal the group or individuals that she is working with cannot be included in this chapter.

It shall be noted that my personal knowledge of counseling and psychology is also limited and based on basic sport psychology courses as well as independent psychology studies. Therefore, the recommendations are only based on these individual experiences and cases in Rwanda.

According to the results of this study, yoga may benefit one living with traumatic experiences and symptoms of PTSD. Yoga being part of the holistic program can be helpful for one living with the HIV/AIDS, since yoga helps to strengthen the body and it is able to calm one's mind. On top of that, the group support seemed to be giving positive benefits socially and strengthened the others' trust. Yoga influenced the men in the program to be more aware of their violent behavior and also seemed to reduce their violent behavior. Therefore, yoga could be seen as beneficial for the perpetuators of domestic violence or people with violent behavior. However, it is impossible to draw conclusions based on this study how sustainable the results are in terms of violent behavior.

More studies need to be done using focus groups with yoga and without yoga. For Project Air, it would be beneficial to include physical tests for the new participants. Frequent physical tests would show how yoga is beneficial for people living with HIV physiologically. Frequent psychological tests or interviews being integrated into the program would create an understanding of yoga's psychological benefits. It would be interesting to analyze the difference between various physical exercises as well, one focus group doing yoga and the second group doing another sport.

Although in general the experiences with yoga were very positive, it is good to note that women's empowerment can be regarded as a threat from the male's perspective. The inclusion of men and creating an understanding of the overall benefits is therefore extremely important. The presence of the trauma counselors and creating a safe environment for the yoga classes is recommended since silent physical exercise, images, or body postures can trigger traumatic experiences. The question of negative effects of yoga was brought up during the interview, but most likely due to the cultural background negative sides were not mentioned, besides some muscle pain. However, similar studies have been done and negative affects have been noted. Geretz (2010, 28) studied yoga's role in transforming trauma in urban youth in Sierra Leone and found that "being aware of their thoughts within a given moment through practicing yoga and mindful breathing that they became more aware of the negative affect they had previously not attended to." Similar findings were done in Norway where yoga was taught for inmates in high security Ringerike jail near Oslo. The prison stopped having yoga classes when they noticed that yoga brought up intense emotions in the prisoners. Prison lacked the recourses to treat emotions unleashed by the deep breathing exercises, reports the BBC (2005).

In general, the participants had very positive experiences with yoga. Being able to laugh and share the joy with others connects people. Learning to respect your body and to find the strength in you helps to build a better self-esteem. Feeling healthier and stronger encouraged one living with HIV to plan ahead and think about the future. Calming your mind during yoga and using the power of breath in everyday work enabled one to stay focused. Better sleep made one feel energetic and young again. It was said "Yoga is like medicine."

Peace

Despite worldwide condemnation of mass rapes in both Rwanda and the former Yugoslavia in the 1990s, the trend toward targeting women has continued. It is perhaps more dangerous to be a woman than a soldier in an armed conflict (Patterson 2011).

Globally, rape has been used as a weapon of war and in fact seems to be getting even more advanced and organized than ever before. A study done by the American Journal of Public Health shows that in the Democratic Republic of Congo 1,100 women are raped everyday (*Sydney Morning Herald* 2011). It is estimated that in South Africa, a woman has a greater chance of being raped than learning how to read (Rape Statistics—South Africa and Worldwide 2011). According to the International Criminal Court (CNN 2011), the security forces in Libya were allegedly using sexual enhancement drugs as a machete and gang-raping women they stopped at checkpoints. There were reports of male sexual enhancement drugs and Viagra used as a tool of massive rape.

Although rape is a common weapon of war and used in conflicts and postconflict areas, the aftermath of rape is not widely recognized. In fact despite extensive documentation on the detrimental effect of trauma on reconstruction, a very small percentage of postconflict reconstruction funding covers programs to address mental health, notes USAID (2007).

Sport has been recognized as an effective tool for peacebuilding, peacekeeping, and conflict management by different organizations, governments, societies, and individuals. However, many of the sports for development and peace programs are targeted for children and adolescents, and especially for boys. In Rwanda, many trauma-healing programs are concentrated primarily on trauma counseling for children (Petersen-Coleman and Swaroop 2011).

The vulnerability of women during and after the conflicts creates a great demand for gender sensitive, holistic reconstruction programs. The research and my personal experiences as a teacher for Project Air proved that yoga is a powerful tool for people living with traumatic experiences. As a teacher, I was often able to see the change in my students' faces every time after the yoga class. The sensations, laugh from the classrooms, smiles, sound of the breath, or the look on the participants' faces during the class never made it into this chapter. The chapter is also missing the effect of a touch. When hands were touched against women's and men's hands during the final relaxation, their bodies went from tensed to relaxed without any worries. Classes were filled with the joy of learning. No matter which ethnical group they represented they all faced challenges in life. Participants cried and laughed, lost family members, had not enough to eat, worried about their children's education, were afraid of their husbands, feared of losing a wife or losing a husband. They were poor, ashamed of HIV+, and some had no place to stay. Yet they never lost their faith, moved on day after day, were able to smile, and work after losing everything. Every week the participants proved how they were able to hop on a mat and allow their bodies to become strong, minds to be free, and hearts to be open.

References

Ashoka's Changemakers. 2008. "Mental Health Care for Youth in Post-Conflict Rwanda: Current Policy and Recommendations." *International Center for Attitudinal Healing.* http://www.corstone.org/html/downloads/CorStoneRWANDA.pdf (accessed July 15, 2011).

Bessel van der Kolk. 2006. "The Limits of Talk Bessel van der Kolk Wants to Transform the Treatment of Trauma." http://www.traumacenter.org/products/pdf_files/Networker. pdf (accessed July 15, 2011).

The British Broadcasting Corporation (BBC). 2005. "Yoga Classes Provoke Prisoners." *News Europe*, August 3. http://news.bbc.co.uk/2/hi/europe/4743741.stm (accessed July 15, 2011).

Brown, Richard P., and Patricia L. Gerbarg. 2005a. "Sudarshan Kriya Yogic Breathing in the Treatment of Stress, Anxiety, and Depression: Part I—Neurophysiologic Model." *The Journal of Alternative and Complementary Medicine* 11, no. 1: 189–201. © Mary Ann Liebert, Inc. http://thevirafoundation.org/images/Trauma_Treatment_Breathwork_Part_I.pdf (accessed July 15, 2011).

———. 2005b. "Sudarshan Kriya Yogic Breathing in the Treatment of Stress, Anxiety, and Depression: Part II—Clinical Applications and Guidelines." *The Journal of Alternative and Complementary Medicine* 11, no. 4: 711–17. © Mary Ann Liebert, Inc. http://www.reconnectwithfood.com/resources/documents/yogaandptsd.pdf (accessed July 15, 2011).

CNN. 2011. "ICC to Investigate Reports of Viagra-Fueled Gang Rapes in Libya." International Edition. http://edition.cnn.com/2011/WORLD/africa/05/17/libya.rapes.icc/index.html (accessed July 15, 2011).

Farlex. 2012. "The Free Dictionary Online." http://medicaldictionary.thefreedictionary.com/Yoga (accessed July 15, 2011).

Geretz, V. J. 2010. *A Case Study on the Role of Yoga in Trauma Transformation: Sierra Leone.* San Diego, CA: University of San Diego.

Handrahan, Lori. 2004. " ." *Security Dialogue* 35: 429–45. http://sdi.sagepub.com/content/35/4/429.refs (accessed July 15, 2011).

Im, E. O. 2001. "Nursing Research on Physical Activity: Feminist Critique." *International Journal of Nursing Studies* 38: 185–94.

Patterson, K. 2011. "Rape as a Weapon of War." *The Vancouver Sun.* http://www.vancouversun.com/entertainment/pne/Rape+weapon/5112855/story.html (accessed July 15, 2011).

Petersen-Coleman, M. N., and S. R. Swaroop. 2011. "Complex Trauma: A Critical Analysis of the Rwandan Fight for Liberation." *The Journal of Pan African Studies* 4, no. 3: 1–19. http://www.faqs.org/periodicals/201103/2323094871.html (accessed July 15, 2011).

Rape Statistics—South Africa and Worldwide. 2011. http://www.rape.co.za/index2.php?do_pdf=1&id=875&option=com_content (accessed July 15, 2011).

Shehreen, K. 2010. "Healing the Hidden Wounds of War." *Daily Star*, December 5. http://archive.thedailystar.net/newDesign/news-details.php?nid=164767 (accessed July 15, 2011).

Siegel, D. J. 2006. "Foreword" In *Trauma and the Body. A Sensorimotor Approach to Psychotherapy.* Ed. P. Ogden, K. Minton, and C. Pain, xiii. New York and London: W. W. Norton & Company.

Sport for Development and Peace International Working Group (SDP IWG). 2007. *Literature Reviews on Sport for Development and Peace.* Canada, Toronto. http://www.righttoplay.com/International/news-and-media/Documents/Policy%20Reports%20docs/Literature%20Reviews%20SDP.pdf (accessed July 15, 2011).

The Sydney Morning Herald. 2011. "1100 Rapes a Day in Congo, Study Finds." http://www.smh.com.au/world/1100-rapes-a-day-in-congo-study-finds-20110511-1ei0m.html (accessed July 15, 2011).

UNAIDS. 2008. "United Nations General Assembly Special Session on HIV/AIDS." Country Progress Report. http://data.unaids.org/pub/Report/2008/rwanda_2008_country_progress_report_en.pdf (accessed July 15, 2011).

United States Agency International Development (USAID). From American People. 2007. "Women & Conflict. Introductory Guide for Programming." http://www.usaid.gov/our_work/cross-cutting_programs/conflict/publications/docs/cmm_women_and_conflict_toolkit_december_2006.pdf (accessed July 15, 2011).

Yoder, C. 2005. *The Little Book of Trauma Healing: When Violence Strikes and Community Security is Threatened.* Intercourse, PA: Good Books.

Sports in the Psychological and Social Demobilization of Child Soldiers

Kim Fletcher and Peter St. Pierre

At the turn of the century, an estimated three hundred thousand children were engaged in organized combat in some capacity (Machel 2001). While the use of child soldiers is not a new phenomenon, it is gaining increased consideration as our understandings of childhood and human rights change (Honwana 2006). In addition to the attention child soldiers are getting from the academic and advocacy communities, service-delivery organizations began to implement child-specific disarmament, demobilization, and reintegration (DDR) programs in the early 2000s (see Morse 2008).

The use of sports in DDR programs for children followed not long after. Sports were first included in an unofficial capacity to fill free time, but later evolved into formal components of the programs as tools to enhance their effectiveness. The problem with the employment of sports in DDR is that they potentially have both positive and negative psychological and social consequences. What is needed is greater theoretical understanding of the aims of DDR and how sports can be used mindfully to enhance their potentially positive effects and mitigate those effects that are potentially negative. In the following chapter, we aim to provide such a theoretical framework for the use of sports in the DDR of child soldiers.

We begin with a brief discussion of the historical use of child soldiers and their recruitment. This history is followed by background information on the DDR process in general and some of the specific challenges faced by those implementing programs for children. We then examine the psychological and social roles sports can play, and conclude by applying the lessons learned to the DDR process for child soldiers.

A Brief History of Child Soldiers

Records of children on the front lines in armed conflict exist from the middle ages (Honwana 2006). While current discussions of child soldiers tend to evoke images of Africa and Southeast Asia, historically the use of child soldiers was not limited to specific geographical areas. During the US Civil War, nine- and ten-year-old "drummer boys" often started as *aides-de-camp* but soon entered the fighting ranks. Some scholars estimate that as many as one-third of the Civil War's combatants were under the age of eighteen (Rosen 2005).

Children continued to fight on behalf of the United States as recently as World War II, when Calvin Graham, the United States' youngest enlisted serviceman, joined the Navy at the age of twelve (Boyer 2011). Legally, enlisted men and women had to be eighteen or older (seventeen with parental consent), but at the time armed service recruiters rarely asked for proof of age. Minors who were caught were sometimes discharged, but many stayed until the war ended or they were killed. Outside the United States, thousands of children took part in the Jewish resistance, the Polish *Szare Szeregi* (Gray Ranks), and the Soviet Red Army.

The number of children in official state militaries has declined since the Convention on the Rights of the Child came into force in 1990. However, the use of children as a percentage of active combatants in irregular forces has increased in recent decades. This rise in recruitment of child soldiers is often credited at least in part to the increased availability of light weapons. The eight-pound AKM is a weapon of choice among rebel groups, and it is argued that it is so simple a ten-year-old can learn to strip and reassemble it (Machel 1996). However, David Rosen points out that the AK-47 has been available since 1949, while the increase in child soldiers is much more recent (Rosen 2005). Rosen also reminds us that rocket propelled grenade launchers, which weigh a significant twenty-two pounds loaded, are popular among groups employing child soldiers. Therefore, the accessibility of light, easily maintained weapons alone is not enough to account for the increase of children in combat. Changes in the nature of warfare, however, may account for much of the change in fighting forces' demographics.

While child soldiers are often seen as victims who are kidnapped or otherwise forced into fighting, this view overlooks two key facts. First, many child soldiers join by choice (Rosen 2005). Second, for children, joining an armed faction in current wars can be the logical decision. During World War I, civilians accounted for approximately 10 percent of the casualties. In World War II, that number rose beyond 50 percent. In today's guerilla wars, more than 90 percent of the casualties may be civilian (UNICEF 2011). The statistics suggest that the shift in the nature of warfare may be more salient than the changes in weaponry when attempting to account for the increased use of child soldiers. While forced recruitment does occur, hostile groups do not have to rely on kidnappings or other means of coercion. Interviews with child soldiers suggest that they choose to fight for their own protection, to protect their villages, or sometimes to avenge friends or relatives (Peters and Richards 1998). Neryl Lewis goes so far as to argue that the "least dangerous place to be in a war today is in the military" (Lewis 1999, 96). Many children may join armed factions because remaining a civilian means almost certain death.

With the rise in child soldiers, a major challenge facing those who work in postconflict reconstruction is the DDR of these children. One needs to only turn on the news to find stories of well-trained adults who have difficulty returning to civilian life. Demobilizing and reintegrating children who lack the training, maturity, and prior experience to deal with the adjustment can be particularly challenging.

Disarmament, Demobilization, and Reintegration

The process of transforming ex-combatants from soldiers into civilians typically consists of three phases: disarmament, demobilization, and reintegration (DDR). In the disarmament phase, small arms and light weapons (SALW) are collected and disposed of. The United Nations Security Council suggests that disarmament is a key step in peacebuilding, arguing that "even if full disarmament and demilitarization prove unachievable, a credible programme of disarmament, demobilization and reintegration may nonetheless make a key contribution to strengthening of confidence between former factions and enhancing the momentum toward stability" (UN Security Council 2000, 1).

While it is a simple idea in theory, disarmament programs face several challenges in practice. Ex-combatants are not always willing to give up their weapons, and often their desire to keep a gun is rational. If the people or groups doing the disarming cannot guarantee the safety of those they wish to disarm, then taking away their means of protection is a disservice at a minimum. In addition to providing security, weapons can be symbolic of prestige or simply of manhood. Removing them in these cases is not as easy as setting up a drop-box and offering one hundred dollars a gun (Ashkenazi February 21, 2012).[1]

The second stage, demobilization, is "the process by which the armed force of the government and/or opposition or factional forces either downsize or completely disband" (Knight and Özerdem 2004, 500). Again, this process sounds simple in theory; the fighting has stopped so soldiers can become civilians again. In practice, however, the "formal" disbandment of military groups is the easy part of the process. The informal social and psychological demobilization of ex-combatants is much more difficult.

Identification with an armed group is more than a formal title. It is a relationship. It is a community to which an individual belongs, whether he or she joined by choice or was forcibly recruited. For an ex-combatant to be considered fully demobilized, the community with which he identifies should be shifted from soldiers to civilians. Social and psychological demobilization also means dismantling the previous hierarchical structures that underlie the militant system. If a former soldier was taught to obey a commander's orders, simply taking him off the battlefield does not remove the inclination toward obedience. The enterprising commander knows that it likely would not be difficult to convince those in his ranks to follow him again in legitimate or illegitimate activities if the need arises (Ashkenazi, February 21, 2012). Therefore, the demobilization phase should be used to undo the hierarchical social structures of the fighting forces, and to teach the ex-combatant that there are times when it is appropriate to question authority.

The final phase in the DDR process is reintegration of the ex-combatant into his home community. Ex-combatants often find little to return to and have varying abilities to deal with the consequences. Reintegrating adults and older children means sending tens of thousands of unemployed people back into an already saturated or nonexistent job market (United Nations Development Programme 2008). In addition, the social services and support structures available in many developing countries are already poor. To exacerbate the problem, ex-combatants are detached from social support networks—kin groups and communities—they would have enjoyed if they had not joined the fighting forces. Challenges differ for younger children.

The Challenges of DDR among Children

Disarming children can prove especially difficult. Child soldiers have been taught that their gun is their "protector," their "provider," and their "safety" (Beah 2007b). As Michael Ashkenazi (February 23, 2011) puts it, "You are talking about a group of kids who have learned to get what they want and need by pointing a gun at someone and saying 'give me.'" Removing their weapon is removing both their means of survival and, for many, a connection to their new "family." While we may think any child would be thrilled to leave the war, it takes a great leap of faith to give up those two things, and the entire process is often accompanied by a high degree of anxiety. In order for any DDR program to be successful, a means of reducing anxiety must be considered and implemented.

As with disarmament, psychologically and socially demobilizing children from the armed forces has its own challenges. During the conflict, the armed group took the place of the child's family in that the force provided food, shelter, and protection. Demobilizing him means removing him from the perceived family environment in an attempt to make him dissociate from that group.

Many children spent their formative years with the armed force. One of the reasons children make excellent soldiers is because, once trained, they may not have the inhibitions that adults have. Their instinct becomes to kill those with whom they have a problem. In trying to turn a child soldier into a civilian, this training is problematic for two reasons. First, the now-instinctual method of problem solving through violence must be unlearned. Second, the children have to learn that many of their actions would be considered wrong by society's standards. They likely engaged in acts that they did not consider particularly extraordinary at the time, but become more traumatizing as they reflect on them through new lenses and standards of behavior. This moral reorientation is an added psychological challenge in demobilizing young ex-combatants.

A consistent critique of child-focused DDR programs is their definition of "child." UNICEF delimits "childhood" using an arbitrary age limit of eighteen. While in the Western context this limit seems almost natural, eighteen-year olds in countries employing child soldiers may have extensive military experience and possibly children of their own. Defining an ex-combatant as a child when he is socially an adult has both psychological and social implications in the demobilization phase. If the former child soldier is also a father, he has to be removed from a position where he could provide for his family to enter a program with younger children leading to an uncertain future.

The final phase of the DDR process, reintegration, can be challenging for former child soldiers in many postconflict societies due to the significant stigma attached to being an ex-combatant.[2] In some rebel forces, an initiation tactic is to have the children commit an atrocity in their home community to make returning more difficult. For example, Sierra Leone's Revolutionary United Front (RUF) was known both for this tactic and for branding their children so that wherever they went people would know with which group they were associated.

Each phase of the DDR process, while relatively straightforward in theory, presents its own dilemmas and challenges in practice. In this chapter, we focus on the role sport can play on the social and psychological demobilization of children. While these steps are critical, it should be kept in mind that they are necessary but not sufficient conditions for successful DDR programs. In the end, the success of the program depends on the coordination of efforts in security sector reform, transitional justice, and perhaps most critically, economic development. If the conditions that led to the original conflict are not improved, it is only a matter of time before the fighting resumes.

Social and Psychological Demobilization of Children

As argued above, demobilization involves formal, social, and psychological processes. Formal demobilization is simply the official disbandment of the fighting force. "Social demobilization" involves changing the community with which an ex-combatant identifies from the military to civilians. This social demobilization can be further subdivided into two related parts. First, with whom does the former child soldier interact? If a child's relationships remain entirely with other soldiers or others associated with fighting forces, he would not be considered socially demobilized. However, if the people he considers his community of reference are from civilian groups, social demobilization may be said to have occurred.

Second, if the child does interact with civilians, does he display the appropriate role behaviors for that group? Has he accepted and adopted the norms and mores of his home community? Michael Ashkenazi (February 25, 2012) argues that one way to measure the success of the demobilization phase is to compare the characteristics of an ex-combatant with those of a civilian in a given society. That is, soldiers are expected to have certain role behaviors. They may be aggressive, disciplined, obedient to those above them in a hierarchy, etc. Civilians, in this case, children, are expected to have a different set of characteristics. Perhaps they are supposed to be passive and more egalitarian than hierarchical. To the degree that the former child soldier consistently displays the latter role behaviors and shuns the former he can be said to be socially demobilized.

Similar to adults, complete demobilization for children involves a psychological component as well. As a soldier, the child was expected to engage in little critical thinking. He was to follow orders when they were given, and in exchange the basic necessities of life were provided. As a civilian, the child must learn to be self-reliant and to question authority to prevent being exploited by a former commander. Due to armed groups becoming an alternative "family" structure for many child soldiers, breaking down the former hierarchies is especially important. If children leave a DDR program still feeling that a former commander is a father or brother figure who should be obeyed, they are vulnerable to reentering negative situations. In this chapter, we explore the ways in which sports may affect both the social and psychological dimensions of demobilization of child soldiers.

Prior Literature on Sports and DDR

At face value, team sports would be particularly well suited to the tasks of both psychological and social demobilization. Conventional wisdom states that participants are socialized into a group, and learn concepts such as teamwork, fair play, aggression management, leadership, discipline, cooperation, and trust to be effective members of the team. However, prior literature on the link between sport and DDR shows a variable effect.

Several success stories relate sports to positive peacebuilding in general and to DDR specifically (e.g., Dyck 2011; Koenen and Stura 2010; Sugden 2006). Koenen and Stura (2010) show that sports are beginning to be used more systematically in postconflict situations throughout the Middle East and Africa for youth to "overcome their emotional stress," "enhance psychosocial rehabilitation," and "break social, economic and religious barriers." They note that "guided sports and play activities can help people to cope with the impacts of a crisis, leading to a number of positive physical, psychological, psychosocial and social health benefits" (Koenen and Stura 2010, 4).

Relating sports to DDR, Dyck (2011) examined the use of football (soccer) in a DDR camp in Sierra Leone and found that the sport was credited with decreasing direct violence within the camp, and it was successful in channeling violent tendencies. However, he cautioned that the sport's role was a "modest" one, and argued that it "must continue to be . . .

but one component of an integrated approach with other activities" (Dyck 2011, 410).

While Dyck (2011) acknowledges that sports can have a modest positive effect in the DDR process, he also notes that sport can affect the process negatively. When children are being taken from a place where "battle" is the norm, football offers an arena for the continuation of wartime divisions rather than their erasure. The rules regulating sports may add some formality to the process, but in their most basic form sports are little more than controlled conflict. In other words, sports alone are not a "magic bullet" that automatically leads to psychosocial changes in ex-combatants.

Simply adding sports into a DDR program with the hopes that the positive outcomes will take care of themselves can result in further ingraining the "soldier" outlook even in civilian activities. What is needed is an understanding of the theoretical links between sports and changes in psychological and social behaviors. What role can sports play to impact psychosocial attitudes and behaviors positively? In what ways might sports negatively affect the process? DDR practitioners must be aware of both the potential positives as well as the negatives in order to gain the most from their use of sports in the process.

Sports as a Vehicle for Social and Psychological Changes

The use of sports to encourage character building and social change had a long history before it was applied to DDR, with perceived social benefits that have become "common knowledge." For example, it is not unusual to hear athletes tout their sports' roles in keeping them "off the streets," or making them "the person they are today." Sports are commonly believed to increase any number of desirable social traits from improved leadership skills to the ability to work in teams, to the ability to handle criticism.

However, the social benefits of participation in sports may not be the result of participation in the activity itself. Using a meta-analysis of literature relating sports to personal characteristics, Stevenson (1975) illustrated this ambiguity. He discovered that the existing literature pointed to positive, negative, and no effects of sports participation on personal characteristics. One of the major limitations of the research at that point was that much of it was cross sectional, meaning there was an assumption that athletes and nonathletes were similar at baseline, and any differences between the groups were attributed to the sports. However, Stevenson argues that the differences may be the result of self-selection into sports rather than the impact the sport had on the participants (Stevenson 1975). He concluded, "There is no valid evidence that participation in sport causes any verifiable socialization effects," and therefore these effects must "remain in the realm of 'belief' and should not be treated as 'fact'" (Stevenson 1975, 299). Frey and Eitzen support this claim in more recent literature arguing, "Despite strong cultural beliefs, there is little evidence to support the claims made for the contribution of sport to the socialization process" (Frey and Eitzen 1991, 506).

While sports may or may not contribute to socialization, it is possible that social processes are still related to sports. Helanko (1958) argues that sports may have developed as a result of social progressions. He suggests that as boys mature they move through three social stages. In the first—pre-gang—stage, play is primarily unstructured and largely noncompetitive. In the second—gang—stage, boys begin to identify and associate with groups. It is this stage and those that follow that will be important to DDR practitioners. Helanko divides the gang stage into two periods. He argues that the first period, when children are nine to twelve years old, is typified by "introversive interaction" (Helanko 1958, 231). That is, the group interacts with its own members to the explicit exclusion of others. In the second gang period, when children are twelve to sixteen years old, "interaction changes and becomes extroversive" (Helanko 1958, 231). Here, one gang may merge with another and grow. It is from the first and second gang stages that sports evolve, as boys' groups seek the opportunity to compete with other groups. In the third stage, the boys break away from the groups as they move into the post-gang phase and socialize increasingly in (nonsexual) pairs.

Sports and Their Potential Effects on DDR

Helanko's phases are relevant to the DDR process for several reasons. If these stages are biological rather than cultural, a boy's life stage may deeply impact the best ways to approach his demobilization. Due to UNICEF's age-delimited definition of "children," everyone under the age of eighteen is sent to the same kind of DDR camp with the same rules, policies, and procedures. However, those boys may span two or even all three of Helanko's phases. It would be fruitful to be aware of those boys who are in the different periods of the gang phase as well as those who have shifted to post-gang. Boys in the first period of the gang phase may attempt to form an in-group quickly in the camp, to the exclusion of others. The formation of this group could be productive or counter-productive depending on its nature. Those running the DDR camp may face more challenges in trying to create sport teams and combine in-groups among the boys in the first period than those in the second. In addition, Helanko argues that in general boys seventeen and older are in the "post-gang" phase. In that case, sport will likely have less of an impact among those boys, as they will be less susceptible to the needs and desires of the "gang." Therefore, approaching older boys one-on-one may have a greater impact than hoping they will succumb to group pressure to conform.

Ishmael Beah's (2007a) account of being a child ex-combatant in a DDR camp provides anecdotal support for this particularistic approach to older children. While Beah speaks highly of the demobilization process he underwent, he gives the most credit for his personal turnaround to one factor—a girl. Of course, those involved in DDR cannot be expected to play matchmaker for each child soldier in the camp. The lesson to be learned is that while group pressure through sport may be influential for those at the "gang" stage of social development, individual attention may be more important for those who have shifted into the "post-gang" phase.

While the research suggests that sports, in and of themselves, do not necessarily impact social processes, that does not mean they cannot be used as "hooks" and vehicles for psychological and social changes. Those who create and implement DDR programs must be aware that because the impact of sports is neither inherently good nor bad, any benefits accrued will be the result of overtly making the connection between positive sports-related skills and desired life skills.

Table 1 lists some of the potential social and psychological benefits and disadvantages of sports in the DDR process. As the prior literature illustrates, none of these arises naturally from the activities. Therefore, those in the field must actively find ways to draw out the positive physical, emotional, and social benefits of sports. Practitioners also must be aware of the potential negative consequences such as isolation, rejection, and lowering of self-esteem and work to combat those effects. While participation in sports without additional support and behavior modification strategies is not the panacea that has come to be accepted as fact, new programs that include behavior management strategies are showing positive results.

Successful Sports-Based Socialization Programs and Their Lessons for DDR

Recent programs using sports as change agents are targeting children in a variety of realms. Some programs provide services to general

Table 1
Potential Benefits and Negative Results of Sport Participation

Potential benefits of sports	Potential negative results of participation
Social:	Social:
Teamwork/cooperation	Sport is "formalized conflict"
Communication	Solidification of in-groups and out-groups
Leadership	Continuation of "command structure"
Conflict resolution	Continuation of hierarchy
Create friendships and peer groups	
Psychological:	Psychological:
Patience/persistence	Isolation
Takes mind off other topics	Rejection
Cope with competition in a positive way	Continued emphasis on winning
Responsibility (actions and consequences) Think critically (solve problems and learn from failure)	
Discipline	

populations of children, while others are targeted toward at-risk groups such as disadvantaged inner-city youth, children from families with low socioeconomic status, refugees, asylum seekers, and gangs. This section will examine some of these programs and discuss how they consciously plan for positive socialization and psychological effects and overcome the inherent negatives that result from sport participation. In the following section, we argue that similar results may occur when using sports as a tool for demobilization and reintegration.

Individual Sports in Demobilization

The First Tee is a program designed to expand the sport of golf by providing access for economically disadvantaged youth. The mission of the program is to "impact the lives of young people by providing educational programs that build character, instill life-enhancing values and provide healthy choices through the game of golf" (First Tee 2012). The program has expanded to include elementary school programs that serve entire school populations through a comprehensive Physical Education curriculum. The First Tee program touts nine core values that are important in golf and in life: honesty, integrity, sportsmanship, respect, confidence, responsibility, perseverance, courtesy, and judgment.

A recent impact assessment on the effectiveness of the program supports the notion that sports participation can affect behavior. An initial study of the effectiveness of the program was conducted in 2003. This snapshot reported a 47 percent increase in the understanding of life skills among participants compared to nonparticipants. Parents noted dramatic improvements among participants in communication skills, confidence, responsibility, school grades, and social skills. The initial study led to a four-year study of the First Tee program, which suggests that life skills taught through sports can be transferred to life after the program. Seventy-eight percent of the children interviewed reported that the skills that they learned in the First Tee program have helped them in future pursuits. "Skills including decision making, self-management, and setting goals were consistently transferred to situations involving school, family, friends, jobs, college, career, and out of school activities" (First Tee 2011).

The First Tee program offers several valuable lessons for those involved in DDR programming. As outlined above, demobilization involves changes in communities of reference, role behaviors, and psychological processes. In the past, the use of sports in DDR focused almost entirely on the perceived benefits of team sports. What the First Tee illustrates is the possible psychological and social benefits of individual sports.

Using Ashkenazi's model for measuring demobilization, the role behaviors and psychological characteristics of child soldiers can be compared with the hypothetically desirable characteristics of civilian children in a community (see Table 2). The goal of the DDR process is then to shift the child from identifying with and acting as a soldier to identifying with and acting as a civilian. While both individual and team sports could be used as vehicles for promoting these changes, individual sports are particularly attractive.

While the basic structure of both team and individual sports is one person or group versus another, it is relatively easy to shift the focus in individual sports from competition against the other to competition against oneself. The goal does not have to be "beat him"; instead, it can be "get a personal record." With that shift, the nature of competition as well as the way in which success is achieved may have profound effects on an ex-combatant. Because the only way to improve in an individual sport is to make individual changes, the door is opened for discussing and altering

Table 2
Possible Differences in Psychological Components: Soldier vs. Civilian

	Child soldier	Civilian child
Conflict resolution	Violent/protect self	Nonviolent/defer to authority
Discipline	Structured	Unstructured
Consequence of competition	Losing = possibility of death	Losing = opportunity to learn
Critical thinking	Follow orders	Evaluate options and make choice

several personal attitudes and characteristics. Due to the inherent focus in individual sports on improving oneself, such sports are uniquely suited for making psychological and behavioral changes among ex-combatants in the DDR program.

Team Sports in Demobilization

While individual sports are an underexploited avenue for personal change in DDR programs, team sports still may have a role to play. Several organizations have found ways of combating the potential negatives in team sports to deliver programs that use sports to engage and alter social behavior and communities of reference. For example, West Texas Swoosh is a nonprofit organization that teaches life skills through basketball in a community in Texas. Most of the participants are from single-parent homes in a small community where "there are a lot of bad influences" (Drinkard 2009). The program stresses education, and participants are required to maintain passing grades in school and to stay out of trouble. Pam Anderson, a codirector of the program, says, "One of the reasons the kids come is it gives them an alternative and it gives them a choice . . . It teaches them commitment, dedication and discipline" and "gives them a choice as opposed to going to the streets" (Drinkard 2009).

While West Texas Swoosh is an effective program for children to learn life skills in a general population or with at-risk youth within a community, child soldiers are not "average" children. Most have been removed from their community and learned to live within a very different kind of community culture. During the DDR process, they must first unlearn violent behaviors and beliefs, and then relearn behaviors suitable for reintegration into their former culture. Moving toward this end are sport programs that cater to groups that are more similar to child soldiers than the general population.

The Australian Institute of Criminology (AIC) has published several reports on the trends and issues in crime prevention and decreasing antisocial behavior through sports and physical activity (e.g., Cameron and MacDougall 2000; Morris, Sallybanks, and Willis 2003). Cameron and MacDougall (2000) make two arguments about the role of sports as a social change agent: first, sports can have beneficial effect in steering youth away from trouble, but second, "sport and physical activity were important, but not sufficient, components of a broader strategy" for the development of values and behaviors. Morris, Sallybanks, and Willis (2003) provide further insight into this broader strategy by including ideas to make sports programs more effective. The authors identified three structural strategies that define successful outcomes. First, successful programs involve youth in the program delivery and provide opportunities for leadership. Second, they create a safe and engaging environment in which "youth felt comfortable about making mistakes without censure." Finally, those programs have opportunities in the community to continue prosocial activities. These cases indicate evidence of sports impacting general and at-risk populations in a positive way, and give general guidelines for how to structure sports-based activities to enhance their positive effects.

In DDR, the primary social goal is for ex-combatants to shift their communities of reference from combatants to civilians. That is, when they enter the program they identify with and as soldiers. When they leave the program the intent is to have them identify with and as civilians. In a program in which the soldiers are cantoned, making this shift can be incredibly difficult because nearly everyone around them is also an ex-combatant. However, the stories reported from Swoosh suggest some strategies that can be employed in order to increase the chances of success.

For the West Texas Swoosh, the goal is to give kids a socially desirable alternative to identifying with gangs or other "troublemakers." Not only is the ability to play basketball an incentive in itself, but the organization also pays for the players to travel and have other experiences through the team. Because the players see the value in being with the team, they are able to do other things that might be considered socially undesirable by their peer group such as focus on academics. That is, if peers ask why they are studying, they can say it is in order to play basketball—a socially acceptable response—while studying only for the sake of an education may be looked down upon. In the same way, in a soldier's eyes, becoming a "civilian" is not always considered a step up, or even a horizontal move (e.g., Beah 2007a). Child combatants often see themselves as capable fighters, independent, and more experienced in life than child civilians.

Team sports, then, can serve two roles in helping children shift their communities of reference. First, sports offer the child an alternative community with which to identify. Galvanek (2009) provides evidence that this tactic can even be effective in combining members of previously opposing forces. After putting children from opposing forces together on a football team, "the children were much more concerned about their teams' names and the goals they had scored than in what force they had previously fought" (Galvanek 2009, 21). This finding suggests that one way to shift the children's self-identity from soldier to civilian is to move them from soldier to teammate to civilian.

In addition, sports can be used as an incentive to promote the desired outcomes of the DDR program. Just as West Texas Swoosh used the threat of not playing to incentivize academics, sport in DDR camps can be used as an incentive for going to classes, following rules, or behaving in other ways associated with civilian behavior. Galvanek (2009) notes that the threat of missing a game was effective in Liberia, as "the children simply did not want to miss out on the day's game" (Galvanek 2009, 21).

A secondary social goal of demobilization is the dismantling of the former command structures and hierarchies. Sports can be troublesome in this regard because, as noted in Table 1, sports lend themselves well to hierarchical structures. Teams often have coaches, captains, and other unofficial leaders. If those sports' structures reinforce the preexisting hierarchical structure, then the sports are not advancing the end-goal of social demobilization.

The suggestions in the AIC reports may be useful in this regard. The AIC suggests involving youth in program delivery and providing op- portunities for leadership. If those leadership opportunities are granted to preexisting leaders, then the former hierarchies will remain in place. However, granting equal access to leadership opportunities may help reduce the impact of the former structures. In addition, the AIC suggests creating an environment in which youth feel they can "[make] mistakes without censure." If the time spent on sports becomes such a "safe place," then it will be an arena in which former commanders cannot criticize or make requests of those lower down in the structure. Again, this space would then be beneficial in reducing the impact and legitimacy of the former hierarchy.

Conclusions

While sports are commonly thought to have inherent social and psychological benefits, research suggests that sports in and of themselves are neither good nor bad. However, sports can have a positive impact when they are used as a tool or a "hook" for certain ends. When considering DDR, sports can be used positively to affect both the psychological and social demobilization of child soldiers.

An ex-combatant may be considered demobilized to the degree that his personal role behaviors match those of a civilian rather than a soldier. While much of the literature relating sport and DDR focuses on the effects team sports can have on socialization, the success of the First Tee suggests that individual sports may be well suited to addressing personal and psychological changes. Individual sports also have the benefit of reframing the competition and conflict that may be present in sports. Rather than the competition being solely external, individual sports allow a competitor to see the ultimate goal as setting a personal best or making individual improvements instead of out-performing his opponent. This shift in the focus of the sport both encourages personal changes and helps mitigate the conflict that may develop from team activities.

Demobilization also involves shifting the community with which an ex-combatant identifies and dismantling the former command structures. Team sports may be well suited for both of these tasks. The team gives the child a new community that can act as an intermediate step between identifying with soldiers and identifying with civilians. As part of a sports team, he can still identify with fellow soldiers but consider himself a teammate first. However, this change in identity does not come simply from playing the game. It must be cultivated through activities and education that are designed to transfer the lessons of the game into the desired life skills.

Organizing team sports also offers the chance for a change in the leadership structure. Those who were commanders in the fighting may not be the leaders on the team. This shift in the power structure may serve the group well after the DDR program is complete and the children reenter civilian life. If these structures remain intact, they may be abused by former commanders. Dismantling them provides those who were subordinate to regain their autonomy.

It is important to note that while UNICEF considers everyone under eighteen years of age to be "children," there is evidence to suggest that the impact of using the pressure of a team may vary depending on the age of the ex-combatant. If Helanko's (1958) social progression holds across cultures, boys in the "post-gang" stage may be influenced more by one-on-one attention and interactions than they are by the group. However, in spite of the limitations of sports outlined above, when structured correctly, they may be effective tools in furthering the goals of the DDR process.

Notes

1. Dr. Mike Ashkenazi is a Senior Researcher at the Bonn International Center for Conversion. In 2007, he conducted the training for South Sudan DDR Commission, including the procedures for disarmament of SALW.
2. There are a growing number of girls serving in armed factions in varying capacities. In many ways the reintegration process for girls can be more complicated than that for boys. Because of the possibility of sexual violence, girls associated with fighting forces may face additional stigmatization which can make the reintegration process for girls more difficult than that for boys. While the DDR of female child soldiers is a critical and integral part of the positive peacebuilding process, the literature suggests that the socialization process is slightly different (see, e.g., Mazurana, McKay, Carlson, and Casper 2002). In addition, in many of the societies in which child soldiers are currently engaged, the values desired for girls and boys are different. Therefore, in this chapter we focus on the DDR of boy soldiers.

References

Beah, Ishmael. 2007a. *A Long Way Gone: Memoirs of a Boy Soldier*. New York: Sarah Crichton Books.
———. 2007b. "Q&A with Ishmael Beah." Television Series Episode. In *Q & A*. Washington, DC: C-SPAN, March 20.
Boyer, Rick. 2011. *Take Back the Land: Inspiring a New Generation to Lead America*. Green Forest, AR: Master Books.
Cameron, Margaret, and Colin MacDougall. 2000. "Crime Prevention through Sport and Physical Activity." In *Trends and Issues in Crime and Criminal Justice 165*. Canberra: Australian Institute of Criminology.
Drinkard, L. 2009. "Basketball Helps Keep Kids off Streets." *Victoria Advocate*. June 30. http://m.victoriaadvocate.com/news/2009/jun/30/bc-tx-west-texas-swoosh/ (accessed February 21, 2012).
Dyck, Christopher B. 2011. "Football and Post-War Reintegration: Exploring the Role of Sport in DDR Processes in Sierra Leone." *Third World Quarterly* 32: 395–415.
Frey, James H., and D. Stanley Eitzen. 1991. "Sport and Society." *Annual Review of Sociology* 17: 503–22.
Galvanek, Janel B. 2009. "The Reintegration Process for Child Soldiers in Liberia." *Conflict Trends* 3: 19–25.
Helanko, Rafael. 1958. "Sports and Socialization." *Acta Sociologica* 2: 229–40.
Honwana, Alcinda. 2006. *Child Soldiers in Africa*. Philadelphia: University of Pennsylvania.
Koenen, Katrin, and Claudia Stura. 2010. "Healing through Sports: Psychosocial Physical Activity Programmes in Crisis Areas." *Coping with Crisis, Newsletter* 3: 4–6.
Lewis, Neryl. 1999. "Social Recovery from Armed Conflict." In *Recovery from Armed Conflict in Developing Countries*, ed. Geoff T. Harris, 95–110. New York: Routledge.
Machel, Graça. 1996. "Impact of Armed Conflict on Children." Report submitted to the UN General Assembly. http://www.unicef.org/graca/ (accessed April 28, 2012).

————. 2001. *The Impact of War on Children: A Review of Progress since the 1996 United Nations Report on the Impact of Armed Conflict on Children.* New York: United Nations Children's Fund.

Mazurana, Dyan E., Susan A. McKay, Khristopher C. Carlson, and Janel C. Kasper. 2002. "Girls in Fighting Forces and Groups: Their Recruitment, Participation, Demobilization, and Reintegration." *Peace and Conflict: Journal of Peace Psychology* 8: 97–123.

Morris, Leesa, Jo Sallybanks, and Katie Willis. 2003. "Sport, Physical Activity, and Anti-Social Behavior in Youth." *Research and Public Policy Series No. 49.* Canberra: Australian Institute of Criminology. http://www.aic.gov.au/documents/9/C/C/%7B-9CC8CDD4-CF5B-4F2C-8D9A-AA1FA76889B8%7DRPP49.pdf (accessed April 13, 2012).

Morse, Jane. 2008. "Programs Help Child Soldiers Return Home." America.gov Archive. February 1, 2008. http://www.america.gov/st/hr-english/2008/February/20080201170846ajesroM0.9215052.html (accessed February 21, 2012).

Peters, Krijn, and Paul Richards. 1998. "'Why We fight': Voices of Youth Combatants in Sierra Leone." *Africa: Journal of the International African Institute* 68: 183–210.

Rosen, David M. 2005. *Armies of the Young: Child Soldiers in War and Terrorism.* Piscataway, NJ: Rutgers University Press.

Stevenson, Christopher L. 1975. "Socialization Effects of Participation in Sport: A Critical Review of the Research." *Research Quarterly* 46: 287–301.

Sugden, John. 2006. "Teaching and Playing Sport for Conflict Resolution and Co-Existence in Israel." *International Review for the Sociology of Sport* 41: 221–40.

The First Tee. 2011. "Impact Report." http://www.vanymca.org/health/pdf/impactreport.pdf (accessed April 8, 2012).

The First Tee. 2012. "Mission Statement." http://www.thefirsttee.org/club/scripts/public/public.asp?GRP=17345&NS=PUBLIC (accessed January 30, 2012).

UNICEF. 2011. "Patterns in Conflict: Civilians Are Now the Target." http://www.unicef.org/graca/patterns.htm (accessed April 21, 2012).

United Nations Development Programme. 2008. *Post-Conflict Economic Recovery: Enabling Local Ingenuity.* New York: United Nations Development Programme.

United Nations Security Council. 2000. *Report of the Secretary General on The Role of the United Nations Peacekeeping in Disarmament, Demobilization and Reintegration.* New York: United Nations.

The Role of Universities in Sport, Development, and Peace: The Case of the University of the Western Cape in South Africa

Marion Keim

Introduction

In 1994, Daniel Sanders (1994, 51) wrote:

The role of universities in peace and social development has to be viewed in the context of pressing global problems and the central issue of human survival in an increasingly interdependent world. We know that concerns such as poverty, homelessness, violence and environmental and developmental crises are no longer confined to one nation. What were once, for example, local incidents of social dislocation or pollution, now involve multiple linkages that transcend national boundaries. It is also presumptuous to think that any one institution or group by itself—be it the United Nations, the non-governmental organisations or the universities—could deal with problems that are unprecedented in terms of increases in rate, scale and complexity.

Eighteen years later, the challenges still exist and in fact have become bigger as the Millennium Development Goals show. We continue to struggle to find better ways to collaborate toward our common goals and even to share resources. The good news is that there are agencies which in the last two decades have begun to look for additional, innovative means to assist in the field of peace and development. The author's concern here is the use of sports for such an end. The United Nations (UN) is one such organization increasingly looking at sports as tool for peacebuilding and development, as are NGOs, CBOs, business, and lately, universities (Keim 2009).

This chapter will explore if and how universities can play a role to harness expertise, promote research, teaching, and community engagement and perform capacity building in the field of sport for development and peace. This includes initiating, forming, or even coordinating partnerships with other stakeholders, universities, NGOs, governments, the private sector, and sport organizations. The University of the Western Cape (UWC) in South Africa, with its recently established Interdisciplinary Centre of Excellence in Sports Science and Development (ICESSD), will serve as an example.

The rationale behind this choice to look in detail at the example of ICESSD is that South Africa has had a unique history of conflict and has been a country in transition for the past decades. It has a unique history of peace and reconciliation and has been home to four Novel Peace Prize winners: Albert Luthuli, Nelson Mandela, Frederik de Klerk, and Archbishop Desmond Tutu (Chancellor of the UWC for twenty-four years from 1996 to 2011).

The UWC, founded in 1960, is itself an institution with a remarkable history of involvement in the struggle for democracy and social transformation, an institution once called the "intellectual home for the left," which has produced great thinkers and leaders over the years, many of whom were called by Nelson Mandela to serve in his original cabinet.

UWC also has a proud and rich sporting tradition that has characterized the development of the institution since its inception, with a Chancellor for many years who believes in the power of sports for peace and reconciliation.

> "Through properly organised sport," stated Archbishop Tutu in 2003, "we can learn to play together with respect and with laughter, we can learn to all be on the same team, and in the process we can contribute to building a new South Africa that is a just nation for all" (Keim 2003, 9).

In 2009, UWC chose to establish the first ICESSD on the continent and worldwide, with a mandate to contribute to the understanding and advancement of sport as a tool for development through high quality research, teaching, community engagement, new technologies, and the application of sport science to advance the physical, social, and economic development and well-being of South African and African communities.

This chapter will consider the historical context of peace, education, and sport in South Africa before looking at the role, mission, and mandate of the university with regard to sports, development, and peace.

Historical Background and Educational Context

The history of education in South Africa in punctuated with expressions like "Bantu education," "gutter education," and "Soweto 1976." A brief review of developments in the education sector may be helpful to establish the context of this chapter and in looking at the role of educational institutions in South Africa over the years.

Separate educational institutions for Black and White South Africans existed since the early twentieth century, but racial segregation was not enforced by law until the 1950s. Education was not compulsory, particularly for the Black population. In the first half of the century, many Black children received no schooling at all, while a small number of Black and Coloured children received a superior education at Mission schools throughout South Africa. Importantly, among these children there were many future leaders in politics, society, and trade.

In 1953, the infamous Bantu Education Act (Act 47 of 1953) was passed by the Nationalist Government. This Act had detrimental effects as it transferred control over education for Africans from the provinces to the National Minister of Native Affairs, Dr. H. F. Verwoerd, one of the main architects of apartheid. Verwoerd openly stated the purpose of the new law as providing for an education which would prepare Black people for inferior and subordinate positions in society:

By blindly producing pupils trained on a European model, the vain hope was created among Natives that they could occupy posts within the European community despite the country's policy of "apartheid."
There is no place for him (i.e. the Black South African) in the European community above the level of certain forms of labour (...) For this reason it is of no avail for him to receive a training which has as its aim an absorption in the European community, where he cannot be absorbed (cf. Rose and Tunmer 1975, 261 and 266; Sparks 1990, 196).

Verwoerd here refers to the White South Africa as "the European community." This alone indicates how poorly the apartheid architects were adapted to Africa.

The apartheid government was extending the principle of segregated education to all "population groups." The Coloured Persons Education Act no. 47 of 1963 puts education for Coloureds under the supervision of the Department of Coloured Affairs, while the Department of Indian

Affairs assumed control over education for "Asians" with the Indian Education Act no. 61 of 1965. The provincial Departments of Education retained responsibility for the education for Whites. The Educational policy was determined by the Minister of National Education, assisted by the National Education Council.

In line with the segregation of administrative structures, separate curricula were developed for the children and youth of the four officially determined "population groups." Education was compulsory only for Whites, while only Black and Coloured children had to pay school fees.

All in all, there were seventeen different departments of education in South Africa under the auspices of the Department of National Education—a proliferation of administrative structures which existed until 1995. The differentiation at bureaucratic level reflected far-reaching differences in the provision of education for the various "population groups."

Within the apartheid framework, White schools and universities had the function of ensuring the continued supremacy of Whites and educating the future leadership. Comparatively speaking, these schools and institutions of higher learning offered education of a high quality, not only in the formal class room situation, but also in terms of extracurricular sports and cultural activities.

In 1968, the Coloured Representative Act (Act no. 52 of 1986) conferred limited decision-making powers on the Coloured Representative Council, that is, regarding "Coloured education." This included not only schools, but also institutions of tertiary education reserved for the "Coloured population," such as the UWC and a number of teacher training colleges. These institutions were allowed to offer limited training for lower to middle level positions in schools, the civil service, and other institutions designed to serve a separated Coloured community (Keim 2003, 23).

The problems experienced in the "Coloured educational system" closely resembled those in schools for Africans, for example, the high number of dropouts, which Niven (1982) attributes to low levels of income and to a lack of opportunities for further training. In addition to this, the absence of the opportunity for Coloured people to participate on an equal footing with Whites in the economic, social, and political life of apartheid, South Africa occasioned a complex negative response, in which apathy tended to alternate with outbursts of resistance.

At UWC, protest action by students and Black academic staff in 1975 led to the appointment of the first Black Rector, Professor Richard E. (Dick) van der Ross, who established a climate hospitable to intellectual debate and internationally respected scholarship.

In its mission statement of 1982, UWC Objectives, the university formally rejected the apartheid ideology on which it was established, adopting a declaration of nonracialism and "a firm commitment to the development of the Third World communities in South Africa." In 1983, through the University of the Western Cape Act of 1983, the University finally gained its autonomy on the same terms as the established "White" institutions (UWC 2009).

In 1987, the University also formalized its "open" admissions policy, providing access to a growing number of African students, and paving the way for rapid growth. Despite severe constraints, students from the disadvantaged communities graduated in increasing numbers, equipped to make a professional contribution to the new South Africa. President Nelson Mandela later lauded UWC for having transformed itself "from an apartheid ethnic institution to a proud national asset" (UWC 2009).

This brief overview demonstrates the administrative and structural fragmentation, as well as the qualitative differences in the education of the various "population groups" in apartheid South Africa. The system was designed to emphasize and strengthen the (assumed or real) cultural differences between these "population groups," to avoid—as far as possible—all opportunity for social contact between the school-going youth of these "groups," and to reinforce and perpetuate the social stratification and political division within South African society.

In 1994, South Africa had eleven universities and eight technikons for White students, and one university and one technikon each for Coloured, Indian, and Black students (South African Communication Service 1994, 282).

For a postapartheid South Africa striving for nation-building and equality, the legacy of the apartheid educational system has been a heavy burden which can still be felt at many levels, including at the universities today. Sport, as considered here, has been offered as one of several means to contribute in its own way to overcoming these wounds of the past.

Historical Background and Sports and Peace Context in South Africa

Traditionally, sports have played an important and powerful role in South African history and society. However, it is the very unique story of sport, peace, and development in a country which defeated apartheid which Allison (2000, 69) refers to when he writes:

. . . in few countries could institutions of civil society (such as sport) outflank and manipulate what appears to be a powerful state in this manner; in no other country, perhaps, could sporting institutions have played so large a part in forming the direction that the state would take.

Under apartheid, it was solely the White sport structures which had governmental support of a White government with the consequent favorable conditions conducive for their development, progress, and growth. The history of non-White sport was an unhappy one of oppression, interference, and forced relocations (particularly in the twentieth century), the effects of which are still to be felt today. The DSR White Paper of 1995 (1995, 2) notes that, "In the apartheid era more than 30 million South Africans were never taken into serious account when it came to sport and recreation." Watson cites an example from the oldest African township, Langa in Cape Town, where thirty-six soccer clubs had to share a single stadium without seating or flood lights (Watson as quoted in Archer and Bouillon 1982, 39; Keim 2003).

Principles such as "Whites and Non-Whites must organize their sport separately," "No mixed sport will be allowed within the borders of South Africa," and "International teams competing in South Africa against White South African teams must be all-White according to South African custom" officially guided government policy until 1971. In reality, however, these principles were instituted far beyond 1971 in an informal manner (Archer and Bouillon 1982).

Over the following years, history changed significantly for South Africa. In 1994, the country had its first democratic election and gained its long desired freedom and its first democratically elected president, Nelson Mandela. The DRS White Paper at the time noted that:

A new era has now dawned in which the fortunes of those 30 million (South Africans) need seriously to be recognised in concrete terms. . . As South Africa enters into a new democratic dispensation the need to entrench that new democratic ethos in sport as part of the transformation process for the upliftment of the quality of life for all South Africans cannot be over-emphasised (1995, 2).

In the time that followed, Nelson Mandela's first Minister for Sport, Mr. Steve Tshwete, stated: "Sport exerts an immeasurable influence as a unifying force for reconciliation and for the process of nation building" (Keim 2003, 171).

Today, South Africa is not only able to invite the world to the biggest sports events such as the Rugby World Cup in 1995 or the Soccer World Cup in 2010, it is a country where the role for sports in conflict resolution and peacebuilding has been documented by Hollywood in the film "Invictus" with director Clint Eastwood showing the world the power sports holds for peace and development. Significantly, South Africa has recently been elected the Chair for Peace and Sport for the UN International Working Group (IWG) in 2011 in Geneva with Russia as vice chair. This is the first time an African country heads an IWG in the field of sports and peace.

What does all the above mean for South Africa and its sports? These questions are complex and not easy to address. It does not mean that for the majority of South Africans and South African sports, particularly in the disadvantaged communities, the situation will change overnight. The legacy of apartheid can be still felt in townships and in sports structures, despite infrastructural benefits the Soccer World Cup might have brought, and despite White papers and political rhetoric. Like the rest of the conti-nent, South Africa continues to face complex challenges. Unlike the rest of the continent, many of these challenges are rooted in a past where ex-treme state violence was used to enforce inequality, leaving South Africa as a nation with both unhealed wounds and extraordinary examples of resilience and determination to create a greater collective society. There are many signs of hope in South Africa today. There are many efforts made within and beyond sport to work together in a new way, in a multistake-holder fashion, a willingness to take on responsibility and make voices heard for the causes of sport, development, and peace. Because universi-ties have always been central to the direction of the state in the twentieth and twenty-first centuries, with certain universities being the original architects of apartheid and others such as UWC committing itself to undo-ing the inhuman and unjust system, it is appropriate here to ask what role universities can play in promoting development and peace through sports.

The Notion of Peace, Peacebuilding, Development, and Sport

Before discussing the potential role of universities in sport, develop-ment, and peace, the concepts of peace and peacebuilding, sports, and development need to be briefly considered.

According the UN document *An Agenda for Peace* (United Nations 1992), peacebuilding consists of a wide range of activities associated with capacity building, reconciliation, and societal transformation. Building peace is seen as a long-term process which includes all activities to build and promote peace and overcome violence (Pfaffenholz 2003). Some authors like Galtung (1964) distinguish between *negative peace*, referring to the absence of violence, and *positive peace*, as the restoration of relationships and the integration of human society through the creation of social systems that serve the needs of the whole population. He proposes a holistic approach to peacebuilding in the form of "3 Rs": *Reconstruction* of people and places, *Reconciliation* of relationships, and *Resolution* of issues and animosities (Galtung 1996). Developing peace therefore includes identifying and understanding the notion and nature of factors obstructing peace within a cross-cultural and multidisciplinary context.

An interesting aspect in this regard is to compare Western and the South African concepts of peace. The term *peace* originally derives from the Latin word "pax." In the West, it is generally understood as a "political condition that ensures justice and social stability through formal and informal institutions, practices and norms" (Miller 2005, 55), or as "a contractual relationship that implies mutual recognition and agreement" (Ibid. 56). In isiXhosa, one of South Africa's eleven official languages, the word for *peace* is *"uxolo"* which not only covers a state of inner tranquillity and an atmosphere of peace, but also implies the promotion of forgiveness and healing.

Development in a South African context can be described as multistakeholder efforts with actors working together for the growth and positive advancement of the whole. There cannot be sustainable development without positive peace.

In 1989, it was clear for Ruckelshaus that if 80 percent of the global community is poor, it is not possible to live in a world of peace (Sanders 1994, 57). Brown called for what was a "new social vision, a social vision of what society could be like, guided by considerations of human values and enhancement of the quality of life of all people" (Sanders 1994, 57). Today the Millennium Development Goals pick up on these thoughts in their call for the development of a global partnership for development focusing on reduction of *extreme poverty*, hunger, *child mortality* rates, and diseases and the promotion of universal primary education, gender equality, improving maternal health, and ensuring environmental sustainability by 2015. The role of sport has been highlighted in this regard by local, national, and international organizations including the UN.[1]

Recently, "Sport for Development and Peace" has been referred to as the "intentional use of sport, physical activity and play to attain specific development and peace objectives, including, most notably, the Millennium Development Goals (MDGs)" (UNOSDP 2008, 6). It is worth noting that in a development context the definition of sport is a broad inclusive one, addressing the spectrum of recreation, play, competitive sport, and indigenous sport and games, in other words "all forms of physical activity that contribute to physical fitness, mental well-being and social interaction," "suitable to people of all ages and abilities, with an emphasis on the positive values of sport" (UNOSDP 2008, 6 ff).

The potential of sport as a tool for development and peace at universities has yet to be realized. There is a lack of awareness that well-designed sports for development initiatives, be they lessons or courses, research, or community outreach initiatives, "hold significant potential to help drive the attainment of the MDGs and related development goals" and that "sport can be used as a highly effective tool applied in a holistic and integrated manner with other interventions and programs to achieve optimal results" (Ibid. 13).

The Role of Universities in Sport, Development, and Peace

When looking at the role of universities with regard to development, Rector and Vice Chancellor of the UWC, Professor Brian O'Connell, emphasizes seven strategic partnerships with our species (2012). "There are at least seven human development challenges," says O'Connell, "that universities must champion. Governments can't or won't." They are:

1. To move humans in developed countries to understand that they have lived beyond their means and they must prepare themselves for a more humble future.
2. To move humans in developing countries to understand that they cannot use the developed nations as points of reference for their material expectations.
3. To move all humans to understand that we must develop a wise relationship with our natural environment.
4. To move all humans to think of ourselves as earthlings who must work together to secure our future. This implies an internationalist perspective.
5. To move all humans to understand that there is a direct relationship between population growth and the availability of resources.
6. To move all humans to understand that there is a direct relationship between ownership, competence, and hard work on the one hand and development on the other.
7. To move all humans to understand that safety lies in knowledge and partnerships.

Ruckelshaus and other analysts emphasized already in 1989 the need to create a *"sustainability consciousness"* in the quest for a peaceful and sustainable world. This would require, at a minimum, the following three conditions (Sanders 1994, 57): (a) the understanding that the human species is part of nature, (b) the acknowledgement that economic development must account for the environmental costs of production, and

(c) the realization that to ensure a liveable peaceful global environment, it is necessary to pursue the goal of sustainable development of the entire human family.

For Sanders, the following are the key elements for universities in their potential for preparing youth who would help to shape an international vision, and a social ethic for peace and social development:

1.   The devotion and pursuit of truth.
2.   Serving as social critic in shaping the vision for the future.
3.   A commitment to an education that introduces an international dimension.
4.   Development of interdisciplinary approaches in dealing with problems and to pursue international issues in a global framework from the standpoint of several disciplines and professions.

According to Sanders, the one common purpose is devotion to truth. Truth may be "provisional or definitive." But if the university does not share the conviction that there is truth worth pursuing "for its own sake" that can be taught and learned—that is objective—then it is found wanting (Sanders 1994, 54). This pursuit of truth, "a defining characteristic" of universities, is a "key element in their potential for preparing youth who would help to shape an international vision, and a social ethic for peace and social development" (Ibid. 54).

When considering the role of universities in sport, peace, and development, the author agrees with Sanders that:

> Any attempt to identify the potential role of universities in shaping a vision for the future and in dealing with common concerns of peace, environment and development is fraught with difficulties. While universities share some basic common attributes, there is considerable variation between countries and regions. There are also issues related to the mission of universities and how this is viewed in the context of particular societies. Universities vary in terms of level of education; educational philosophy; tradition; and degree of emphasis on research, teaching and service. Universities also vary regarding the extent to which they are international, regional or parochial. Despite these variations and difficulties, it is necessary in the current global context to examine the potential of universities in dealing with the interconnected global issues of peace, environmental protection and sustainable development (Ibid. 52 ff).

In this task, it is necessary first of all to examine the fundamental and distinctive mission of universities. The unique mission of the university (especially the western university) has been the pursuit of truth, *manifold but finally unitary* probing the universe and our place in it. An essential aspect of this quest for truth is the commitment to objectivity and openness to diverse values, interpretations, and frames of reference. Ideally then, the university is an intellectual and moral community (Sanders 1994, 53).

I believe that Sanders' thoughts on universities and their role in peace and social development are transferrable to the field of sport, development, and peace and should be further discussed when looking at the UWC where ICESSD has been established.

The Case of the University of the Western Cape

To understand UWC's context and activities as an "engaged university," one has to take its history and the history of education and sports in South Africa into consideration. The history of UWC has been deeply intertwined with the history and present situation of South Africa. The UWC established by the apartheid government as "Bush University" for Coloured students only developed quickly into a university involved in the struggle against oppression, discrimination, and disadvantage. Among academic institutions, it has been in the vanguard of South Africa's historic change, playing a distinctive academic role in helping to build an equitable and dynamic nation. UWC's key concerns with access, equity, and quality in higher education arise from extensive practical engagement in helping the historically marginalized participate fully in the life of the nation (UWC 2009).

Today the UWC, as a national university, is alert to its African and international context as it strives to be "a place of quality, a place to grow from hope to action through knowledge." It provides opportunities for an excellent teaching and learning experience that is contextually responsive to the challenges of globalization and a society in transition, which enhances students' capacity as change agents (Mission of UWC). UWC's aim is to enhance itself as a significant research and innovation university, regionally and internationally. Its Institutional Operating Plan (IOP) gives substance to UWC's distinctive role as a public university in South Africa's emerging democracy and as a leading centre of higher learning. At the same time, UWC is an engaged university, connected to the public sphere, committed to being an effective partner in the larger national project of building an equitable society, and striving to give effective leadership at all levels.

UWC's Recent Peace and Development Initiatives

The special role that the UWC has played over the decades in its commitment to the creative resolution of conflict and peacebuilding in a context of social transformation, inspired by the example of its

Chancellor, Emeritus Archbishop Desmond Tutu, winner of the Nobel Peace Prize in 1984, denotes the appropriateness of UWC as the location for a special Nelson Mandela Seminar on the Role of Universities in Conflict Transformation, Reconstruction, and Peace Building in Africa in September 2005. The organizers of this first International Nelson Mandela Seminar dedicated to the role of universities in the promotion of conflict transformation, reconstruction, and peacebuilding in Africa saw conflict resolution and peacebuilding as part of the larger issue of social transformation. The seminar brought together sixty-five selected representatives from thirteen nations, from African and international universities, governments, and civil society involved in the field of conflict management and peacebuilding. The participants had been acutely aware of the barriers conflict and violence present to development in Africa, and the importance of universities in educating socially engaged change agents to help resolve conflict and to further reconstruction and peacebuilding on the continent. For two days, discussions evolved around the tremendous potential of universities for leadership in the area of conflict resolution and peacebuilding in Africa and beyond and the cooperation between tertiary institutions and civil society in this regard.

During the seminar, the delegates looked at specific questions focusing on their respective areas of work such as NGOs, academia, government, or business and the specific role they see themselves and others playing in the promotion of conflict transformation, reconstruction, and peacebuilding; how they can support and strengthen each other; and foster better cooperation. The different group outcomes were discussed in great detail in the larger forum and comprised part of the outcomes of the conference proceedings (Keim 2007).

Of the many outcomes is the call for institutions of higher learning to include conflict resolution instruments as a central part of the intellectual environment of students and to build an ethos of conflict resolution into the lives and functions of these institutions. Also, noted is the need to expand this discourse into interactive learning that serves as a double entry to inform practice and practitioners and to provide academics and students the space to draw lessons from experience and practice.

Overall, the seminar called for a strong collaboration between universities, governments, and civil society to address conflict transformation and peacebuilding in Africa and beyond. Participants also called for linking civil society practitioners with tertiary institutions and government departments to broaden research opportunities, expand training resources, promote field work collaborations, and to develop the capacity of community leadership. Participants recognized the potential of strengthening the conflict prevention and peacebuilding links between universities and civil society. It was felt that these links were missing in the past in the field of peacebuilding in the (South) African context but that they are vital for many bridges to be built in Africa and beyond (Keim 2007, 29).

One of the keynote speakers, Professor Amr Abdalla, now Vice Rector of the University for Peace in Costa Rica, summarized the spirit and aim of the conference in his closing words: "Peace educators of the worlds unite. We need to work together and build bridges so that we can make peace education an integral part of universities and communities" (Abdalla 2005).

Achmat Dangor, CEO of the Nelson Mandela Foundation, stated: "Global realities make it imperative that universities discard the vestiges of their 'ivory tower' pasts—they must be robust players together with the state and civil society in engaging broader societal dynamics and in building democratic polities. In this context we couldn't have chosen a better institutional partner than the University of the Western Cape. It has a proud history of resistance to injustice and of making a difference in the world" (Keim 2007).

The seminar participants saw the need for a special focus to be placed on youth participation in community development and peacebuilding efforts and made a call to look at alternative methods to address and involve them. One of the developments as a direct result of the seminar has been the establishment and work of the Western Cape Network for Community Peace and Development in 2005 which consisted then of six and to date of over forty NGOs, a tertiary institution (UWC as one of the founder members of the Network), and local government departments working in the field of conflict resolution, youth, women, development, peacebuilding, and sports in South Africa. In the same year, the Network started with its Sport for Peace program and the development of its Kicking for Peace Program, a multicultural sport development program for children and youth in South Africa (which later, in 2010, was awarded the Beyond Sport Award). In the following year, UWC hosted the 2006 International Conference on Unlocking the Potential of Sport for Youth Wellness and Development. At that time, sport had gained quite a momentum and started to become more recognized locally, nationally, and internationally, even by the UN as a beacon of hope for peacebuilding or postconflict intervention.

There are no quick fixes for any county's problems with regard to peace and development, but there are opportunities. In our case, the time seems to be right for the university to leave a legacy for South Africa, Africa, and beyond. The establishment of ICESSD can be seen as a significant and visionary step by the UWC to promote peace and development using sport in an interdisciplinary way.

ICESSD

UWC has always been an important sports development node for South Africa. Sports development in and through UWC is a key component in giving effect to the University's mission and is embedded in its strategic plan. Sports are seen as part of the general education of students, and a way of enabling them to engage with the wider community productively.

ICESSD was established to contribute to the relatively new research niche area of sports for development. It is the first of its kind on the African continent and has the potential to have a significant impact in this crucial research area nationally, on the continent and internationally.

ICESSD aligns itself with the goals set out in the University's mission statement and the project of building a better society. It identifies with and seeks through its work to advance the University's commitment to excellence in teaching, learning, and research; the nurturing of cultural diversity; and responding in critical and creative ways to the needs of a society in transition by using sports as a vehicle. ICESSD's vision is to be Africa's leading interdisciplinary centre for sports and development promoting sports as a powerful tool for health, well-being, peace, and social change through high quality research and combining the areas of sports and health sciences and community development. Although ICESSD has only been in existence for two years, it already has a growing network of active partners locally, nationally, from academia, civil society, and governments as well as the UN committed to work together to achieve this vision.

Early in its process of creation, ICESSD values were identified by locating itself within the ethos of UWC. The Centre is committed to:

- seeking cross faculty and transformative approaches to sport and development;
- multidisciplinarity;
- communal and social engagement, both internally (within the University) and externally (reaching out to other institutions and civil society);
- locating itself within the African reality and acknowledging the lessons to be learned from the continent;
- promotion of socioeconomic transformation and sustainable development;

- upliftment and empowerment of previously disadvantaged groups;
- accountability, transparency, inclusivity, and participatory decision making in all its practices;
- academic rigor and excellence in teaching, research, and direct community engagement;
- respecting diversity, in terms of race, sex, sexual orientation, age, religion, and culture;
- a human-centered approach in research, teaching, training, and outreach; and
- continuously striving for improvement (ICESSD Constitution 2009).

The Role of ICESSD in Sports for Development and Peace

ICESSD as an interdisciplinary center of an "engaged university" continuously strives for quality engagement in generating and transmitting knowledge in the field of sports and development. This includes excellence in teaching, learning, and research which is accessible, efficient, responsive lifelong, and includes developing and empowering initiatives. ICESSD's approaches may vary according to different needs, demands, and interests. However, they always take the past, present, and future into consideration, consider urban and rural, and are shaped by a seriousness with regards to the socioeconomic issues of the communities we serve. Through a transformative approach and engagement in local, continent-wide, and global sport and development issues, ICESSD's main aim is to make a sustainable difference for a better society using sports as a tool.

ICESSD conducts multidisciplinary research and service programs, offers capacity building in form of short courses and training for the next generation of sport and development leaders through continuing education, and conducts interdisciplinary research with local, African, and international partners.

ICESSD runs a prestige scholarship program, and a regular conference program with partners such as the UN Office on Sport for Development and Peace, ICSSPE (International Council of Sport Science and Physical Education), provincial government, Jacobs Foundation, Nelson Mandela Foundation, and the Western Cape Network for Community Peace and Development, the University for Peace Africa Program, and others. Latest international research conferences and seminars focusing on sports and development hosted by ICESSD include the First International Sport and Development Conference titled "Beyond 2010" in 2010 with three hundred participants from eighteen countries and the Second International Sport and Development Conference in December 2011 with two hundred participants from thirty-three countries discussing the topic of Strategic Planning and Networking for Sports, Development, and Peace.

ICESSD has a strong commitment to hosting seminars which stimulate debates around peacebuilding and social transformation. ICESSD hosted the seminar "Mahatma Gandhi's Legacy for Peace and Development in South African Communities" in March 2010 with his grandson, Professor Rajmohan Gandhi. ICESSD also hosted the International INWENT Dialogue on Violence and Crime Prevention in 2010; the Annual Healing of Memory Lecture with Mrs. Ela Gandhi (Gandhi's grandaughter) as keynote speaker talking on "Restoring Humanity" in August 2011; and the Global Peace Youth Summit in cooperation with the National Peace Alliance in October 2011. All ICESSD events, whether workshops, trainings, conferences, or seminars, are attended by a mix of delegates from NGOs, academia, government, and other organizations.

The center has also established an interdisciplinary research group on sport for development for postgraduate students at UWC and held young researcher's days and writing workshops in 2010 and 2011. ICESSD has been involved in curriculum development in the form of accredited short courses which offer students, university staff, teachers, coaches, government representatives, and community members opportunities for developing skills in the field of leadership, social transformation, and community development using sport as a vehicle. Presently, the program has thirteen registered courses in Life Skills and Community Peacebuilding; Conflict Management and Transformation; Leadership, Sport, Peace, and Development; Sport and Recreation for Community Development; and Monitoring and Evaluation for Sport and Development. Furthermore, UWC envisages starting a multidisciplinary MA degree in Sports for Development and a Postgraduate Diploma in Sport, Development, and Peace in January 2013.

The experience of having an Interdisciplinary Sport and Development Center at a university can be extremely positive and beneficial for the advancement of the field. However, it also can lead to many questions, discussions, and reflections about the role of universities in sport, development, and peace as outlined below.

Discussion

Although theoretical deliberations around aims and objectives of sport for development and peace as well as implementation of practical programs have lately been very much a topic at national and international gatherings of governments, civil society, and funding organizations, the role of universities in sport, development, and peace in this regard has been neglected and has only lately been getting more attention (Keim, Jordaan, Barrio, Chikwanda, Grover, Bouah, Asihel, Cabral, and Ley 2011).

Despite the call for the development of a global partnership in the MDGs focusing on awareness raising and knowledge exchange, academics are not listed with regards to key people working on multiple levels in sports for peace initiatives, according to the "Recommendations to Governments" as outlined in the Right to Play Report "Harnessing the Power of Sport for Development and Peace." Key people listed in the peace-building matrix include: community leaders, teachers, coaches, and top athletes, heads of NGOs/UN and Government organizations (Right to Play 2008, 234). Universities are also not mentioned in any of the twenty-five recommendations for government in the field of Sport and Peace.

Looking at the global effect of sports for development and peace programs, there seems to be a lack of qualitative and quantitative assessment at a local, national, and global level to ensure that internationally stated social and transformational goals for sports, peacebuilding, and community development are met. The strengths of universities in sports, peace, and development have been lately pointed out (Keim, Jordaan, Barrio, Chikwanda, Grover, Bouah, Asihel, Cabral and Ley 2011, 78) as the following:

- Research in and for peace and human development.
- Teaching, capacity building, and equipping the next generation of researchers.
- Community engagement: transfer of knowledge to the civil society and local communities (including adaptation of knowledge to the local context).
- Technical assistance.
- Awareness creation and education for sustainable development (including promotion of critical thinking and reflection).
- Outreach and development programs.
- Networking and collaboration among and between universities and groups of civil society.
- Publication of evidence-based recommendations in the field.
- Academic freedom (Ibid. 2011, 78).

In addition, universities can provide the following to partners in the field:

- Expertise in terms of human resources and research capacities.
- Knowledge production and transfer through teaching and training in the field. Forms of assessment and methods of evaluation to ensure that stated social and transformational goals for sport and community development are met.

With regards to national and international Policies and Governance, academics could play a more coordinated role in sports, development, and peace as they are able to:

- Inform and evaluate government policies for sports, development, and peace.
- Provide skills for implementation and meeting of goals of international protocols.
- Assist in building cooperative governance.
- Monitor and evaluate.
- Be consistent representatives at the table.
- Bridge the gap between academia, civil society, and government.

The above has the potential to build much needed evidence in the emerging area of sports and development, which universities can share widely with sport organizations, federations civil society, business, and government initiatives. In addition, regular events such as international conferences on sports for development and peace issues should be promoted and supported.

Looking at the work ICESSD is doing and its vision for further involvement for others universities, additional thoughts come to mind including:

(a) Difficult questions requiring honest answers.
(b) Sports, peace, and sustainable development.
(c) North–South collaboration.
(d) Lessons learned: sport as a tool for peacebuilding.

Difficult Questions Requiring Honest Answers

If we want to use sports as a means for peace and development particularly at the university context, we must not be afraid to ask—and honestly answer—some difficult questions:

- Are we all on the same page when we discuss concepts of sports, development, and peace?
- Is there a common understanding of the key concepts of sports, peace, and development, social transformation, and communities?
- Is there a common understanding of what players in the field see as sports, peace, and development? Is it their field of work, a project, a business, or a study?
- Are universities actively promoting sport as a tool for social transformation, development, and peace emphasizing its potential to address discrimination, inequity, stereotypes, and on their campuses and in the communities where they work?

- What can universities do and what are universities doing in terms of their human and other resources to promote sports, peace, and development in their teaching, research, and community engagement?
- Are and if so how are universities contributing to the transformation and development of their communities using sports?
- What new kinds of sporting opportunities are being created for students and young people?

Additional Challenges

- How can sports, development, and peace fit into a university whose strength and core business are seen as conducting research, delivering publications, and teaching in higher education?
- Are universities seen as institutions of higher learning which have objectivity and academic freedom or are they seen as ivory towers removed from the people and local realities when it comes to sports, development, and peace issues?
- What are the challenges for research approaches which claim to look at sports, development, and peace in participatory way but do not keep their promise to research subjects?
- How can researchers in the field of sports, development, and peace improve their approach in taking the needs and contexts of disadvantaged communities into consideration?
- How can we ensure that outcomes of research focused on sports, development, and peace are disseminated to empower communities and that applied research can be used as a tool for community development and sports?
- Conferences, workshops, and seminars give lately more and more feedback about individual academic research, teaching, and outreach results. However, what does the university do as collective or as an institution of higher learning?

North–South Collaboration

Can we as universities play a part to create awareness for more suitable and sensitive approaches from the North, regarding the approach to research and training in the development context?

Can the South Teach the North?

How can we assist the next generation of sports and development leaders (researchers, practitioners, and academics) through postgraduate training programs which have a developmental and cross-cultural emphasis, to become interdisciplinary skilled "pracademics" with the necessary sensitivity for multicultural and global issues.

These are only meant to be some preliminary questions which point out some of the challenges which impact on the role universities play or can play in the field of sports, development, peace, and which might be food for thought and should be seen as an encouragement to expand the list and to get involved in debates and discussions around them.

Lessons Learned: Sport as a Tool for Peacebuilding

If one wants to examine the role of universities in the field of sports, development, and peace, the starting point needs to be that the role of universities as institutions of higher learning has to be viewed in their individual contexts, below is an example using South Africa.

In South Africa, obstacles to community development and peace-building include attitudes which were ingrained by the apartheid system but which continue to exist even after the transition to democracy and undermine efforts for building more caring communities such as ethnic prejudices, racism, and xenophobia, and fear of the other.

In terms of sports, development, and peace in South Africa, it is crucial to establish first, what are the impediments to creating peaceful communities in the country? It is then essential to look at the role a university can play in the promotion of conflict transformation, reconstruction, and peacebuilding in South Africa in relationship to local governance structures, national governance structures, civil society, and each other using sports.

In the South African context, it is important to ask how can universities support and strengthen the work of NGOs and Civil Society in the area of conflict transformation, reconstruction, and peacebuilding in Africa using sports as a tool and how can NGOs and Civil Society strengthen the work of universities in the area of conflict transformation, reconstruction, and peacebuilding using sports as a tool. To include universities in the discussions and implementation of programs on sports and peace is about cooperative governance. There is a global demand for multistakeholder networks to foster good cooperative governance and partnerships, and thus inclusion which is a very important African approach as it adheres to the principles of transparency and fairness.

At ICESSD, the aim is to reinvigorate the culture of engagement that South Africa is famous for, using the examples set by Desmond Tutu, Nelson Mandela, and others. We also feel that *important lessons* can be drawn from the experiences of practitioners and from models which have been developed within communities to manage local conflicts as they arise and to promote peacebuilding. There is a need to expand the academic and intellectual discourse into interactive learning (and possibly joint curricula development) that serves to inform practice and practitioners and to provide academics with the space to draw lessons from experience and practice. This kind of cross-fertilization could address the shortcomings of the many uncoordinated initiatives in this field in South Africa, and address the need for networking and information sharing, as well as the interconnectedness of institutions of tertiary education with the rest of civil society, and the need for partnerships with other civil society organizations.

In this way, material causes of conflicts around access to resources and economic factors as well as the nonmaterial causes of community conflict that include racism, culture, ethnicity, tradition, religion, gender, and differences in value systems can be addressed in a more holistic and systematic manner.

The questions posed above show that there are challenges to the role of universities in sports, development, and peace, and to making relationships and projects in sports, development, and peace sustainable and mutually beneficial. Different visions, values, ethics, world views, approaches to teaching, research, and community engagement in the field of sports, development, and peace can undermine the success of even the best intentions to programs. Thus, the careful consideration of broader national contexts, histories, and meanings needs to ground sports, development, and peace initiatives no matter where they take place.

Sports are a reflection of any society's success stories and its miseries, its socioeconomic challenges, and its values. How we play our part as universities working in the field of sports, development, and peace need not be constrained as a reflection of what is. For sports to be transformative, for sports to bring peace within and between individuals and communities, the research, teaching, and community outreach sport programs we create must be a reflection of where we want to go, of who we want to be, as people and as a nation and as global citizens. The decision remains up to us.

Note

1.   See: http://www.un.org/sport2005/a_year/mill_goals.html.

References

Abdalla, Amr. 2005. "Keynote Speech at the Nelson Mandela Seminar on the Role of Universities in Conflict Transformation, Reconstruction, and Peace Building in Africa, September 2005." In *Role of Universities in Conflict Transformation, Reconstruction and Development*, ed. Marion Kein, 55–71. Leuven: Uitgeverij Lannoo Press.

124   Sports, Peacebuilding and Ethics

Allison, Lincoln, ed. 2000. *Taking Sport Seriously.* 2nd ed. Oxford: Meyer & Meyer Sport.
Archer, Robert, and Antoine Bouillon. 1982. *The South African Game: Sport and Racism.* London: Zed Press.
DSR Department of Sport and Recreation, South Africa, ed. 1995. *Sport and Recreation in South Africa: A National Policy Framework.* White paper (Draft). Pretoria: Government Printer.
Galtung, Johan. 1964. "An Editorial." *Journal of Peace Research* 1: 1–4.
———. 1996. *Peace by Peaceful Means: Peace and Conflict, Development and Civilization.* Oslo: International Peace Research Institute.
Keim, Marion. 2003. *Nation-Building at Play—Sport as a Tool for Social Integration in Post-Apartheid South Africa.* Oxford: Meyer & Meyer Sport.
———, ed. 2007. *The Role of Universities in Conflict Transformation, Reconstruction and Development.* Leuven: Uitgeverij Lannoo Press.
———. 2009. "Translating Olympic Truce into Community Action in South Africa—Myth or Possibility." In *Olympic Truce-Peace and Sport.* Athens: International Olympic Truce Centre.
Keim, Marion, Gerard Jordaan, Maria Rato Barrio, Clever Chikwanda, Tarminder Grover, Lyndon Bouah, Solomon Asihel, Jose Cabral, and Clemens Ley. 2011. "Sport and Development from the Perspective of University." In *Sport und Internationale Entwicklungszusammenarbeit,* ed. Karen Petry and Michael Gross, 75–96. Köln: Sportverlag Strauss.
Miller, Christopher E. 2005. *A Glossary of Terms and Concepts in Peace and Conflict Studies.* University for Peace, Africa Programme. San Jose, Costa Rica: University for Peace.
Niven, John McGregor. 1982. *The Educational System in the Republic of South Africa.* Occasional Paper No. 4. Pietermaritzburg: Departmant of Education, University of Natal.
O'Connell, Brian. 2012. *Mandela Day Presentation,* July 13, 2012. UWC, Bellville, South Africa.
Pfaffenholz, Thania. 2003. *Community-Based Bottom-Up Peacebuilding.* Nairobi, Kenya: Life and Peace Institute, Modern Lithographic.
Right to Play. 2008. "Harnessing the Power of Sport for Development and Peace, Recommendations to Government." Toronto. Sport for Development and Peace International Working Group (accessed April 5, 2012).
Rose, Brian, and Raymond Tunmer. 1975. *Documents in South African Education.* Johannesburg: Donker.
Sanders, Daniel. 1994. "The Role of Universities in Peace and Social Development." *Journal of Social Development in Africa* 9, no. 1: 51–58.
South African Communication Service, ed. 1994. *South Africa Yearbook.* Pretoria: South African Communication Service.
Sparks, Alister. 1990. *The Mind of South Africa.* New York: Ballantine Books. 196 ff.
United Nations. 1992. "An Agenda for Peace, Preventive Diplomacy, Peacemaking and Peace-keeping." Report of the Secretary-General Pursuant to the Statement Adopted by the Summit, Meeting of the Security Council, New York.
United Nations Office on Sport for Development and Peace (UNOSDP). 2008. "Harnessing the Power of Sport for Development and Peace: Recommendations to Governments." Final Report, SDP International Working Group. http://www.un.org/wcm/webdav/site/sport/shared/sport/pdfs/SDP%20IWG/Final%20SDP%20IWG%20Report.pdf (accessed April 5, 2012).
UWC. 2009. "UWC History." http://www.uwc.ac.za/index.php?module=cms&action=-showfulltext&id=gen11Srv7Nme54_8987_1210050562&menustate=about (accessed March 30, 2012).

Protection through Corporate Marketing in Professional Sports

M. Lee Brooks and Michael B. Shapiro

> *"Every kid around the world who plays soccer wants
> to be Pele. I have a great responsibility to show them
> not just how to be like a soccer player, but how to be
> like a man."*
>
> —Pele, Brazilian soccer player,
> considered possibly the world's greatest

Introduction

As members of society, we require rules to live by. This is true in both war and peace, in our general social interactions and, most certainly, in athletics. These rules govern our behavior, telling us when our actions are fair play or out of bounds. Beyond the rules themselves, ethics is an overarching concept that applies to all forms of human conduct and relations.

While the gladiatorial "win at any cost" way might have suited the ancient arenas, that approach is not acceptable in modern sports or in real-life situations. Instead, we have established limits on our actions. In sports, these are contained both within the game rules and the organizational guidelines. Coaches apply these rules, often quite visibly. Indeed, good coaches not only apply game rules established by leagues or associations, but also apply these separate rules that benefit the teams and the individual players themselves. When this happens, exceptionally talented athletes may find that they never enter the arena, ball field, or court because of

125

violations of internal rules. A referee, umpire, or on-field official may never blow a whistle or cite an infraction if coaches or team administrators publicize and both conspicuously and uniformly apply rules of good conduct and professional behavior. In short, clearly established rules avoid and prevent unnecessary conflict and promote peace, they ensure that there is no conflict unrelated to the contest at hand.

It is well documented that professional sports teams, including the leagues, owners, staff that have a direct impact on the game itself, and the players, enjoy protection and privileges generally not extended to other major corporations. This is demonstrated in the fact professional sports teams are protected from the laws in the United States associated with monopolies and portions of the antitrust laws Congress has passed.[1] It is vital to the interests of the professional athletic corporations and the various professional athletic leagues that they govern themselves in a manner consistent with the expectations of lawmakers, fans, and other corporations that rely on the corporation or league to market their products. Furthermore, product protection dictates that leagues market their product in a manner consistent with generally accepted rates of growth in revenue for that product. Business models anticipate market growth, streams of revenue, and sustaining market levels that ensure long-term viability.

Professional athletic leagues invest heavily in merchandize, arenas, amenities for fans, scholarships, social, and community commitments, but the single largest investment, as with most corporations, is the human resources side of the business—here the players. It is important to note here that the players are the products that are generally identified, by both the avid fan and the casual observer, as the product of the sport, rather than all of the other assorted business aspects of professional athletics. The players are the face of the organizations and have to represent the product that is being marketed. Policies and procedures are in place to protect the product, and are weighted heavily toward the players' conduct, both on and off the field, so as not to damage the product they represent. These policies and procedures are designed to project an image that has been introduced into the business model by the corporations. Ultimately, the product protection is image.

The development of the policies and procedures has been examined, and any significant developments or evolutions of the policies have been compared and noted. Each league or corporation enters into collective bargaining agreements that govern and bind both parties to acceptable levels of conduct. A large portion of the collective bargaining agreements addresses player conduct, administrative procedures for disciplinary action, grievances, and appeals of actions taken by the league for conduct that may have an adverse impact on the image of the product.

While individual teams fall under the collective bargaining agreements, with certain limitations, they each reserve the right to develop and implement additional policies that may be more restrictive than the collective bargaining agreements. The purpose of these additional policies is to protect the image of the specific team. For example, the New York Yankees, as a team policy, do not allow facial hair (Rozell 2009), something that is not addressed by Major League Baseball's collective bargaining agreement.

As the players are the image of the teams and the league, they assume a celebrity status. This necessarily means that the media will cover their activities, in the athletic arena and beyond. On- and off-field exploits will affect, positively or negatively, the teams', the league's, and the public's attitudes. Thus, it is in the teams' and the corporations' best interests to educate each of the players, as well as monitor and sanction inappropriate behavior, all while emphasizing, rewarding, and publicizing positive community commitments.

Growth rates over the past ten years have demonstrated a significant rise in the value of individual teams, significant increases in player salaries, and a generally held perception by the public that players belong to a "millionaires club." This has been an era of prosperity. With few exceptions, everyone associated with these sports in the United States have benefited monetarily. The team owners have seen a rise in the value and financial viability of their investments. Players' compensation has grown to unprecedented levels, both for star players and as a result of substantial increases in league-minimum pay. Public money has been used for construction of new arenas, some costing a billion dollars or more, in demonstration of the value that a major league team has on a community.[2]

Player selection, retention, and marketing are critical to the success of the operation of not only the team, but also the league as well. Because of this, risk assessment and management have become important issues. Who will be the team's star and the face of the team affects fan support, merchandizing, attendance, and viewership, all of which directly affect the bottom line of the teams and leagues. Potential employees (players) are subjected to batteries of psychological testing, medical examinations which include screening for the use of illegal or banned substances, IQ tests, background investigations by private investigators which may include interviews with friends, family, and others associated with the player, and canvassing of their social networking and media posts. Negative findings may result in the player being moved further down in the draft order, which translates to a lower entry-level salary, but minimizes the risk of selecting a player who may have significant character flaws that could jeopardize the image of the team and league, potentially damaging the overall product. Even experienced players are subjected to a vetting process with a heavy emphasis on character issues and fitting into the community.

Athletes who reach this level are competitive by their very nature. Certainly, the financial rewards are a potential motivator. Generally, professional athletes may also be motivated by a deeper commitment to the sport; however, this may not be universal (Gregory 2012). The culmination of a professional career may be induction in that sport's Hall of Fame. There is clearly a code of conduct for such admission, and the teams market their Hall of Fame members extensively. Players who excelled in their sports over a professional lifetime have been denied access for conduct, on- or off-field, that damaged the image of the game.[3] Simply being great at the sport is not enough, the player has taken on a larger role than merely demonstrating athletic prowess. He or she has been charged with protecting the product, and failure to do so may have everlasting consequences.

Definitions

For the purpose of this chapter, because the different sports use different terminology, these definitions will be used interchangeably as each organization is discussed.

Collective Bargaining Agreement—Mutually accepted contract that binds employer and employee, generally for a specific term and with specific conditions relating to compensation, benefits, rules and regulations, and performance standards.

Corporation (Athletic)—For the purposes of this chapter, an athletic corporation is the governing body for a professional sport. Examples would include Major League Baseball (MLB), the National Football League (NFL), the National Basketball Association (NBA), the National Hockey League (NHL), and the Professional Golf Association (PGA).

Corporation (Nonathletic)—For the purposes of this chapter, a nonathletic corporation is a for-profit organization generally governed by a Board of Directors that may be publically or privately held.

Hall of Fame—An organization that recognizes players who have met the criteria for admittance generally based upon player performance, character, community involvement, and "ambassadorship" for their sport.

Leagues—Subdivisions generally for the purpose of balancing schedules, geographic distribution, and maintenance of fan interest through rivalries, and for determining play beyond the regular season.

Legal Precedent—Statutory law or binding case law precedent, such as decisions of the US Supreme Court.

Media—Print, audio, or video generated either by the athletic corporations themselves, or the news or entertainment industries.

Off-Field Conduct—That conduct which may rise to the level of illegality, or involving moral turpitude, serious lapses in judgment, or for any other reason deemed to be unbecoming of a professional athlete.

On-Field Conduct—Conduct outside the rules generally accepted for the efficiency and play of the game. Examples would include unsportsmanlike or egregious conduct determined not to be in the best interest of the sport.

Owners—The person or persons who have a majority or controlling interest in a team that is a member of an individual league and/or athletic corporation.

Player Associations—A group of professional athletes that have formed an organization to advocate for conditions of employment.

Player Contracts—Binding agreements entered into by employer and employee that identify individual conditions of employment, compensation, and performance, as opposed to general terms covered in the collective bargaining agreement.

Players—Participants in the professional athletic endeavors, not including the administrative, coaching, or support staff.

Policies and Procedures—Principles that govern the management of organizations.

Product—That which is being produced by the corporations. For nonathletic corporations this may be as simple as goods and/or services, however, for athletic corporations and the purposes of this chapter we will use a very broad definition including the game itself, the marketing, merchandize, vending, athletes, etc.

Product Protection Strategy—Any decision, policy, or procedure designed with the specific intent of minimizing critical assessments of the product.

Risk Analysis/Risk Management—A process or strategy designed to maximize investment and minimize loss.

Staff That Have a Direct Impact on the Game Itself—Owners, senior management, managers, coaches, and player evaluators or scouts.

Team (or Member or Club)—The individual professional sports groups that make up either the "leagues" or the "athletic corporations."

Literature Review

In 1982, Thomas J. Peters and Robert H. Waterman, Jr. wrote:

> Our research told us that any intelligent approach to organizing had to encompass and treat as interdependent at least seven variables: structure, strategy, people, management style, systems and procedures, guiding concepts and shared values (i.e., culture), and the present and hoped for corporate strengths or skills (Peters and Waterman 1982, 9).

Peters and Waterman's book, *In Search of Excellence*, was an examination of sixty-two companies covering a broad spectrum of American corporations in the service, technology, consumer goods, general industrial, product management, and resource-based fields. Performance from 1961 through 1980 was analyzed. Companies that passed all of the authors' hurdles for excellent performance were identified. Six different criteria were used and qualifying companies were in the top half of all of their industry's competitors in at least four of the six over the twenty-year period. Indeed, seventeen companies ranked in the top half of all six measures, while an additional six companies met five of the six benchmarks.

The criteria used to identify these superlative companies were only the first step. They were economic measurements that examined investment and return. Further analysis of these top companies focused not on the economics, but rather on the methodologies of how these corporations succeeded. The common themes that ran through all of the successful corporations were placed into eight categories: bias for action, close to the customer, autonomy and entrepreneurship, productivity through people, hands-on value driven, stick to the knitting, simple form lean staff, and simultaneous loose-tight properties. "Above all, the *intensity* itself, stemming from strongly held beliefs marks these companies. The love of the product and customer was palpable" (Ibid., 16).

A "bias for action" means identifying and addressing problems or issues without delay. In professional athletics, automatic review of scoring plays by the National Football League and the National Hockey League exemplifies this. Fans, indeed the industry itself, mandate that plays that result in a score or which may have resulted in a score but for the on-field call of the officials are immediately examined using "instant replay" to ensure the accuracy of the call. Similarly, the National Basketball Association uses these video replays to confirm whether a shot was inside or outside the "three point" line or to determine whether time remained when the shot was taken. Substance abuse policies implemented not only by the major professional leagues, but also throughout athletics including cycling, swimming, and the Olympics, also evidence a "bias for action" and the need to protect the product. In the middle of the 2011–2012 season, the National Football League responded to the potential for on-field injuries by adding trainers to league booths and watching for players exhibiting symptoms or conditions that would require a medical response.

> The project showed more clearly than could have been hoped for that the excellent companies were, above all, brilliant on the basics. Tools didn't substitute for thinking, intellect didn't overpower wisdom, analysis didn't impede action (Ibid., 13).

To the uninitiated observer, it is quite apparent that there are leaders in the various markets, to those who study the markets it is obvious why certain companies excel while others maintain the status quo. While there are numerous theories why some flourish while others flounder, research has identified aspects of the leading companies that make them successful. That is not to say that there is a simple formula that makes one company successful and another unsuccessful. It is not a matter of either/or when it comes to being successful. Certain companies are successful when measured against certain market variables, but they do not rise to the next level of success. When examining the level of success of the four professional sports organizations, it is difficult to argue that they have not been successful. Each, in its own right, has surpassed financial success, enjoys wide spread viewer support, and has expanded to markets generally not known as large media centers. As has been argued in other places, this may be a product of noncompetition for that particular sport, but the success that has been enjoyed cannot be dismissed as a function of the product.

Treacy and Wiersema (1995) conducted a three-year study of eighty corporations in thirty-six different markets in an attempt to identify variables that made them market leaders. These variables were identified as values exhibited by the company that allowed them to lead their markets in success as measured by a share of the market, customer satisfaction, and financial success. The values displayed resulted in four rules that govern the management of the company. These four rules are:

1. Provide the best offering in the marketplace by excelling in a specific dimension of value.
2. Maintain threshold standards on other dimensions.
3. Dominate your market by improving value year after year.
4. Build a well-tuned operating model dedicated to delivering unmatched value.

The authors identified three value disciplines, a philosophy, and way of operation that describes how a business is run. The first value discipline was "operational excellence," which is illustrated by a general model that executes well with guaranteed low prices and hassle-free customer service. Waste is minimized and efficiency in operations is rewarded. Companies that demonstrated this value are Wal-Mart, McDonald's, and GE. The second value discipline demonstrated by market leaders was "product leadership." These companies offer the best product and continuously innovate to make the product better. Companies identified in this group included Sony, Johnson & Johnson, Apple Computer, and Nike Footwear. The third value identified was "customer intimacy," which was defined as focusing on a specific customer need, cultivating that relationship, and satisfying that need with the best solution. The axiom here is never lose a customer and to increase your business with the client. Examples of these values were IBM and Nordstrom. The lesson to be learned from this is that a company cannot be all things to all customers, which suggests that a company should select a value system that best suits their product. The culture developed from adopting one of the values will propel the company to the next level of success.

During the research for *The Discipline of Market Leaders* (Ibid.), the authors discovered that the market places in the 1990s were different from market places in the past. There was increased competition and new models had to be developed to maintain or increase a share of the market. As they discovered truisms about the market place, they developed rules to apply to these changes.

The first new imperative they found was, "Different Customers Buy Different Kinds of Value." This led to rules one and two, which state, one, provide the best offering in the market place by excelling in a specific dimension of the value, and, two, maintain threshold standards on other dimensions. Another rule was developed based on the concept of, "As Value Standards Rise, So Do Customer Expectations." This led to the idea that companies must dominate the market by improving value year after year. Finally, "Producing Unsurpassed, Ever-Improving Value Requires a Superior, Dedicated Operating Model." Companies must build a well-tuned operating model dedicated to delivering unmatched value. An examination of the four professional sports organizations reveals that each developed value oriented cultures, maintained adherence to the rules, and enjoyed a great deal of success beginning in the 1990s.

When is success simply not the standard for which organizations are measured and should organizations be satisfied with being successful?

Are organizations capable of making the leap to a level beyond success as measured by market share, financial stability, long-term viability, and sustainability in the market place? As has been discussed earlier, research has identified companies that excel at what they do based on specific economic indicators, but what of those companies or organizations that go beyond just being successful. There are organizations that exceed the economic indicators on a consistent basis and have reached a different level of success that places them in the category of having gone from an excellent performing company to be a great company performing at unsurpassed levels of success.

In *Good to Great*, Jim Collins (2001) sets out to identify factors that were present in companies that made the leap from being a very good organization to being a great organization. Again, economic variables were used to measure and define great companies. While many companies are on the cusp of greatness, there are clearly identifiable factors that allow certain companies to make the leap while others remain good. Being good is no longer the standard of measurement for an organization; companies strive to become great.

The first factor identified in the research was what was called having a Level 5 leader. This was having a leader of a company who was dynamic and could lead the company to the next level. What was particularly interesting was that the Level 5 leader is not a person who seeks the media attention, is larger than life, and who is egotistical in their approach. Rather the Level 5 leader is more self-effacing, quiet, reserved to the point of being shy, who has personal humility, and professional will.

Secondly, the popular trend for organizations is to set a vision, develop a mission statement, and create a five-year business plan that directs the organization. Many fail because they do not recognize the second fundamental aspect of great companies that is to first get the right people on board and get the wrong people off the bus before determining where the bus is going. Level 5 leaders typically assess the management staff to determine if the right people are in place to lead the organization to the next level. Once the right people are selected and placed in the right positions, the organization can move in the right direction to obtain greatness.

Thirdly, great companies confront the brutal facts but never lose faith. The basis for developing this revelation came from a prisoner of war who confronted the reality of his situation, but never lost faith in the fact that he would be rescued or released one day. Great companies recognize the reality they face, confront it, and have an attitude that they will succeed.

This faith, that in the end you will prevail, must never waiver regardless of the difficulties you face.

Great companies or organizations have a "culture of discipline," which is quite different from having discipline. Most organizations have discipline as it relates to a process of maintaining order and structure, but great companies have a culture of discipline. This is demonstrated by basic concepts such as when you have disciplined people, you do not need a hierarchy. If you have disciplined thoughts, you do not need a bureaucracy; when you have disciplined actions, you do not need excessive controls. A culture of discipline creates an environment where people are allowed freedom to be creative because they are disciplined in their life. This approach is nurtured and permeates the organization.

Great companies also think differently about technology and the application of technology. They do not use technology as the primary means for transformation, but they are pioneers in the application of carefully selected technology. Collins discovered that technology by itself was never the root cause of either greatness or decline.

Great companies and great organizations simply think and act differently than companies that are good. The transformation takes place for several reasons, but it takes passion and commitment on the part of the entire organization. To waste time on actions that are not purpose driven is simply not going to produce rewards. The degree to which the company excels is directly related to the actions of the Level 5 leader. Insuring the right people are on board the bus, while removing the wrong people, will create a culture of discipline necessary for transformation to occur.

The four professional sports organizations, as a whole, have flourished over the years, but conversely, some individual franchises have not enjoyed the same level of success. Indeed, the National Basketball Association currently owns the New Orleans franchise because of poor management of that franchise. The National Hockey League allowed the Atlanta franchise to relocate to Canada because of poor management, and currently owns the Phoenix franchise. Major League Baseball is currently accepting bids for the Los Angeles Dodgers franchise because the owner went into bankruptcy. Yet, as a league, each of these has enjoyed great success over the past decade as measured by viewership, financial success, and share of the market place.

Applications of Crisis Management to Product Protection

Generally, the application of product protection policies, procedures, models, strategies, and decision making are precipitated by circumstances typically described as a crisis. Critical Incident Management, Integrated Command Structure, Emergency Operations Command, Disaster Preparedness, and various other monikers have been applied to the process of dealing with situations beyond the norm. Public safety, along with the military, has utilized these methods for many years and the process is accepted as a best practices methodology. While the procedures have been around for many years, they have gained popularity in the past decade because of the events of September 11, 2001, and the subsequent awareness of potential disasters. The concepts are extended from man-caused events, to natural disasters, as well as any event falling outside the norm. Many public safety agencies employ the methods on every event to which a response is required.

For public safety agencies or any agency that has a responsibility to save lives, critical incident management is a vital organizational function on which they will be evaluated. Any loss of life, while tragic, will be the standard for which the agency will be held accountable and evaluated. Slow response, ill-conceived plans, irrational decisions, or a perception that the event was simply overwhelming will result in a negative image that will persist for many years.

For organizations that produce a product, or provide a service that is dependent on the public for the survival of that product, critical incident management has become a mainstay of their existence. Failure to address a crisis can have far-reaching implications for the organization and in some instances, threaten the very viability of the organization. The term crisis has various connotations depending on the manner in which it is applied. For public safety personnel or military personnel under hostile situations, the term crisis has a significantly different meaning than when applied by someone who cannot find their car keys. Both may represent a crisis for the individuals, but the differences in scope should be apparent.

Organizations have become more adept at dealing with crises as they have become more familiar with the consequences of not handling them properly. For the discussion here, the term crisis is defined as a significant threat to operations that may have a negative impact on the product if not handled efficiently. While purposefully broad, the definition encompasses events or situations that are outside the normal operations of an organization and will have a negative impact on that organization. A significant threat is represented by the potential damage that can be inflicted on the organization or those dependent on the organization. This damage may be financial, harm to public safety, or the loss of a reputation that was developed over the years. Any threat to the organization must be perceived as a threat to the product, which is the lifeline of the organization. Thusly, product protection is merely a survival technique employed by way of crisis management. "Crisis can create financial loss by disrupting operations, creating a loss of market share/purchase intentions, or spawning lawsuits related to the crisis" (Coombs 2007, 1–14). Professional sports organizations are somewhat insulated from the loss of market share because of a lack of competition from other similar sports; however, failure to protect the product through crisis management could result in a loss of viewership or fan support as people turn to other options. It is important to note that a crisis can stem not only from team, staff, or player action, but also from acts by fans.[4] A subsequent shift by followers and enthusiasts would result in a loss of revenue, along with a loss of reputation.

Although the damage associated with any crisis is varied, the loss of reputation may be the most difficult to overcome and may result in sustained losses for extended periods: "A crisis reflects poorly on an organization and will damage a reputation to some degree. All crises threaten to tarnish an organization's reputation" (Dilenschneider 2000). It should be apparent that any crisis to an organization would have a financial impact on the organization. The goal of the organization is to handle the crisis in an efficient manner, minimizing the damage to the reputation, and reducing the financial loss to the organization. The lessons gleaned from the public safety environment suggest that crisis management is a process and not simply a "one approach fits all" technique. While specific aspects of the process have to be identified and implemented by the organization's hierarchy, it is generally accepted that there are critical measures that should be employed.

There are three points that should be emphasized during the initial response to any crisis: (1) be quick, (2) be accurate, and (3) be consistent. "A quick response is active and shows an organization is in control" (Carney and Jordan 1993, 34–35). Conversely, research indicates how silence is too passive (Hearit 2006). This is a clear indication that the organization is not in control and it allows others to control the crisis. A quick response creates credibility for the organization, allows the process to continue, and results in the organization gaining control of the situation. The application of this concept was illustrated during the 2011 football season when there were several violent collisions that resulted in concussions for players. In one particular incident, a player was not properly diagnosed with a concussion and was allowed to reenter the game. The National Football League was heavily criticized for not taking a much stronger approach to closed head injuries. The National Football League responded quickly by placing a medical staff person in a booth that would allow observation of players exhibiting closed head injury symptoms. A failure to respond quickly, accurately, and consistently with stated policies would have resulted in damage to the product by way of its reputation.

While preparation, along with the initial response, is vital to minimizing the damage to an organization, it would be disingenuous to believe a crisis will not leave some mark on the product. To not plan for the recovery of reputation or credibility is to plan for failure and long-term loss financially. Bill Benoit has identified strategies to repair the damage to the organization's reputation (1997a, 1997b, 177–80). These strategies are identified as follows:

1. Attack the accuser: crisis manager confronts the person or group claiming something is wrong with the organization.
2. Denial: crisis manager asserts that there is no crisis.
3. Scapegoat: crisis manager blames some person or group outside of the organization for the crisis.
4. Excuse: crisis manager minimizes organizational responsibility by denying intent to do harm and/or claiming inability to control the events that triggered the crisis.
    *   Provocation: crisis was a result of response to someone else's actions.
    *   Defeasibility: lack of information about events leading to the crisis situation.
    *   Accidental: lack of control over events leading to the crisis situation.
    *   Good intentions: organization meant to do well.
5. Justification: crisis manager minimizes the perceived damage caused by the crisis.
6. Reminder: crisis managers tell stakeholders about the past good works of the organization.
7. Ingratiation: crisis manager praises stakeholders for their actions.
8. Compensation: crisis manager offers money or other gifts to victims.
9. Apology: crisis manager indicates the organization takes full responsibility for the crisis and asks stakeholders for forgiveness.

This is not to suggest that every crisis warrants a strategy to repair or restore the organization's reputation, but having them in the tool box allows for an efficient response to the entire event and not just the initial phases. The four major professional sports organizations have a unique business model for controlling activities, both inside and outside the workplace, which might lead to a negative perception regarding the product.

138   Sports, Peacebuilding and Ethics

Collective Bargaining Agreements, Contracts, and Disciplinary Procedures

As a part of the collective bargaining agreements between the players' unions and management, each sport has included a variety of clauses that not only describe performance measures, but also in many cases include oaths of loyalty to fans and the ever-nebulous game. While the four major sports organizations are indeed businesses, and therefore follow a business model that ensures financial success, unlike traditional corporations, they must also employ standards of conduct in recognition of the position they occupy in the public's eye. It is clear through the collective bargaining agreements, individual player contracts, and team rules that the integrity of the game, therefore the product, is or strived to be of the highest concern.

Major League Baseball addresses these concerns in Article XII, which is the Discipline article, and various other subsections in the Major League Baseball Players Association Collective Bargaining Agreement, dated 2007–2011. Not only is player conduct addressed, but also loyalty to the teams and League and even the American public are demanded.[5] It is clear, through the loyalty clause, that not only are there performance standards, but also personal conduct standards as well.

The National Football League similarly addresses personal conduct and behavior.[6] In the NFL Collective Bargaining Agreement, dated 2006–2012, one finds a significantly more detailed set of rules, including "conduct detrimental to [a c]lub"[7] and actions "detrimental to the integrity of, or public confidence in, the game of professional football."[8] The Agreement is so detailed that it even outlines a letter of termination based on personal conduct.[9]

The National Hockey League addresses personal conduct in the NHL-NHLPA-2005 Collective Bargaining Agreement Article 18, Commissioner Discipline, which is unique because it differentiates between on-ice and off-ice conduct, and in the individual player contracts. The National Hockey League also gives significant attention to performance-enhancing substances in Article 47, Performance-Enhancing Substances Program.[10]

Finally, the National Basketball Association is unique in and of itself because it has, in addition to a player code of conduct, a separate fan code of conduct (NBA 2012). The intimacy of the basketball court, unlike the forced physical separation of fans and players in a baseball or football stadium, or at an ice rink, combined with "fan frenzy," increases the likelihood of inappropriate behavior. Further, the NBA Collective Bargaining

Agreement, dated 2005, includes a clause addressing the issue of firearm possession,[11] as well off-court, nonbusiness related, violent behavior.[12] The National Basketball Association also requires that each player should take mandatory life skills programming[13] to address issues where crises tend to develop, as well as skill-enhancement programs in both "media training and the business of basketball."[14] While certainly seen as a benevolent attempt at assisting players with necessary skills, one would be naïve to believe that it is not designed to protect the league as well.[15]

Examples of the Application of Product Protection Policies and Procedures

One Man—One Sport

In 1996, Eldrick Tont "Tiger" Woods turned pro. The game of golf and the Professional Golf Association have never been the same. Certainly over the years there have been a myriad of star players. Names like Robert T. "Bobby" Jones, Sam Snead, Arnold Palmer, and Jack Nicklaus come to mind, but none have taken the game by storm the way Woods has done. He is the highest-paid professional athlete in the world, having earned an estimated $90.5 million from winnings and endorsements in 2010 (*BBC Sport* 2010). These earnings were in spite of his failure to win any of the three majors he played that year since he returned from a self-imposed break from golf following revelations about extramarital affairs. During his career, Woods has earned, from game play alone, nearly $95 million dollars, and has won some seventy-one PGA events (*PGA Tour*). In 2010, *Forbes* estimated his net worth at $600 million (Badenhausen 2010).

Between December of 2009 and early April of 2010, Woods took leave from professional golf. Later in 2010, he lost the world number one ranking and his ranking gradually fell to a low of #58 in November 2011 (*ESPN Golf* 2011). While, at one time, his endorsements included General Motors, Titleist, General Mills, American Express, Accenture, and Nike, Inc., following his admission of infidelity, several companies reevaluated their relationships with him. Accenture, AT&T (The Associated Press 2010), Gatorade (*BBC News* 2010a), and General Motors (*BBC News* 2010b) completely ended their sponsorship deals, while Gillette suspended advertising featuring Woods. Even the magazine *Golf Digest* suspended Woods' monthly column as of the February 2010 issue (Kelly 2009). *Business Wire* magazine reported that shareholders in his company lost up to $12 billion (UC Davis Graduate School of Management 2009).

For the PGA, the scandal could not have been worse. For more than ten years, the PGA and the name of Tiger Woods had been inextricably linked. The PGA went into crisis mode, seeking to boost the image of clean cut, family man Phil Mickelson (Kay 2009). Other fresh young faces were also promoted by the PGA, but, in the end, they found that their television ratings suffered (Rishe 2011). Marketing industry pioneer, Nielsen, once waxed poetic about Woods' effect on golf's television ratings when he returned in February of 2009 following rehabilitation after knee surgery (Nielsen 2009).

As expected, PGA television viewership dropped precipitously during Woods' prolonged absence (Klayman 2009). According to Michael Bamberger, senior writer at *Sports Illustrated*, "TV ratings basically double when Tiger is playing in a Tour event" (SI Golf Group 2009; Gorman 2009). Bamberger called this the "Tiger Effect." Prior to Woods' return to professional golf, David Dusek, deputy editor for Golf.com was quoted ". . . it's going to be a circus like golf has never seen before. Ratings for that event will be huge. In the long run, if Tiger wins as he has in previous years, he'll still draw eyeballs to televisions" (Gorman 2009).

Protect the Player

NFL/NHL Concussions

Responding to reports of serious closed-head injuries and concussions, the National Football League continues to amend its rules in an effort to safeguard the players. In December of 2010, the League announced that it would require "certified athletic trainers in the press box to help monitor head injuries" (*Fox Sports* 2011). The purpose of adding the trainers to the elevated site is to "monitor the entire game without distraction and inform medical personnel on the sideline of any potential head injuries" (Ibid.), and it was implemented after Cleveland Browns quarterback Colt McCoy sustained a concussion earlier in the month after an illegal helmet-to-face mask hit by Pittsburgh linebacker James Harrison. McCoy was knocked out of the game by the hit, but returned after only two plays and was not tested for a concussion on the sidelines.

Harrison received a penalty for roughing the passer on the play, and later became the first player since 1986 to receive a suspension for making a tackle on the field (Ulrich 2011), and the first player to be suspended for a helmet-to-helmet hit at a time when the NFL Commissioner Roger Goodell and the entire League were attempting to enforce enhanced player safety rules (Schefter and The Associated Press 2011). The NFL has modified its rules to include Article 13(3) in Section 2 of Rule 12, prohibiting defensive players from using their helmet against a passer who is in a defenseless posture, including by "forcibly hitting the passer's head or neck area with the helmet or facemask, regardless of whether the defensive player also uses his arms to tackle the passer by encircling or grasping him."[16]

For the 2011 season, the NFL modified its rules, including several for the purpose of protecting its players. These changes included Rule 12-2-8 to prohibit illegal "launching" into a defenseless opponent and Rule 12-2-9 which incorporated former rules regarding "defenseless players" into a new article with standardized protection.[17]

The NFL also requires its teams to use a "Sideline Concussion Assessment Tool (SCAT),"[18] at the beginning of a season, and again after a possible injury.[19] This test is an adaptation of the Sports Concussion Assessment Tool 2 (SCAT2).[20] While the assessment is only a tool, in February of 2011 (NFL 2011a), the NFL revised its policies and practices to address possible concussive incidents (NFL 2011b).

Following the implementation of the concussive assessment tool, more than three hundred former NFL players have filed suit against the League alleging significant injuries (Simon 2012). On a motion made by the NFL, four of the cases have been consolidated in the Eastern District of Pennsylvania (Needles 2012). Famed Dallas Cowboy's running back Tony Dorsett is one of the litigants, claiming that more "should have been done in the past to warn about the dangers of concussions" (Armour 2012).

The NFL, a $9 billion per year industry, and its member teams are alleged to have had "a culture of indifference . . . toward concussions and other injuries." In response, and using Super Bowl XLVI's global stage where one-minute commercials cost $3 million, the NFL aired a one-minute TV commercial highlighting rule changes over the years designed to make the sport safer. John Mara, owner of the New York Giants, was quoted "None of us want to put players in perilous situations . . . I don't want to see guys that are on this team, 20 years from now, with debilitating injuries, no matter what they are" (Ibid.).

The NFL issued a statement in December of 2012 denying responsibility for the players' injuries alleged in the suit. "The NFL has long made player safety a priority and continues to do so. Any allegation that the NFL intentionally sought to mislead players has no merit. It stands in contrast to the league's actions to better protect players and advance the science and medical understanding of the management and treatment of concussions" (The Associated Press 2012a).

The National Hockey League is also dealing with concussive injuries. Between May and August of 2011, three NHL "enforcers," players known for their aggressive play and intimidation of opponents, died. One, Derek Boogaard, who died as a result of a toxic combination of painkillers and alcohol that police ruled an accident, hadn't played for months while trying to recover from concussions sustained in on-ice bouts (Cohen 2011).

In 2010, former NHL enforcer Bob Probert died suddenly at age forty-five. During his autopsy, it was discovered that he had Chronic Traumatic Encephalopathy, a degenerative brain disease. Probert, a legendary tough guy who had a history of alcohol and drug abuse, died of heart failure while on a family boat outing. The NHL and NHL Players' Association have jointly run a behavioral program to help players dealing with personal problems, including substance abuse and other issues. Following one of the more recent deaths, NHL Commissioner Gary Bettman said he expected the program to be reviewed, "I don't think any sports league does more than we do, but maybe there's more, as we focus on it, that we need to focus on" (*Yahoo!Sports* 2011).

Hockey concussions aren't only factors in deaths. The League's "poster child," Sidney Crosby, has suffered from them since at least the 2010–2011 season. Crosby, who entered the League in the 2005 draft, has been featured by the NHL repeatedly. At a time when interest in hockey was waning, the NHL actively sought to use him in marketing efforts. The entire 2004–2005 season had been lost to a labor stoppage. Crosby burst onto the scene, setting franchise records for assists and points as a rookie, and was named an alternate captain of the Pittsburgh Penguins that year, rising to team captain in 2007 and leading them to the Stanley Cup two years later. As the youngest captain ever to win the Cup, the NHL continued an unabashed campaign featuring Crosby.

During the 2010–2011 season, Crosby sustained a concussion as a result of hits to the head in back-to-back games. He was sidelined for ten and a half months, and after playing only eight games in the 2011–2012 season, the concussion-like symptoms returned in December 2011. He has not played since (Cotsonika 2012).

As the aptly titled article "NHL's problem with concussions goes far beyond Crosby" (Rossi 2012) states, "Seventy-two players missed at least one game because of a concussion or concussion-like symptoms. That's an average of 2.4 players for each of the NHL's 30 clubs, which have 23-man rosters." This is clearly a problem for the entire NHL. Indeed, the League and the NHL Players' Association officials meet no less than three times each year for a "concussion summit," a practice that began in 2009 (NHL 2009). The NHL has also adopted Rule 48, defining an "Illegal Check to the Head."[21] Further, the League prohibits players who show symptoms of a concussion from returning to game action before they are taken to a dark room and evaluated by a team physician, though few professional teams' physicians are neurological experts.

Banned Substances

There is confusion across sports regarding which drugs should be banned since the spectators themselves could legally purchase certain performance-enhancing training supplements at the local supermarket while the athletes could be punished for using the same supplements (Epstein 2003). It is noteworthy to examine how some sports have dealt with banned substances violations: "Major professional sports in the United States coordinate their own drug testing and use policies through collective bargaining agreements (CBAs) or consent from the professional athletes from their individual professional contract" (Ibid.). Unlike the Olympic Games where both punishment and deterrence are the major foci, professional sports use drug testing primarily to identify and initiate treatment of the offending athlete. Compounding the problem is the lack of a "uniform standard that applies to the NFL, NBA, NHL, and MLB. Each has different testing for a variety of drugs and punishments and treatment are different in each league" (Ibid., 179–80).

Major League Baseball

In 1998, Mark McGwire, of the St. Louis Cardinals and Sammy Sosa, playing for the Chicago Cubs, both broke New York Yankees' icon Roger Maris' long-standing record for the most home runs in a single season. Maris set the mark in 1961 with sixty-one "long balls" and the record stood for nearly forty years. McGwire ended the season with seventy home runs, and Sosa finished with sixty-six. Both have subsequently been linked to the use of "performance enhancing drugs" or PEDs. Sosa reportedly failed a test for such drugs in 2003 (Schmidt 2009), and had long been rumored to use anabolic steroids, although he consistently denied such use (Congressional Hearing 2005).[22] In 2010, McGwire admitted "that he used steroids on and off for nearly a decade" including "when he broke baseball's home run record in 1998." McGwire also admitted to using human growth hormone (Weinbaum and The Associated Press 2010).

For Major League Baseball, this is a critical problem. Six of the top fifteen all-time home run hitters have been linked to performance-enhancing drugs, including McGwire and Sosa, as well as Barry Bonds, Alex Rodriguez, Rafael Palmeiro, and Manny Ramirez (Ibid.). Prior to McGwire's admission, MLB Commissioner Bud Selig had commissioned former United States Senator George Mitchell to conduct an investigation into the use of PEDs in baseball.

Baseball certainly benefited from McGwire's and Sosa's home run battle. Only four years earlier, in 1994, the game suffered from a strike that ultimately lasted some 232 days, and which caused the cancellation of the entire postseason including the 1994 World Series. The home run derby revitalized fan interest in Major League Baseball even while the players were under a cloud of suspicion for the use of PEDs (Bodley 2006).

National Football League

As recently as October of 2011, and despite the best efforts of the National Football League and with the encouragement of members of Congress, the National Football League Players Association has declined to "begin testing for human growth hormone," claiming that "it needs more scientific information before it will consent to such a program" (Battista 2011). The union balked and has indicated that it wants to independently examine the accuracy of the blood test for human growth hormone, a test which has been used by the World Anti-Doping Agency since 2004. An agreement between the NFL, represented by Commissioner Roger Goodell, and the players' union had suggested that testing would begin in the 2011–2012 season, but "stipulated that the union had to agree to procedures for testing, and the union has raised concerns about whether the established ratio for a positive human growth hormone test is appropriate for professional football players" (Ibid.).

The Olympic Games

The International Olympic Committee (IOC) has taken perhaps the most proactive stance on the prevention of the use of performance-enhancing drugs of any athletic organization in the world. In 1968, the IOC established the first testing of forty International Olympic Committee athletes in the Grenoble, France Winter Olympic Games. Twenty years later, celebrated Canadian track star Ben Johnson was cited for his use of illegal steroids during the Seoul, Korea Games. Johnson was stripped of his gold medal in the one hundred-meter race and also was disqualified from the World Championships where he'd finished first the year earlier (*Agence France-Presse* 2008). The Olympic Movement has set the standard for both competition drug testing and out-of-competition testing; however, enforcement is often left to each country's national Olympic committee and the individual national governing body for the particular Olympic sport (Epstein 2003). Despite long-standing efforts to detect and prevent substance abuse, the Olympics continue to be marred by such behavior. Marion Jones was an American sprinter. She won five medals at the 2000 Summer Olympics in Sydney, Australia, including three gold medals. Ultimately, the medals were taken away after she admitted to taking steroids before the Games and later lying to federal agents about her drug use. She was suspended from competing in track and field events for two years and sentenced to serve six months in jail (Beresini 2011).

Cycling

Perhaps no major sport has faced such persistent allegations of the rampant use of performance-enhancing drug (PED) as has professional cycling. The Union Cycliste Internationale (International Cycling Union or UCI) is cycling's international federation as recognized by the International Olympic Committee (IOC). The UCI's Mission Statement includes a reference to its fight "against doping."[23]

Lance Armstrong, the seven-time winner of the famed Tour de France bicycling event was dogged by allegations of the use of performance-enhancing drugs throughout his career. Armstrong steadfastly denied the rumors. In fact, he tested positive once, for cortisone during the 1999 Tour, but he later produced a physician's note indicating the drug was necessary to treat saddle sores. A former teammate, Floyd Landis, accused Armstrong and other top cyclists of doping (Schmidt and Macur 2010).

Landis won the 2006 Tour De France only to have his victory nullified after a positive doping test. He subsequently sent "a series of emails to cycling officials and sponsors admitting to, and detailing, his systematic use of blood transfusions and performance-enhancing drugs during his career" (Albergotti and O'Connell 2010). The US Anti-Doping Agency also banned him from the sport for two years.

In May of 2011, former Armstrong teammate Tyler Hamilton also accused Armstrong of injecting a banned performance-enhancing drug "many times" during their cycling careers on the CBS television show

60 Minutes (Keteyian 2011; Overtime Staff *CBS News* 2011). That same month Hamilton voluntarily surrendered his 2004 Olympic cycling gold medal "after admitting to doping during his cycling career" (Macur 2011). Hamilton had been sanctioned twice for doping prior to his retirement.

Beginning in 2006, the UCI conducted tests of athletes' blood, both in and out of competition. Annual tests have increased each year, from an initial 8,253 to 13,516 in 2010.[24] In 2011, twenty-eight infractions were reported.[25] This compares with forty-three incidents reported in 2006.[26] The dramatic reduction led Ettore Torri, the anti-doping prosecutor for the Italian National Olympic Committee (CONI) to report that while doping "has not been eliminated [it has been] reduced 'a great deal'" (Benson 2011). Torri noted that in 2011 only one doping case was instituted from the cycling grand tours. His positive sentiments were echoed by the International Cycling Union's anti-doping manager, Francesca Rossi, who said that cycling's approach to the doping problem "should be taken as an example. Other sports do a lot of testing but in terms of quality they don't compare to us. Cycling is always in the spotlight but today it's at the vanguard of anti-doping" (Ibid.).

Torri's comment might have been a bit premature. In October 2010, barely a year before his claim that doping has been reduced when he stated: "The longer I'm involved in this the more I marvel at how widespread doping is . . . [a]nd I don't think it will be eradicated. Because it just evolves continuously. There are new substances coming out that can't be tested for" (Farrand 2010). On February 3, 2012, US Attorney André Birotte, Jr. announced that he was "closing an investigation into allegations of federal criminal conduct by members and associates of a professional bicycle racing team owned in part by Lance Armstrong" (The Associated Press 2012b), just days later the Court of Arbitration for Sport, sport's highest court, stripped fellow cyclist Alberto Contador of his 2010 Tour de France title and banned him for two years after they found him guilty of doping (Logothetis 2012). This made Contador only the second Tour de France champion to be disqualified and stripped of victory for doping, following American Floyd Landis who lost his 2006 title after testing positive for testosterone.

The prosecutor's decision to end the Armstrong investigation follows the failure to secure a conviction for lying about the use of steroids by baseball's home run king Barry Bonds. Bonds, who was found guilty of obstruction of justice and sentenced in December of 2011 to two years of probation including thirty days of home detention, is appealing his conviction (Mintz 2011). The steroid-related trial of another baseball star, former pitcher Roger Clemens, is scheduled to begin in mid-April 2012, after a judge declared a mistrial in the summer of 2011 when prosecutors showed jurors inadmissible evidence (Courson 2011).

In contrast to the ending of the criminal case, US anti-doping officials have indicated that they will not be dissuaded by the government's decision to close the Armstrong probe. Travis Tygart, the chief executive officer of the US Anti-Doping Agency has stated that "Unlike the US Attorney, USADA's job is to protect clean sport rather than enforce specific criminal laws . . . [o]ur investigation into doping in the sport of cycling is continuing and we look forward to obtaining the information developed during the federal investigation" (Shipley 2012).

Criminal/Violent Behavior

What if an athletic corporation fails to adequately discipline on-field egregious behavior? Similarly, when should civil authorities take action regarding off-field conduct and what is the corporate responsibility for punishment in such situations? These issues have been discussed for many years.[27]

On March 8, 2011, Montreal Canadiens' player Max Pacioretty received a hard check from Boston Bruins' defenseman Zdeno Chara during a NHL hockey game. Pacioretty hit his head on the glass partition between the benches, was rendered unconscious, fractured his fourth cervical vertebra, and suffered a severe concussion. While the on-ice officials ejected Chara from the game on an interference call, the NHL declined to suspend or fine him for the hit. Fans in Montreal, where the game was played, were irate and Montreal police began investigating the possibility of criminal charges (Jones 2011). Ultimately, the provincial prosecutors' office announced that it did "not believe a court would find Chara guilty of a crime and . . . closed the case" (Brehm 2011).

Precedent existed for the filing of criminal charges for hockey-related action. In October of 2010, then minor league player Patrice Cormier pled guilty to a charge of assault causing bodily harm following an elbow to the head of Quebec Remparts defenseman Mikael Tam. After the hit, Tam was convulsing on the ice, and suffered brain trauma and damage to his teeth. While in court, Cormier received an unconditional discharge, he had been suspended from play for the remainder of the 2009–2010 season (Vivlamore 2010). Cormier's sentence was identical to that received by the son of former Montreal Canadiens' goaltender Patrick Roy, Jonathan Roy, who was criminally charged after beating rival goalie Bobby Nadeau during an on-ice brawl in March of 2008 (*Postmedia News* 2010).

Perhaps the most celebrated on-ice incident of excessive violence in the modern era of hockey involved Marty McSorley of the Boston Bruins. On February 21, 2000, after losing an on-ice fight to Vancouver Canucks' player Donald Brashear, McSorley was unable to engage Brashear in another fight. Time was running out and the Bruins were behind in the score. McSorley skated toward Brashear and struck his head from behind with his stick. Brashear's head crashed into the ice and he went into convulsions. The NHL immediately suspended McSorley for the remainder of the season, and he was later convicted of criminal assault and given an eighteen-month conditional discharge by the court (USLegal, Inc., 2010–2013).

In one of the most famous, or perhaps infamous, incidents of violence in modern sports, former NBA player Latrell Sprewell choked his then Golden States Warriors' coach, P. J. Carlesimo, during a 1987 practice: "When he assaulted and threatened to kill his coach, P. J. Carlesimo, during a Dec. 1 practice, he committed one of the most outrageous acts on the court or field of play that American professional sports in the modern era has known, and that act will surely follow him for the rest of his life" (Taylor 1997). Not only did Sprewell threaten to kill Carlesimo and grab him by the throat and drag him to the ground, requiring other players to pull him away, about twenty minutes later Sprewell returned and went after Carlesimo again, throwing punches before he could again be hauled away: "Golden State responded to Sprewell's attack by first suspending him for 10 games, then, two days later, terminating his four-year, $32 million contract, which had nearly three years and about $25 million remaining, citing the conduct clause in the basic player agreement. That clause says players must conform to standards of good citizenship" (Ibid.). Only after the team had acted did the NBA finally step in when NBA Commissioner David Stern suspended Sprewell for one year, during which time he could not be paid by any NBA team. Ultimately, an arbitrator reduced the suspension from eighty-two to sixty-eight games, which cost Sprewell $6.4 million and his shoe endorsement contract with Converse (Puma 2004).

Seven years later, fighting in the NBA once again took center stage. This time it was a brawl not during a practice or between player and coach, but on the court during and after a regulation game, a fight that ended up in the stands. The Indiana Pacers and Detroit Pistons were already brawling during the 2004 game, but when a plastic cup was thrown at a player, the fight extended into the stands (Hoopedia 2004).[28] The fight, now known as "The Malice at the Palace" or "The Basketbrawl," caused significant changes by the NBA and even action by legal authorities; "The brawl was compared to some of the worst fan incidents in American sports history, such as Disco Demolition Night at Comiskey Park in 1979, as well as the hooliganism that is more prevalent in Europe" (Ibid.).

Eventually, the NBA handed down record suspensions following the incident. In all, nine players received suspensions from one day to the remainder of the 2004–2005 NBA season, a total of eighty-six games (seventy-three regular season, thirteen postseason), which was the longest in the history of the NBA for an infraction not related to drugs or gambling (Ibid.). The NBA invoked, under a pre-2005 Collective Bargaining Agreement, Rule 12-A-VII-c, "During an altercation, all players not participating in the game must remain in the immediate vicinity of their bench. Violators will be suspended, without pay, for a minimum of one game and fined up to $35,000" (Ibid.).

Recognizing fan involvement in the fight, the league said that it would review security procedures and alcohol policies at all arenas, and Commissioner David Stern vowed to impose lifetime, league wide bans on spectators who cause trouble. On February 17, 2005, the NBA imposed a new alcohol policy for all NBA arenas, including a size limit of 700 ml (24 ounces) for alcohol purchases and a maximum of two alcoholic beverage purchases for any individual person. Alcohol sales were also banned after the end of the third quarter (Ibid.). The league is the only major sport to have a "Fan Code of Conduct."[29]

While the NBA is often depicted as the edgiest of the four major sports, historically it has disciplined players for on-court altercations. Several incidents occurred prior to the "Basketbrawl" including in 2002 between the Portland Trailblazers and the Golden State Warriors (ESPN Research 2006),[30] and in a remarkable 1995 game between the Indiana Pacers and Sacramento Kings, where the NBA suspended sixteen players for fighting (Ibid.). Following the "Basketbrawl," the NBA has continued to address on-court fighting. In 2006, NBA Commissioner David Stern suspended Denver Nuggets' player Carmelo Anthony for fifteen games, while his teammate, J. R. Smith, and New York Knicks' player Nate Robinson each drew ten game suspensions. Four other players received suspensions, and both teams were fined $500,000 (Ibid.).

The NFL has dealt with off-field violence for years. Prior to 2000, most incidents involved alcohol and minor bar-room scuffles. That all changed in 2000 when two NFL players were charged with murder, and others were suspected of breaking and entering, drunken driving, and spousal abuse (*CBC News* 2000; Donatelli and O'Toole 2000). The incidents prompted then NFL Commissioner Paul Tagliabue to hand down the League's first suspensions for off-field violence—two-game suspensions to Jumbo Elliott of the New York Jets and Matt O'Dwyer of Cincinnati Bengals for their part in a bar fight and to Denard Walker of the Tennessee Titans, who pleaded guilty to assault on the mother of his child (Ibid.).

The incidents also prompted NFL coaches Mike Holmgren, Brian Billick, and Tony Dungy of the Tampa Bay Buccaneers to hold a seminar for NFL team owners and other coaches about how to deal with players who show the potential for violent behavior. They discussed the possibility of more intensive background screening on players eligible for the draft and cautioned players about reasons to stay out of trouble (Ibid.).

These words could not have been more prophetic in the case of former Atlanta Falcons and current Philadelphia Eagles' quarterback Michael Vick. In 2007, Vick and three codefendants were charged by a federal grand jury in Virginia with conspiring to engage in competitive dog-fighting, procuring, and training pit bulls for fighting, and conducting the enterprise across state lines (The Associated Press 2009a). After signing a plea agreement in which he admitted to conspiring with the codefendants, who were Vick's childhood friends, NFL Commissioner Roger Goodell suspended Vick indefinitely without pay. Vick ultimately plead guilty and was sentenced to spend twenty-three months in a federal prison. In 2009, the NFL's Goodell said that Vick would have to show genuine remorse to get a chance at resuming his career in the NFL. Later that same year, Vick was conditionally (The Associated Press 2009b), and subsequently fully (Adams 2009), reinstated by Goodell.

One-time NFL player Plaxico Burress was a Super Bowl hero. He caught the winning touchdown pass in the last minute of the New York Giants' 17-14 upset win over the previously unbeaten New England Patriots in Super Bowl XLII (2008). A year later, he was sentenced to two years in prison for violating New York's stringent gun laws having pled guilty to a firearms charge stemming from an incident in which Burress accidentally shot himself in the thigh at a Manhattan nightclub with a gun that had not been licensed in New York. He had already been cut by the Giants (Vacchiano 2009): "Hours after Burress pleaded guilty, the NFL announced that [C]ommissioner Roger Goodell had suspended [him and he was] ineligible to sign with any team until [completion of] his prison term. After that, Burress [would be eligible to] sign with an NFL team without further review" (Paolantonio and The Associated Press 2009). Following twenty months in prison, Burress was reinstated by the League (*CBS Sports* 2011) and subsequently signed with the New York Jets (Cimini 2011).

Gambling

In 1919, eight Chicago White Sox baseball players were allegedly involved in a conspiracy that fixed the World Series, and all the players were banned for life. The White Sox players, including "Shoeless" Joe Jackson, became known as the Black Sox. The 1919 Chicago White Sox had the best record in the American League, but were possibly the most unhappy team, as owner Charles Comiskey paid them some of the lowest wages in professional baseball. Comiskey used the "reserve clause" in players' contracts, which prevented them from changing teams without the permission of the owners, to keep salaries low. At that time there was no players' union to give them bargaining power.

During World War I, interest in baseball had dropped to an all-time low. The 1919 World Series was the first national championship after the war. Postwar enthusiasm for baseball took everyone by surprise. Indeed, national interest, which had reached its nadir only one year before, caused baseball officials to make the World Series a best of nine, instead of the traditional best of seven (*Chicago Historical Society*). Perhaps the most famous scandal in baseball history, eight of the players were accused of throwing the 1919 Series against the Cincinnati Reds.

The incident might never have been publicized except that the 1920 season was also marred by gamblers' payments to players: "In September 1920, a Cook County, Illinois, grand jury convened to look into allegations that the Chicago Cubs had thrown games against the Philadelphia Phillies. The investigation soon extended to the 1919 World Series and baseball gambling in general" (Ibid.). It was revealed that gambler Joseph Sullivan had approached White Sox player "Chick" Gandis and had offered players $100,000 to lose to Cincinnati Reds in 1919. "Shoeless" Joe Jackson had admitted to the grand jury that he had been promised $20,000 and paid $5,000, but those records were missing during the 1921 trial, only to be discovered in the possession of Comiskey's lawyer, George Hudnall, four years later. Eventually, all the players were acquitted.

"After the 1920 season, fearing baseball might not survive the gambling scandal, club owners decided to clean up their act. The three-man national commission, headed by Ban Johnson, was replaced by a single, independent commissioner with dictatorial power over baseball" (Ibid.).

Renowned federal judge Kennesaw Mountain Landis was named Major League Baseball's first Commissioner. In spite of the acquittals, Landis banned all eight players from the game for life. He said it was important to restore the public's faith in baseball, "regardless of the verdict of the juries, no player who throws a ball game, no player who undertakes or promises to throw a ball game, no player who sits in confidence with a bunch of crooked players and does not promptly tell his club about it, will ever play professional baseball" (Lowitt 1999).

Another notable victim of gambling impropriety is baseball player Pete Rose. Rose's alleged gambling problem led Major League Baseball to ban him from eligibility to baseball's Hall of Fame. In 1989, rumors of Rose having gambled on baseball games while a player with the Cincinnati Reds caused then outgoing MLB Commissioner Peter Ueberroth and his successor, A. Bartlett ("Bart") Giamatti, to retain attorney John Dowd to investigate the gambling charges. The official 225-page report, which Giamatti asserted was confidential, was released to the media by court officials and detailed a pattern of betting on baseball games between 1985 and 1987, including on fifty-two Reds' games. In August of 1989, an agreement banning Rose from baseball for life was reached, declaring Rose "permanently ineligible," but permitting him to apply for reinstatement after one year (Brioso and Barzilai 2004). The following year Rose pled guilty to concealing income on his tax returns and was sentenced to five months in prison followed by three months in a half-way house and one thousand hours of community service. In February of 1991, the National Baseball Hall of Fame adopted a rule stating that "any player on baseball's ineligible list shall not be an eligible candidate" for induction.[31] Rose has subsequently admitted to gambling on baseball multiple times, including in a 2002 meeting with MLB Commissioner Allan Huber "Bud" Selig, on ABC's Good Morning America in 2004, and on a sports radio program in 2007 where he said "I bet on my team to win every night because I love my team . . . I made a big mistake. It's my fault, it's nobody's else's fault . . . " (Lampert 1997).

Gambling is not limited to spectators and players. In 2007, former NBA referee Tim Donaghy pled guilty to two felony charges related to providing picks to co-conspirators. Donaghy had resigned from the league earlier that year while being investigated by the Federal Bureau of Investigation (FBI) for betting on games that he officiated over, thus avoiding a League suspension. It was alleged that he made calls affecting the point spread in those games (National Basketball Association). Donaghy served thirteen months in custody (*Fox News* 2009).

Tying It All Together

This chapter has taken a compressive look at the premise that major professional sports are businesses, albeit ones operating in a slightly different environment than traditional businesses. While a component of any business model addresses product protection, the professional sports institutions address it through participant behavior and general codes of conduct. They must protect their product, the image of the various sports, while promoting the merchandize, the event, and of course the players who often are the face of the individual organizations and the sport itself. In ordinary terms, sports marketing and profits have continued an upward trend over recent years, but how do we compare professional athletics with our customary business measurement tools?

Ownership interest, investors, or stockholders, are different from stake-holders. In sports, the stakeholders are clearly the fans, but the concept also includes the various vendors and sponsors, and perhaps even the local residents, taxpayers who may have funded outright, or at least subsidized, the sport and perhaps the sporting venue. Some residents may be unwilling stakeholders, because their local government made the decision to invest in the team, seeking long-term return on that investment, while others, the true local "fans," are stakeholders in both senses.

Turning to the businesses themselves and the leaders of the sports organizations, how do they measure up to our earlier business assess-ments? Are any of the four major sport commissioners Collins' *Good to Great* Level 5 leaders (Collins 2001)? One could argue that baseball's first commissioner, Judge Kennesaw Mountain Landis, was one, years before the concept was even created. Landis chose to "clean house" in baseball, declaring that "No player who throws a ball game, no player who undertakes or promises to throw a ball game, no player who sits in confidence with a bunch of crooked players and does not promptly tell his club about it, will ever play professional baseball" (Lowitt 1999). History remembers "Shoeless" Joe Jackson as a player who exceeded his season excellence during the 1919 World Series, but he too took money outside the game and suffered a lifetime ban.

Was Bart Giamatti a Level 5 leader when he banned Pete Rose, baseball's all-time hit leader (Davis 2000–2013), from the game for life (Brioso and Barzilai 2004)? Rose has not been inducted into baseball's Hall of Fame, and many argue he will never be inducted. Both Landis and Giamatti acted in what they perceived to be the best interest of their busi-ness, baseball, but did they meet the other criteria of being "self-effacing, quiet, and reserved to the point of being shy, who has personal humility and professional will?" How will NFL Commissioner Roger Goodell deal with the recent New Orleans Saints "bounty scandal" (Floyd Engel 2012)?

Peters and Waterman (1982) might agree that their *In Search of Excellence* seven variables (structure, strategy, people, management style, systems, procedures, guiding concepts, and shared values or culture) are evident in each of the major sports. We have already demonstrated that each of the sports, and others such as cycling and golf, have a "bias for action," quickly identifying and addressing problems or issues. Indeed, this is part of crisis management given the fickleness of fans and sponsors in the twenty-first century. Any organization, sports or otherwise, that fails to anticipate the potential for crisis and develop an anticipatory response to it is being remiss. Professional athletics have the tremendous potential for crisis given the wide variety of individuals involved and the media attention to their activities, both on and off the athletic fields.

Have these sports displayed Treacy and Wiersema's (1995) four rules governing management? It can certainly be argued that modern sports provide the "best offering in the marketplace by excelling in a specific dimension of value" (21), and that they "dominate [the] market [seeking to improve] value year after year" (21). However, can sports "maintain threshold standards on other dimensions" (22)? Without true competition, can they "[b]uild a well-tuned operating model dedicated to delivering unmatched value" (25)? Perhaps these are not adequate measurements given the uniqueness of sports in today's business markets. Treacy and Wiersema's value disciplines, "operational excellence" (xii), "product leadership" (xiii), and "customer intimacy" (xiii) might be better tools to gauge success.

One final distinction remains. While the traditional businesses operate in spheres governed by customers, stockholders, and lawmakers, professional sports may not have such restrictions. Clearly, the fans and sponsors can withhold their financial support; however, there is no "consumer protection agency" to protect them in ways that ordinary customers are safeguarded. Further, is there any avenue to "appeal" decisions of league commissioners? The business of sport clearly differs significantly from other businesses.

Conflicting Views

Perhaps former NBA star Charles Barkley said it best in his Nike commercial, "I am not a role model" (*Nike Air Commercial Charles Barkley* 2007). "He went on to say that parents, not someone who can dunk a basketball, should be the ones setting an example for their children" (*Morris Daily Herald* 2012). His friend and former basketball opponent, Karl Malone, who played for the Utah Jazz, while Barkley starred on the Phoenix Suns, retorted "Charles, you can deny being a role model all you want, but I don't think it's your decision to make. We don't choose to be role models, we are chosen. Our only choice is whether to be a good role model or a bad one" (Malone 1993).

Individuals, teams, and professional athletic leagues do not choose to be role models. They become them. It is inescapable that athletes and the teams they play for will be revered, not only by little children, but by fans and spectators of all ages. We want to see the incredible play. We show our enthusiasm and support by donning the colors appropriate to our favorite team. All the while, the owners and league management are working tirelessly, some more effectively than others, to safeguard the name, brand, and of course the image of that particular sport.

Conclusion

We have shown that there are many similarities between traditional corporations and the four major professional sports organizations, while at the same time demonstrating the uniqueness associated with the sporting industry (Wrage 2012). Common variables would include financial health, market share, viewership, and long-term viability. Differences would include a lack of competition in the true sense of business competition. The industry that the sports organizations find themselves in is entertainment, while being the only show in town. Marketplaces are defined by supply and demand using a traditional business model, whereas for the four sports organizations the marketplace is defined by the fan base, which oftentimes equates to large media markets or geographical bases.

As noted in the review of the literature, organizations survive by protecting the product that is offered to the customer. We have also seen that successful companies or the successful business models adhere to very well-defined strategies, policies and procedures, and management principles. What is abundantly clear is that those companies who practice specific management philosophies are extremely successful. Those that go beyond merely being "good" companies excel to a level of greatness. This, of course, begs the question, what is beyond greatness? Is there a next level that can be reached by applying management principles specifically designed to ensure long-term market growth? Major League Baseball has addressed this through participation in an Industry Growth Fund.

This chapter has also examined the application of crisis management principles in a nonlaw enforcement or public safety environment. Again, it is quite clear that those companies who practice anticipatory crisis management and who embrace crisis management principles are more likely to be prepared for, and thereafter restore their image and reputation after, a crisis. Crises will happen, they are inevitable, and the failure or inability to address them is a formula for business disaster. Because sports are part of an entertainment industry, it is people-oriented, and the odds of a crisis developing are undoubtedly higher than in a traditional business environment.

As a society, we revere our athletes and the teams they represent. We can argue that sports, in its various forms, have almost become a "sixth institution" for society. It is certainly, to some, as significant as education, government, religion, economics, and family. Sports consume our time and attention. We adjust our schedules around games or related events. Oftentimes, the sport defines who we are. The four major sports have made that transition from good to great, they have practiced market strategies that protect their image and reputation, and have become market leaders in their entertainment industry by practicing sound management principles that are designed specifically to protect the product they represent. This is reflected in the collective bargaining agreements, the players' conduct codes and the players' contracts.[32]One might conclude that all of these are in place, not to educate or protect the player, but primarily to protect the product.

Future Research

This chapter begins an introductory examination of the four major sports in the United States in terms of all of the things they have done to protect their product. Medical issues that must be addressed related to player injuries and the long-term health care necessary to meet their physical needs, remain to be examined. Players are now faster, stronger, and more physically fit than in the past. The games have gone from what was essentially a part-time employment opportunity to a year-round, 24/7/365, endeavor with an economic impact in excess of $10 billion for a single day's sporting event. To suggest that this is not big business which helps drive the economic engine of the United States, or any country, would be less than truthful.

The collective bargaining agreements, player conduct codes, and player contracts address and speak to what is in the best interest of the sport. Clauses such as "detrimental to the game," "in the best interests of," and "the highest standards of honesty, morality, fair play and sportsmanship" speak to subjective interpretation by those in positions of authority and responsibility. Analysis of discipline associated with a perceived violation of one of these clauses would be of interest to determine if disparate application of the policies was in place. Incidences where the use of the "best interests" clauses to discipline players, versus instances where similar conduct resulted in different action, might suggest an underlying principle for product protection.

Notes

1. See: Floyd v. Kuhn. 1972. 407 U.S. 258; *Sherman Antitrust Act*. 1890. Title 15 *U.S. Code*, §§ 1–7; and Federal Baseball Club v. National League. 1922. 259 U.S. 200.
2. For example, Minnesota Vikings (Arden Hills, Minnesota), Arizona Cardinals and Phoenix Coyotes (Glendale, Arizona), St. Louis Rams (St. Louis, Missouri), Indianapolis Colts (Indianapolis, Indiana). See, for example: (Williams 2008, 4; Florida State University Newsroom 2003; Udstrand 2011).
3. See: Peter E. Rose v. A. Bartlett Giamatti, et al. 1989. 721 F. Supp. 906 (S. D. Ohio); and the People of the State of Illinois v. Edward V. Cicotte, et al. 1921. Indictment No. 23912 (the Chicago "Black Sox" case).
4. See: (Pearson 2007; Stott and Pearson 2007; Cacciottolo 2007; Voices Editorials *The Independent* 2004).
5. See, for example, MLB. ARTICLE XII—Discipline, subsection A. Just Cause, SCHEDULE A, MAJOR LEAGUE, UNIFORM PLAYER'S CONTRACT, Section 3 (a), Loyalty, Section 3(b), Baseball Promotion, Section 7 (b) (1), Termination by Club, and SCHEDULE A, MAJOR LEAGUE, REGULATIONS, Section 5 dealing with fines and suspensions.
6. See, for example, NFL. ARTICLE VIII, CLUB DISCIPLINE, Section 1. Maximum Discipline, Section 2. Published Lists, Section 3. Uniformity, Section 7. Cumulative Fines, as well as ARTICLE XI, COMMISSIONER DISCIPLINE, Section 1. League Discipline, Section 5. One Penalty, APPENDIX C, NFL PLAYER CONTRACT, Section 11. SKILL, PERFORMANCE AND CONDUCT, Section 15. INTEGRITY OF GAME, and APPENDIX G, NOTICE OF TERMINATION.
7. See: National Football League Players Association. (2006). *NFL Collective Bargaining Agreement* 2006–2012, Article VIII, Club Discipline, Section 1. Maximum Discipline.
8. See: National Football League Players Association. (2006). *NFL Collective Bargaining Agreement* 2006–2012, Article XI, Commissioner Discipline, Section 1. League Discipline.
9. See: National Football League Players Association. (2006). *NFL Collective Bargaining Agreement* 2006–2012, Appendix G, Notice of Termination.
10. See, for example, NHL. ARTICLE 18, COMMISSIONER DISCIPLINE, Section 18.1 On-Ice Discipline and Section 18.2 Off-Ice Discipline, ARTICLE 47 PERFORMANCE ENHANCING-SUBSTANCES PROGRAM, Section 47.6 Testing Procedures and Section 47.7 Disciplinary Procedures, and the National Hockey League. 2005. *League Standard Player's Contract* (2005 FORM); wherein it states that "[t] he Player further agrees, . . . (e) to conduct himself on and off the rink according to the highest standards of honesty, morality, fair play and sportsmanship, and to refrain from conduct detrimental to the best interest of the Club, the League or professional hockey generally."

11. See: National Basketball Association. (2005). *NBA Collective Bargaining Agreement 2005*, Article VI Player Conduct, Section 9. Firearms.
12. See: National Basketball Association. (2005). *NBA Collective Bargaining Agreement 2005*, Article VI Player Conduct, Section 8. Counseling for Violent Misconduct.
13. See: National Basketball Association. (2005). *NBA Collective Bargaining Agreement 2005*, Article VI Player Conduct, Section 4. Mandatory Programs.
14. See: National Basketball Association. (2005). *NBA Collective Bargaining Agreement 2005*, Article VI Player Conduct, Section 5. Media Training and Business of Basketball.
15. See, for example, NBA. ARTICLE VI PLAYER CONDUCT, Section 4. Mandatory Programs, Section 5. Media Training and Business of Basketball, Section 8. Counseling for Violent Misconduct, Section 9. Firearms, Section 10. One Penalty, Section 11. League Investigations, and the NBA Fan Code of Conduct.
16. See: NFL 2011 Rule Changes. http://static.nfl.com/static/content/public/image/rulebook/pdfs/2_2011_Rule_Changes.pdf (accessed February 3, 2012).
17. See: NFL 2011 Rule Changes. http://static.nfl.com/static/content/public/image/rulebook/pdfs/2_2011_Rule_Changes.pdf (accessed February 3, 2012).
18. See: NFL Sideline Concussion Assessment Tool: *Baseline Test.* http://nflhealthandsafety.files.wordpress.com/2011/01/nfl-sideline-tool-baseline.pdf (accessed February 17, 2012).
19. See: NFL Sideline Concussion Assessment Tool: *Healthcare Professional Section.* http://nflhealthandsafety.files.wordpress.com/2011/01/nfl-concussion-tool-post-injury.pdf (accessed February 17, 2012).
20. See: *Sport Concussion Assessment Tool 2.* http://www.sportconcussions.com/html/SCAT2.pdf (accessed February 3, 2011).
21. See: NHL Official Rules, Rule 48 Illegal Check to the Head. http://www.nhl.com/ice/page.htm?id=64063 (accessed February 3, 2012).
22. "To be clear, I have never taken illegal performance-enhancing drugs. I have never injected myself or had anyone inject me with anything. I have not broken the laws of the United States or the laws of the Dominican Republic. I have been tested as recently as 2004, and I am clean" (Congressional Hearing 2005).
23. See: Union Cyclist Internationale (International Cycling Union) *Mission Statement.* http://www.uci.ch/templates/UCI/UCI1/layout.asp?MenuId=MTI2NjA&LangId=1 (accessed February 3, 2012).
24. See: Union Cyclist Internationale (International Cycling Union). *Testing Statistics.* http://www.uci.ch/templates/UCI/UCI1/layout.asp?MenuId=MTU2NjQ&LangId=1 (accessed February 3, 2012).
25. See: Union Cyclist Internationale (International Cycling Union). *Sanctions, Period of Ineligibility, Disqualification* [2011]. http://www.uci.ch/Modules/BUILTIN/getObject.asp?MenuId=MTU3Mjg&ObjTypeCode=FILE&type=FILE&id=NjY5M-TE&LangId=1 (accessed February 3, 2012).
26. See: Union Cyclist Internationale (International Cycling Union). *Decisions on Anti-Doping Rule Violations made in 2006.* http://www.uci.ch/Modules/BUILTIN/getObject.asp?MenuId=MTU3Mjg&ObjTypeCode=FILE&type=FILE&id=MzQ2N-zY&LangId=1 (accessed February 3, 2012).
27. For example: (Barry and Fox 2005, 1–25; Harary 2002, 197–217; Hechter 1976–1977, 425–53; Landry 2006; Samson 2005, 949–72; Yates and Gillespie 2002, 145–68).
28. See Hoopedia (2004), "Pacers-Pistons Brawl," *NBA.com.* http://hoopedia.nba.com/index.php?title=Pacers-Pistons_Brawl (accessed February 11, 2012).
29. See: NBA Fan Code of Conduct, National Basketball Association. http://www.nba.com/celtics/tickets_NBACodeConduct.html (accessed July 8, 2011).

30. Portland's Rasheed Wallace tried to go after a fan who threw something at him and was fined, two other players were suspended for two and three games, respectively, for fighting and other misbehavior after the game (ESPN Research 2006).
31. National Baseball Hall of Fame Rule 3 (e) "Any player on Baseball's ineligible list shall not be an eligible candidate." http://baseballhall.org/hall-famers/rules-election/bbwaa (accessed February 3, 2012).
32. See: Major League Baseball Players Association Collective Bargaining Agreement dated 2007–2011, Article XXV, *Industry Growth Fund.*

References

Adams, Cindy. 2009. "Eagles Quarterback Michael Vick Fully Reinstated to NFL." *Examiner.com*, September 3. http://www.examiner.com/us-headlines-in-national/eagles-quarterback-michael-vick-fully-reinstated-to-nfl (accessed February 11, 2012).

Agence France-Presse. 2008. "Olympics Fan Guide: Ben Johnson." http://sports.espn.go.com/oly/summer08/fanguide/athlete?athlete=6301 (accessed February 3, 2012).

Albergotti, Reed, and Vanessa O'Connell. 2010. "Cyclist Armstrong Denies Doping." *The Wall Street Journal*, May 20. http://online.wsj.com/article/SB10001424052748703691804575255410855321120.html (accessed February 3, 2012).

Armour, Nancy. 2012. "They Use You Up: Hall of Famer Dorsett Suing NFL." *Foxnews.com*, February 2. http://www.foxnews.com/sports/2012/02/02/use-up-hall-famer-dorsett-suing-nfl/ (accessed February 2, 2012).

Badenhausen, Kurt. 2010. "Tiger's Other Disaster." *Forbes*, June 25. http://www.forbes.com/2010/06/25/tiger-woods-golf-course-design-business-entertainment-celeb-tiger.html (accessed February 11, 2012).

Barry, Matthew P., and Richard L. Fox. 2005. "Judicial Opinion on the Criminality of Sports Violence in the United States." *Seton Hall Journal of Sports Law* 15: 1–25.

Battista, Judy. 2011. "Union Says Not Yet to Test for H.G.H." *The New York Times*, October 14. http://www.nytimes.com/2011/10/15/sports/football/nfl-union-not-ready-to-allow-blood-testing-for-hgh.html?ref=unitedstatesantidopingagency (accessed February 3, 2012).

BBC News. 2010a. "Tiger Woods Loses Gatorade Sponsorship." February 27. http://news.bbc.co.uk/2/hi/business/8540167.stm (accessed February 11, 2012).

———. 2010b. "GM Ends Car Loans for Tiger Woods." *BBC News*, January 13. http://news.bbc.co.uk/1/hi/business/8458194.stm (accessed February 11, 2012).

BBC Sport. 2010. "Tiger Woods Stays Top of Sport Earnings List." July 21. Accessed February 11, 2012, from.

BBWAA Election Rules. 2007. "National Baseball Hall of Fame and Museum." http://baseballhall.org/hall-famers/rules-election/bbwaa (accessed February 3, 2012).

Benoit, William L. 1997a. *Accounts, Excuses and Apologies: A Theory of Image Restoration*. Albany: State University of New York Press.

———. 1997b. "Image Repair Discourse and Crisis Communication." *Public Relations Review* 23: 177–80.

Benson, Daniel. 2011. "Doping in Cycling Greatly Reduced Says CONI Boss." *Cycling News*, November 20. http://www.cyclingnews.com/news/doping-in-cycling-greatly-reduced-says-coni-boss (accessed February 3, 2012).

Beresini, Erin. 2011. "The Top 10 Running Doping Scandals of All Time." *Competitor*, May 25. http://running.competitor.com/2011/05/news/the-top-10-running-doping-scandals-of-all-time_28190 (accessed February 3, 2012).

Bodley, Hal. 2006. "Baseball's Steroids Issue Remains in the News." *USA Today*, March 17. http://www.usatoday.com/sports/baseball/columnist/bodley/2006-03-16-bodley-steroids_x.htm (accessed February 3, 2012).

Brehm, Mike. 2011. "Bruins' Zdeno Chara Not Charged for Hit on Max Pacioretty." *USA Today*, November 17. http://www.usatoday.com/sports/hockey/nhl/story/2011-11-17/no-charge-for-chara/51270586/1 (accessed February 3, 2012).

Brioso, Cesar, and Peter Barzilai. 2004. "The Rose Scandal." *USA Today*, January 5. http://www.usatoday.com/sports/baseball/2004-01-05-rose-timeline_x.htm (accessed February 3, 2012).

Cacciottolo, Mario. 2007. "The Return of the English Disease?" *BBC*, April 6. http://news.bbc.co.uk/2/hi/uk_news/6532989.stm (accessed March 20, 2011).

Carney, Ann, and Amy Jordan. 1993. "Prepare for Business Related Crises." *Public Relations Journal* 49: 34–35.

CBC News. 2000. "NFL Grapples with Off-Field Violence, Crime." April 5. http://www.cbc.ca/sports/story/2000/04/05/f040105.html (accessed February 11, 2012).

CBS Sports. 2011. "Reports: Burress Reinstated, to Meet with Giants, Steelers." July 29. http://www.cbssports.com/nfl/story/15369551/reports-burress-resinstated-to-meet-with-giants-steelers/rss (accessed February 11, 2012).

Chicago Historical Society. "Charles Comiskey and the White Sox." http://chicagohs.org/history/blacksox/blk1a.html (accessed February 3, 2012).

Cimini, Rich. 2011. "Plaxico Burress Signs with Jets." *ESPN*, August 1. http://espn.go.com/new-york/nfl/story/_/id/6820679/plaxico-burress-new-york-jets-agree-one-year-deal-sources-say (accessed February 11, 2012).

Cohen, Tom. 2011. "Three Hockey Enforcers Die Young in Four Months, Raising Questions." *CNN*, September 2. http://edition.cnn.com/2011/SPORT/09/01/nhl.enforcers.deaths/index.html (accessed February 3, 2012).

Collins, Jim. 2001. *Good to Great: Why Some Companies Make the Leap . . . and Others Don't.* New York: Harper Business.

Congressional Hearing. 2005. "Restoring Faith in America's Pastime: Evaluating Major League Baseball's Efforts to Eradicate Steroid Use." House Committee on Oversight and Government Reform, 109th Congress, Testimony of Sammy Sosa, March 17, Serial No. 109-8. https://bulk.resource.org/gpo.gov/hearings/109h/20323.txt (accessed February 3, 2012).

Coombs, W. Timothy. 2007. "Protecting Organization Reputations during a Crisis: The Development and Application of Situational Crisis Communication Theory." *Corporate Reputation Review* 10: 1–14.

Cotsonika, Nicholas J. 2012. "How Sidney Crosby's Lost Year Changed Hockey." *Yahoo!Sports*, January 5. http://sports.yahoo.com/nhl/news?slug=nc-3periods-crosby-concussions-power-rankings-010512 (accessed February 3, 2012).

Courson, Paul. 2011. "Judge Sets New Trial for Clemens in April." *CNN*, September 2. http://articles.cnn.com/2011-09-02/justice/us.baseball.clemens_1_michael-attanasio-laura-pettitte-clemens-defense-attorney?_s=PM:CRIME (accessed February 11, 2012).

Davis, David. 2000–2013. "Career Leaders & Records for Hits." Sports Reference LLC. http://www.baseball-reference.com/leaders/H_career.shtml (accessed March 6, 2012).

Dilenschneider, Robert L. 2000. *The Corporate Communications Bible: Everything You Need to Know to Become Public Relations Expert.* Beverly Hills: New Millenium.

Donatelli, Joe, and Thomas O'Toole. 2000. "Wake Up, NFL: You've Got a Violence Problem." *ESPN*, February 1. http://assets.espn.go.com/nfl/s/2000/0201/329054.html (accessed February 11, 2012).

Epstein, Adam. 2003. *Sports Law.* Clifton Park, New York: Delmar Cengage Leaning; cited in: "Drugs and Testing." http://sportslaw.uslegal.com/drugs-and-testing/ (accessed February 3, 2012).

ESPN Golf. 2011. "Tiger Woods Moves to 50th in Rankings." November 13. http://espn.go.com/golf/story/_/id/7231583/tiger-woods-moves-50th-official-world-golf-rankings (accessed February 11, 2012).

ESPN Research. 2006. "Notable Brawls in NBA History." *ESPN*, December 18. http://sports.espn.go.com/nba/news/story?id=2701111 (accessed February 11, 2012).

Farrand, Stephen. 2010. "Torri Suggests Doping is Rife in Cycling." *Cycling News*, October 6. http://www.cyclingnews.com/news/torri-suggests-doping-is-rife-in-cycling (accessed February 11, 2012).

Federal Baseball Club v. National League. 1922. 259 U.S. 200.

Florida State University Newsroom. 2003. "Publicly Funded Stadiums Don't Pay Off." *Newswise*, May, 8. http://www.newswise.com/articles/publicly-funded-stadiums-dont-pay-off (accessed February 17, 2012).

Floyd Engel, Jen. 2012. "Blaming Saints is Height of Hypocrisy." *FoxSports*, March 6. http://msn.foxsports.com/nfl/story/New-Orleans-Saints-bounty-scandal-nature-of-game-roger-goodell-hypocrisy-030512 (accessed March 6, 2012).

Floyd v. Kuhn. 1972. 407 U.S. 258.

Fox News. 2009. "Tales of Personal Fouls: Disgraced Ex-NBA Referee Tim Donaghy Goes 'On the Record.'" *Fox News*, December 11. http://www.foxnews.com/story/0,2933,579988,00.html#ixzz1m70RB9qJ (accessed February 11, 2012).

Fox Sports. 2011. "NFL Will Have Trainers Help with Concussions." *Foxsports.com*, December 20. http://msn.foxsports.com/nfl/story/NFL-will-have-trainers-help-with-concussions-after-Cleveland-Browns-Colt-McCoy-incident-122011 (accessed February 3, 2012).

Gorman, Bill. 2009. "Tiger Woods Doubles TV Ratings, PGA Happy to Have Him Back." *TV by the Numbers*, February 25. http://tvbythenumbers.zap2it.com/2009/02/25/tiger-woods-doubles-tv-ratings-pga-happy-to-have-him-back/13497/ (accessed February 11, 2012).

Gregory, Sean. 2012. "Why Doesn't Serena Williams Love Tennis." *Time*, January 4. http://newsfeed.time.com/2012/01/04/why-doesnt-serena-williams-love-tennis/#ix-zz1mNKP8A7y (accessed February 14, 2012).

Harary, Charles. 2002. "Panel Discussion: Aggressive Play or Criminal Assault? An In Depth Look at Sports Violence and Criminal Liability." *Columbia Journal of Law and Arts* 25: 197–217.

Hearit, Keith Michael. 2006. *Crisis Management by Apology: Corporate Response to Allegations of Wrongdoing*. Mahwah: Lawrence Erlbaum Associates.

Hechter, William. 1976–1977. "The Criminal Law and Violence in Sports." *Criminal Law Quarterly* 19: 425–53.

Hoopedia. 2004. "Pacers-Pistons Brawl." *NBA.com*. http://hoopedia.nba.com/index.php?title=Pacers-Pistons_Brawl (accessed February 11, 2012).

Jones, Ashby. 2011. "Criminal Charges Mulled Over Hit in Bruins-Canadiens Game." *The Wall Street Journal*, March 11. http://blogs.wsj.com/law/2011/03/11/criminal-charges-mulled-over-hit-in-bruins-canadiens-game/ (accessed February 3, 2012).

Kay, Emily. 2009. "Tiger Woods' Sex Scandal Boosts PGA Tour Golf Star Phil Mickelson's Popularity." *Examiner.com*, December 22. http://www.examiner.com/golf-in-boston/tiger-woods-sex-scandal-boosts-pga-tour-golf-star-phil-mickelson-s-popularity (accessed February 11, 2012).

Kelly, Keith J. 2009. "Tiger Gets a Timeout: Golf Digest Suspends Column." *New York Post*, December 24. http://www.nypost.com/p/news/business/tiger_gets_timeout_fXvCsCQeU1OivyjBcOtstJ#ixzz1m77naljj (accessed February 11, 2012).

Keteyian, Armen. 2011. "Teammate: Lance ArmstrongCheated." *CBS News*, May 19. http://www.cbsnews.com/video/watch/?id=7366634n&tag=mncol;lst;3#ixzz1lLd-jvwKV (accessed February 3, 2012).

Klayman, Ben. 2009. "Toothless PGA with No Tiger." *New York Post*, December 11. http://www.nypost.com/p/news/national/toothless_pga_with_no_tiger_dU8sj86D-qWScSwkpmHqSDK (accessed February 11, 2012).

Lampert, Andrew. 1997. "The Pete Rose Hall-of-Fame Controversy." *Cosmic Baseball*. http://www.cosmicbaseball.com/prhof.html (accessed February 3, 2012).

Landry, James. 2006. "Sorting through the Legal Implications of Athlete on Athlete Violence." *Sports Litigation Alert Archives*, November 24. http://www.hackneypub-lications.com/sla/archive/000381.php (accessed February 3, 2012).

Logothetis, Paul. 2012. "CAS Strips Contador of 2010 Tour Title." *USA Today*, February 6. http://www.usatoday.com/sports/cycling/tourdefrance/story/2012-02-06/contador-doping-2010-tour-de-france/52986232/1 (accessed February 11, 2012).

Lowitt, Bruce. 1999. "Black Sox Scandal: Chicago Throws 1919 World Series." *St. Petersburg Times*, December 22. http://www.sptimes.com/News/122299/news_pf/Sports/Black_Sox_scandal__Ch.shtml (accessed February 3, 2012).

Macur, Juliet. 2011. "Hamilton Surrenders Cycling Gold Medal." *The New York Times*, May 20. http://www.nytimes.com/2011/05/21/sports/hamilton-surrender-ing-his-gold-medal.html (accessed February 3, 2012).

Major League Baseball Players Association Collective Bargaining Agreement dated 2007–2011, Article XXV, Industry Growth Fund.

Malone, Karl. 1993. "One Role Model to Another." *Sports Illustrated*, June 14. http://sportsillustrated.cnn.com/vault/article/magazine/MAG1138690/index.htm (accessed February 11, 2012).

Mintz, Howard. 2011. "Barry Bonds Sentenced to Two Years Probation, 30 Days Home Confinement." *Mercury News*, December 16. http://www.mercurynews.com/barry-bonds/ci_19563453?source=rss (accessed February 11, 2012).

MLB. ARTICLE XII—Discipline, subsection A. Just Cause, SCHEDULE A, MAJOR LEAGUE, UNIFORM PLAYER'S CONTRACT, Section 3 (a), Loyalty, Section 3(b), Baseball Promotion, Section 7 (b) (1), Termination by Club, and SCHEDULE A, MAJOR LEAGUE, REGULATIONS, Section 5 dealing with fines and suspensions.

Morris Daily Herald. 2012. "Not Model Behavior: Kids Need Their Role Models to Behave Like Role Models." January 27. http://www.morrisdailyherald.com/2012/01/27/not-model-behavior/axaaumf/ (accessed February 11, 2012).

National Basketball Association. 2005. "NBA Collective Bargaining Agreement 2005." Article VI Player Conduct, Section 4. Mandatory Programs.

———. 2005. "NBA Collective Bargaining Agreement 2005." Article VI Player Conduct, Section 5. Media Training and Business of Basketball.

———. 2005. "NBA Collective Bargaining Agreement 2005." Article VI Player Conduct, Section 8. Counseling for Violent Misconduct.

———. 2005. "NBA Collective Bargaining Agreement 2005." Article VI Player Conduct, Section 9. Firearms.

———. "Tim Donaghy." *National Basketball Association*. http://hoopedia.nba.com/index.php?title=Tim_Donaghy (accessed February 11, 2012).

National Football League Players Association. 2006. "NFL Collective Bargaining Agreement 2006–2012." Article VIII, Club Discipline, Section 1. Maximum Discipline.

———. 2006. "NFL Collective Bargaining Agreement 2006–2012." Article XI, Commissioner Discipline, Section 1. League Discipline.

———. 2006. "NFL Collective Bargaining Agreement 2006–2012." Appendix G, Notice of Termination.

National Hockey League. 2005. *League Standard Player's Contract* (2005 FORM).

NBA. 2012. "NBA Fan Code of Conduct." National Basketball Association. http://www.nba.com/sixers/news/NBA_fan_code_of_conduct.html (accessed February 14, 2012).

———. ARTICLE VI PLAYER CONDUCT, Section 4. Mandatory Programs, Section 5. Media Training and Business of Basketball, Section 8. Counseling for Violent Miscon-duct, Section 9. Firearms, Section 10. One Penalty, Section 11. League Investigations.

NBA Fan Code of Conduct, National Basketball Association. http://www.nba.com/celtics/tickets_NBACodeConduct.html (accessed July 8, 2011).

Needles, Zack. 2012. "NFL Concussion Suits Consolidated in Eastern District." February 1. http://www.law.com/jsp/pa/PubArticleFriendlyPA.jsp?id=1202540814651 (accessed February 1, 2012).

NFL 2011 Rule Changes. http://static.nfl.com/static/content/public/image/rulebook/pdfs/2_2011_Rule_Changes.pdf (accessed February 3, 2012).

NFL. 2011a. "NFL Announces New NFL Sideline Concussion Assessment Protocol." *Official Site of the New Orleans Saints*, February 25. http://www.neworleanssaints.com/news-and-events/article-1/NFL-Announces-New-NFL-Sideline-Concussion-Assessment-Protocol/b17c0f3c-edde-4d9d-a46d-5720bd958867 (accessed February 3, 2012).

————. 2011b. "The NFL's SCAT: Sideline Concussion Assessment Tool." December 11. http://www.sportsconcussions.org/ibaseline/the-nfls-scat-sideline-concussion-assessment-tool (accessed February 3, 2012).

————. ARTICLE VIII, CLUB DISCIPLINE, Section 1. Maximum Discipline, Section 2. Published Lists, Section 3. Uniformity, Section 7. Cumulative Fines, as well as ARTICLE XI, COMMISSIONER DISCIPLINE, Section 1. League Discipline, Section 5. One Penalty, APPENDIX C, NFL PLAYER CONTRACT, Section 11. SKILL, PERFORMANCE AND CONDUCT, Section 15. INTEGRITY OF GAME, and APPENDIX G, NOTICE OF TERMINATION.

NFL Sideline Concussion Assessment Tool: *Baseline Test*, http://nflhealthandsafety.files.wordpress.com/2011/01/nfl-sideline-tool-baseline.pdf (accessed February 17, 2012).

NFL Sideline Concussion Assessment Tool: *Healthcare Professional Section*. http://nflhealthandsafety.files.wordpress.com/2011/01/nfl-concussion-tool-post-injury.pdf (accessed February 17, 2012).

NHL. 2009. "Former Hockey Stars and Medical Professionals Debate Concussions at Summit." *NHL.com*, January 18. http://www.nhl.com/ice/news.htm?id=404975 (accessed February 3, 2012).

————. ARTICLE 18, COMMISSIONER DISCIPLINE, Section 18.1 On-Ice Discipline and Section 18.2 Off-Ice Discipline, ARTICLE 47 PERFORMANCE ENHANC-ING-SUBSTANCES PROGRAM, Section 47.6 Testing Procedures and Section 47.7 Disciplinary Procedures.

NHL Official Rules, Rule 48 Illegal Check to the Head. http://www.nhl.com/ice/page.htm?id=64063 (accessed February 3, 2012).

Nielsen. 2009. "Tiger's Return Expected to Make PGA Ratings Roar." *NielsenWire*, February 25. http://blog.nielsen.com/nielsenwire/online_mobile/tigers-return-expected-to-make-pga-ratings-roar/ (accessed February 11, 2012).

Nike Air Commercial Charles Barkley. 2007. Uploaded by DaniBoxx. http://www.youtube.com/watch?v=nMzdAZ3TjCA (accessed February 11, 2012).

Overtime Staff *CBS News*. 2011. "Ex-Teammate: I Saw Lance Armstrong Use EPO." *CBS News*, May 19. http://www.cbsnews.com/8301-504803_162-20064406-10391709.html?tag=stack (accessed February 3, 2012).

Paolantonio, Sal, and The Associated Press. 2009. "Burress Begins Sentence in Gun Case." *ESPN*, September 23. http://sports.espn.go.com/nfl/news/story?id=4493887 (accessed February 11, 2012).

Pearson, Geoff. 2007. "FIG Fact-Sheet Four: Hooliganism." Football Industry Group, University of Liverpool. http://www.liv.ac.uk/footballindustry/hooligan.html (accessed March 16, 2012).

Peter E. Rose v. A. Bartlett Giamatti, et al. 1989. 721 F. Supp. 906 (S.D. Ohio).

Peters, Tom, and Robert H. Waterman, Jr. 1982. *In Search of Excellence*. New York: Harper and Row.

PGA Tour. "Tiger Woods." http://www.pgatour.com/golfers/008793/tiger-woods (accessed February 11, 2012).

Postmedia News. 2010. "Patrice Cormier Pleads Guilty to Assault, Gets Discharge." *National Post,* October 19. http://sports.nationalpost.com/2010/10/19/patrice-cormier-pleads-guilty-to-assault-gets-discharge/ (accessed February 3, 2012).

Puma, Mike. 2004. "Sprewell's Image Remains in a Chokehold." *ESPN,* December 10. http://espn.go.com/classic/biography/s/Sprewell_Latrell.html (accessed February 11, 2012).

Rishe, Patrick. 2011. "PGA Tour Still Needs Tiger Woods to Drive Ratings." *Forbes,* August 16. http://www.forbes.com/sites/prishe/2011/08/16/pga-tour-still-needs-tiger-woods-to-drive-ratings/ (accessed February 11, 2012).

Rossi, Rob. 2012. "NHL's Problem with Concussions Goes Far beyond Crosby." *Pittsburgh Tribune-Review,* January 29. http://www.pittsburghlive.com/x/pittsburghtrib/sports/penguins/s_778973.html (accessed February 3, 2012).

Rozell, Kevin. 2009. "Steinbrenner's Facial Hair Policy and Those Famous Stache's." *Bleacher Report,* April 29. http://bleacherreport.com/articles/164919-steinbrenners-facial-hair-policy-those-famous-staches (accessed February 17, 2012).

Samson, Clete. 2005. "No Time Like the Present: Why Recent Events Should Spur Congress to Enact a Sports Violence Act." *Arizona State Law Journal* 37: 949–72.

Schefter, Adam, and The Associated Press. 2011. "James Harrison Suspended 1 Game." *ESPN,* December 14. http://espn.go.com/nfl/story/_/id/7348112/pittsburgh-steelers-james-harrison-banned-1-game-hit-cleveland-browns-colt-mccoy (accessed February 3, 2012).

Schmidt, Michael S. 2009. "Sosa is Said to Have Tested Positive in 2003." *The New York Times,* June 17. http://www.nytimes.com/2009/06/17/sports/baseball/17doping.html (accessed February 3, 2012).

Schmidt, Michael S., and Juliet Macur. 2010. "Cycling Doping Inquiry May Broaden." *The New York Times,* May 25. http://www.nytimes.com/2010/05/26/sports/cycling/26cycling.html (accessed February 3, 2012).

Sherman Antitrust Act. 1890. Title 15 *U.S. Code,* §§ 1–7.

Shipley, Amy. 2012. "Lance Armstrong Will Not Face Charges as Federal Doping Investigation is Shut Down." *The Washington Post,* February 3. http://www.washingtonpost.com/sports/cycling/lance-armstrong-federal-case-is-closed-as-us-attorneys-office-ends-probe/2012/02/03/gIQARWk5nQ_story.html (accessed February 11, 2012).

SI Golf Group. 2009. "PGA Tour Confidential: The Tiger Woods Scandal." *Golf.com,* December 6. http://www.golf.com/tour-and-news/pga-tour-confidential-tiger-woods-scandal (accessed February 11, 2012).

Simon, Scott. 2012. "A Fan's Notes on Pro Sports, Brain Damage." *NPR,* January 28. http://www.npr.org/2012/01/28/146022510/a-fans-notes-on-pro-sports-brain-damage (accessed January 28, 2012).

Sport Concussion Assessment Tool 2. http://www.sportconcussions.com/html/SCAT2.pdf (accessed February 3, 2011).

Stott, Clifford, and Geoff Pearson. 2007. *Football Hooliganism: Policing the War on the English Disease.* London: Pennant Books.

Taylor, Phil. 1997. "Centre of the Storm." *Sports Illustrated,* December 15. http://sportsillustrated.cnn.com/vault/article/magazine/MAG1011658/index.htm (accessed February 11, 2012).

The Associated Press. 2009a. "Timeline of Michael Vick Dogfighting Case." *The Virginian-Pilot,* July 27. http://hamptonroads.com/2009/07/timeline-michael-vick-dogfighting-case (accessed February 11, 2012).

————. 2009b. "Vick Cleared for Preseason Participation." *ESPN*, July 28. http://sports. espn.go.com/nfl/news/story?id=4359354 (accessed February 11, 2012).

————. 2010. "AT&T Cuts Connection with Woods." *ESPN Golf*, January 1. http://sports. espn.go.com/golf/news/story?id=4784720 (accessed February 11, 2012).

————. 2012a. "NFL: Concussion Claims Don't Belong in Courts." *ESPN*, January 26. http://sports.espn.go.com/espn/wire?section=nfl&id=7505542 (accessed February 3, 2012).

————. 2012b. "Prosecutors Won't Charge Cyclist Lance Armstrong." *Foxnews.com*, February 4. http://www.foxnews.com/sports/2012/02/04/prosecutors-wont-charge-cyclist-lance-armstrong/ (accessed February 4, 2012).

The People of the State of Illinois v. Edward V. Cicotte, et al. 1921. Indictment No. 23912 (the Chicago "Black Sox" case).

Treacy, Michael, and Fred Wiersema. 1995. *The Discipline of Market Leaders*. Reading: Addison-Wesley Publishing.

UC Davis Graduate School of Management. 2009. "Tiger Woods Scandal Cost Share-holders Up to $12 Billion, UC Davis Study Says." *Business Wire*, December 28. http://www.businesswire.com/portal/site/home/permalink/?ndmViewId=news_view&newsId=20091228005221&newsLang=en (accessed February 11, 2012).

Udstrand, Paul C. 2011. "Sports Subsidies Don't Add Up for Taxpayers. An Analysis of Minnesota Stadium/Arena Subsidies." *Twin Cities Indymedia*, May 1. http://www. tc.indymedia.org/2011/may/sports-subsidies-dont-add-taxpayers-analysis-minnesota-stadiumarena-subsidies (accessed February 17, 2012).

Ulrich, Nate. 2011. "NFL, Union Reps Meet with Browns to Review Concussion Protocol." *Ohio.com*, December 14. http://www.ohio.com/sports/browns/nfl-union-reps-meet-with-browns-to-review-concussion-protocol-league-suspends-steelers-harrison-for-hit-1.250298 (accessed February 3, 2012).

Union Cyclist Internationale (International Cycling Union). *Decisions on Anti-Doping Rule Violations Made in 2006*. http://www.uci.ch/Modules/BUILTIN/getObject.asp?MenuId=MTU3Mjg&ObjTypeCode=FILE&type=FILE&id=MzQ2NzY&LangId=1 (accessed February 3, 2012).

————. *Mission Statement*. http://www.uci.ch/templates/UCI/UCI1/layout.asp?MenuId=MTI2NjA&LangId=1 (accessed February 3, 2012).

————. *Testing Statistics*. http://www.uci.ch/templates/UCI/UCI1/layout.asp?MenuId=MTU2NjQ&LangId=1 (accessed February 3, 2012).

————. *Sanctions, Period of Ineligibility, Disqualification* [2011]. http://www.uci.ch/Modules/BUILTIN/getObject.asp?MenuId=MTU3Mjg&ObjTypeCode=FILE&type=FILE&id=NjY5MTE&LangId=1 (accessed February 3, 2012).

USLegal, Inc. 2010–2013. "Sports Violence." http://sportslaw.uslegal.com/sports-violence/ (accessed February 3, 2012).

Vacchiano, Ralph. 2009. "Giants Cut Plaxico Burress." *New York Daily News*, April 3. http://www.nydailynews.com/blogs/giants/2009/04/giants-cut-plaxico-burress.html (accessed February 11, 2012).

Vivlamore, Chris. 2010. "Cormier Pleads Guilty, Gets Unconditional Discharge." *Atlanta Journal-Constitution*, October 19. http://blogs.ajc.com/atlanta-thrashers-blog/2010/10/19/bogosian-modin-at-practice/?cxntfid=blogs_atlanta_thrashers_blog (accessed February 3, 2012).

Voices Editorials *The Independent*. 2004. "Another Sorry Outbreak of the English Disease." *The Independent*, June 17. http://www.independent.co.uk/opinion/leading-articles/another-sorry-outbreak-of-the-english-disease-730590.html (accessed March 20, 2011).

Weinbaum, Willie, and The Associated Press. 2010. "McGwire Apologizes to La Russa, Selig." *ESPN*, January 12. http://sports.espn.go.com/mlb/news/story?id=4816607 (accessed February 3, 2012).

Williams, Sarah. 2008. "Public Funding of Sports Stadiums." *Policy Perspectives* 4: 4. http://www.imakenews.com/cppa/e_article001083889.cfm?x=b11,0,w (accessed February 17, 2012).

Wrage, Alexandra. 2012. "Compliance Lessons for the Sports and Business Worlds." Law.com Corporate Counsel, April 5. http://www.law.com/jsp/cc/PubArticleCC.jsp?id=1202547978828 (accessed April 6, 2012).

Yates, Jeff, and William Gillespie. 2002. "The Problem of Sports Violence and the Criminal Prosecution Solution." *Cornell Journal of Law and Public Policy* 12: 145–68.

Yahoo!Sports. 2011. "Bettman: NHL to Look at Behavioral Programs." August 17. http://sports.yahoo.com/nhl/news?slug=txbettmanrypien (accessed February 3, 2012).

The Backbone for Success: A Study of Factors Influencing the Team Cohesion of a Division I Volleyball Team

Claudia Stura

*"If you don't have passion and pride, and connection
with the person standing next to you, then there's
really no team at all."*

Introduction

Sport is a unifying factor and a valuable method to promote peaceful
coexistence (Tokarski 2009). It can help to foster trust, team spirit, and
social bonding. Furthermore, it promotes (re)building cohesion (Henley
and Colliard 2005) that has been considered to be one of the most important variables in group dynamics (Carron, Eys, and Burke 2007). Without
cohesion, there is no group development and maintenance (Mullen and
Copper 1994). Thus, it is important to gain an in-depth understanding
of which factors influence team cohesion. As the microcosm sport may
offer important implications for building cohesion among groups not only
through sports but also in other, nonsport settings, this study used a sports
team to examine factors influencing team cohesion. For them, a strong
team cohesion, or the tendency for a group to stick together, has been found
to be important for one reason in particular: it crucially influences effective
teams (Carron and Dennis 1998) and team performance (NurFarah 2003;
Carron and Hausenblas 1998; Widmeyer and Williams 1991).

Studying factors influencing team cohesion is not new. Surprisingly, most prior studies have been quantitative. Hence, this study used direct observations and interviews to gain an in-depth understanding of factors influencing sport team cohesion. Aiming to identify unanticipated phenomena and influences as well as to understand the processes that led to team cohesion and the contexts in which it takes place (Maxwell 2005), the author looked at two factors in particular: the influence of conflict and the influence of the leadership. The study distinguished group cohesiveness between task and social cohesion (Chang and Bordia 2001; Widmeyer, Brawley, and Carron 1985), and "conflict" between task and social conflict. The variable "leadership" referred to the coaches of the team.

The chosen case was the volleyball team of a large, state-funded university, which plays at the NCAA Division I level in the United States. Volleyball was chosen because it requires team members to coordinate their efforts and performances to achieve success. As Kamphoff, Gill, and Huddleston (2005) argued, in volleyball, strong team cohesion may be more important to team success than individual player's skills.

The general research question for this study is the following: What factors impact the team cohesion of this Division I volleyball team? The team was observed for one semester during practice, games, and meetings. Furthermore, nine team members were interviewed in-depth. At the end of the study period, the participants took the Group Environment Questionnaire (GEQ) to determine the members' perception of their team's cohesion.

Major findings included that the head coach's behavior was a decisive factor, which positively impacts the team's cohesion. In addition to her way of facilitating communication, her direct communication style and her confrontational conflict management style seemed to be crucial in this regard. Moreover, the conflict avoidance management style the players mainly used seemed to influence the team's task cohesion in a negative way, while the rules the players followed when someone violated certain group rules seemed to influence the social cohesion positively. The GEQ scores indicated that the individual team members perceived their team's cohesion on a medium to high level. Furthermore, the study also discovered factors influencing the volleyball team's cohesion in a positive way that had not been reported yet, such as the use of rituals and the influence of holding each other accountable.

Literature Review

Studying factors influencing team cohesion among teams is not new. Especially in teams requiring combined efforts to perform well, fostering stronger team cohesion may be more important to team success than individual player identity (NurFarah 2003). Furthermore, Spink (1992) found that teams that had the smallest different understandings in terms of cohesiveness were also the ones that were the most successful. This positive influence of a sports team's cohesion on its performance was supported by many scholars (Carron, Hausenblas, and Eys 2005; Widmeyer and Williams 1991). In the exercise and sports settings in particular, team cohesion also affects the team success (Carron, Colman, Wheeler, and Stevens 2002), being loyal among the team members (Carron and Spink 1993), the team's compliance (Frasier and Spink 2002), and certain group norms, such as "supporting each other" and "sticking to the training schedule" (Prapavessis and Carron 1997). However, scholars lack agreement about how to conceptualize team cohesion. In accordance with Carron, Brawley, and Widmeyer (1998), cohesion is a "dynamic process, which is reflected in the tendency of a group to stick together and remain united in thepursuit of its instrumental objectives as well as for the satisfaction of member affective needs" (213). In this study, cohesion is understood as the sum of all forces influencing and motivating a group to remain united (Festinger, Schachter, and Back 1950).

As improving group performance is more likely to increase from targeting behavior that enhances commitment to the group task rather than liking another, Carless and De Paola (2000) argued that task cohesion is more closely related to performance than interpersonal cohesion. Hence, Chang and Bordia (2001), Carron, Brawley, and Widmeyer (1998), Cota, Evans, Dion, Kilik, and Longman (1995) as well as Carron (1985) identified that team cohesion, the dependant variable of this study, has to be distinguished between task and social cohesion. While task cohesiveness is understood as "the extent of motivation towards achieving the organization's goals and objectives," social cohesiveness refers to "the motivation to develop and maintain social relationships within the group" (Widmeyer, Brawley, and Carron 1985, 17). For this study, the author used this applied distinction of group-level task and social cohesion.

Factors Influencing Team Cohesion

Due to the importance of team cohesiveness, scholars have researched factors influencing sports team cohesion. Several factors have been found to influence team cohesion, such as team building, team size, and team goals. While Widmeyer, Brawley, and Carron (1985) found that pursuing shared goals was a decisive component for cohesion, Widmeyer and

Williams (1991) found team goals related only to the task and not to the social aspects of cohesion. From their longitudinal study of exercise classes, Widmeyer, Brawley, and Carron (1990) reported that perceived cohesion decreased as group size increased due to more opportunities in quality interaction in smaller rather than in larger groups. Conversely, Widmeyer and Williams (1991) found a positive relationship between both variables by examining golfers from intercollegiate teams. The relationship between team building and team cohesion was studied by Carron and Spink (1993) as well as by Estabrooks and Carron (1999). The scholars found that team building in exercise settings improved cohesion. Bosselut, Heuze, Eys, and Bouthier (2010) as well as Eys and Carron (2001) studied the relationship between team cohesion and role ambiguity. They reported that athletes who had a greater tendency to be unclear about the scope of their responsibilities also held lower perceptions of their team's task cohesiveness. By examining the relationship between role ambiguity and group cohesiveness in youth interdependent sport teams, Bosselut, McLaren, Eys, and Heuze (2012) found that early perception of role ambiguity would predict different perceptions of group cohesion between mid and end of season among youth athletes.

Other prerequisites for cohesion have also been the subject of research. Stokes (1983) stated that interpersonal attraction between the individual group members, the individual's risk taking behavior in the form of intimate self-disclosure, and the value a group has for its members appear to be important constituents. While Carron (1988) reported prior performance success to be linked to team cohesion, Widmeyer and Williams (1991) emphasized the role of time in cohesion building. To them cohesion needs time to develop and initial cohesion is often based on previous developed liking of teammates before joining the team. Carron (1988) defined a conceptual system of aspects influencing a team's task and social cohesion. The model consists of environmental factors as the group size, and personal factors as the similarity of the group members. Moreover, his system includes team factors, such as their overall satisfaction with the team, their roles, and communication with each other, as well as leadership factors.

While studies focused mainly on certain aspects and to what extent they influenced team cohesion, the author aimed to find out if former findings may be supported, and examined the contexts in which team cohesion is built and its processes, in order to develop causal explanations.

The Influence of Coaches' Behavior on Team Cohesion

The leadership factors Carron (1988) identified include the relationship the coaches established with their groups, their leadership style, and
behaviors. In particular, clear, consistent, unambiguous communication
from coaches and captains regarding team goals influenced the team's
social and task cohesion positively.

Other scholars have also researched the influence of the coach on team
cohesion. From their quantitative study of basketball players and wres-
tlers, Carron and Chelladurai (1981) reported a statistically significant
relationship between team cohesion and several important factors related
to the coach. Aside from the coach's ability to clarify group goals and
recognize members' contributions, the scholars reported involving members in the decision-making process as a significant, positive influence.
Widmeyer and Williams (1991) reported a similar finding from their study
of golfers. They stressed the importance of the leader's recognition of the
significance of team cohesion as well as the coach's conscious steps to
develop cohesion within the group as main factors in success.

Gardner, Shields, Bredemeier, and Bostrom (1996) reported a significant
relationship between perceived coaching behavior and team cohesion among
baseball and softball players at school levels. In particular, they reported
that coaches who were perceived by their players as providing social support
and who emphasized democratic behavior indicated a higher level of task and
social cohesion. Furthermore, Turman (2003) found that the coach played
a valuable role in the development of a team's cohesion. By studying how
specific types of motivational techniques promoted or deterred a team's
cohesion, the scholar found that bragging, sarcasm, teasing, motivational
speeches, and team prayer as well as dedication especially promoted the
team's cohesion among men as well as female sport teams, while inequity,
embarrassment, and ridicule behavior influenced it in a negative way.

As research has shown, the role of the coach is an important influence
to a team's cohesion. Hence, the author examined this aspect in particular, referring to the four coaches of the team: the head coach and three
assistant coaches, and their behavior toward the group as a whole and its
members, such as their verbal and nonverbal communication.

The Impact of Conflicts on Team Cohesion

In the traditional literature, intrateam conflict has been viewed as the
antithesis of team cohesion (Murrell and Gaertner 1992). Widmeyer,

Brawley, and Carron (1985) reported that the more cohesive teams are more resistant to intrateam conflicts, and that extremely high and low cohesive teams could be predicted to be resistant to conflict. Other scholars, however, found that teams experiencing in-group disruptions may still be effective and referred to task conflict (disagreements about procedures, policies, ideas, and opinions about the task being performed) in particular. For instance, Simons and Peterson (2000) observed that task conflict can be beneficial to team effectiveness, while De Dreu and Weingart (2003) reported that it can also have negative effects, such as distracting team members from their goals.

While all of the formerly mentioned studies referred to male and female teams, Sullivan and Feltz (2001) studied male hockey teams in particular and explained the significance of constructive conflict with their results. In their study of the relationship between intrateam conflict and cohesion, the scholars stated that constructive conflict management was positively related to the team's cohesion while negative conflict management was negatively related to team unity, and destructive styles of conflict management were negatively related to the team's cohesion.

As former studies have shown, conflicts impact a team's cohesion. As a consequence, the author examined this aspect in particular as well. In order to analyze the complex structure of conflict, the author differentiated the independent variable "conflict" between task and relational conflicts. Task conflict is understood in accordance with Jehn (1995) as well as with Chou and Yeh (2007) as members' disagreements about procedures, policies, ideas, and opinions about the task being performed. Relational conflict, on the other hand, will be understood as tension, animosity, and annoyance among team members (Chou and Yeh 2007).

Importance of the Study

As the reviewed literature has shown, the previously conducted studies neither sufficiently researched the relationship between task conflict and task and social cohesion nor the link between social conflict and social cohesion. These specific distinctions, however, may be crucial for a complete understanding of the interdependence between these variables. Furthermore, only certain aspects in the influence of the behavior of the coach on the team's cohesion were examined. Surprisingly, the influence of the coach on task and social cohesion as well as task and social conflict on task and social cohesion were mainly examined through the use of a quantitative approach. Hence, a qualitative approach was used in this study to gain a more in-depth understanding of factors influencing team cohesion, by examining its process and the context in which it takes place. Moreover, the strength of qualitative research was used to identify unanticipated influences (Maxwell 2005).

Methodology

Procedure

The data was collected over a period of three months (started six weeks after the season had started) in various kinds of environments. The direct observations were made on a regular basis during team practice, games, at meetings before and after the games, as well as during extraordinary meetings to make sure that the observations reflected genuine situations.

The author interviewed three coaches because of their different roles and perceptions on how their behavior may influence the team's cohesion. In addition, the author interviewed six players based on two criteria: their roles as players on the court and the length of time they have been on the team. The fact that some team members may understand the influential factors better than others due to having been much longer on the team than others, was considered by choosing three players who have been on the team for at least two years. The study participants took the GEQ at the end of the study period.

Sampling

For the present study, the author chose nonprobability sampling, because the study consisted of in-depth research on a sensitive topic that required informants (Bernard 2006). The author purposefully selected a sport team that played at the collegiate level. Based on Carron and Chelladurai's (1981) theory that the relationship between cohesion and performance is most critical when the amount of mutual interaction is high, the author decided to look at volleyball because of its great amount of mutual interaction and its high importance of combined efforts in order to be successful. The population the author chose to study is the Division I women's volleyball team.

The team played in the competitive Division I league. At this high level, the teams are not only under a lot of pressure to perform well, but each team member is also expected to commit a lot of time to her sport.

The average of two games, three practices per week, the meetings before and after the games, as well as some extraordinary meetings provided the author with plenty of opportunities to collect data via direct observations and interviews. The team consisted of thirteen female players, a female head coach, and two female assistant coaches, as well as two male assistant coaches.

Qualitative Research Methods

Since team cohesion has predominantly been researched quantitatively before, this study encompassed qualitative research methods, direct observations, and interviews. It is accompanied by the quantitative GEQ questionnaire.

The research question of this study was the following: What factors impact the team cohesion of this volleyball team? For the empirical examination of the influence of the coaches' behavior on the team's cohesion, the following subquestions were examined: How do the coaches' behaviors affect the social cohesion of the team? How do the coaches' behaviors affect the task cohesion of the team? To gain a more complete understanding of how different kinds of conflict affect the team's cohesion, the following subquestions were studied: How does the way task conflict is managed influence the team's task cohesion? How does the way social conflict is managed influence the team's social cohesion?

Direct Observations

Bernard (2006) stressed that, "When you want to know what people actually do, there is no substitute for watching them" (413). Hence, observations were key in studying the aspects that impact team cohesion among the volleyball team, and in particular, when examining the influence of task-related and social-related conflict as well as the coaches' behavior. For instance, casual remarks or comments may reveal much information about an occurring conflict between individuals and how it influences team cohesion. Since interactions have to be understood in context, observations were a crucial research method for this study.

The author also chose the direct observation method because of its objectivity, and was very thankful when this unique opportunity was afforded to her. If she had been a participant, her own expectations might have impaired her judgment and thus influenced the outcome of the study. Obtrusive observation was the other method of choice. The author tried to act as nonreactive as possible in order not to influence the team members in any way.

By continuously monitoring the team, the author could record their behavior as precisely as possible and thus gain insight into their interactions and ways of communication, both verbally and nonverbally. She did not only focus her attention on what the team members did, but also on what they did *not* do. For example, the author noticed that some team members refrained from saying "That's okay" to a teammate who made a mistake. She watched people and recorded their behavior on the spot by using a notebook.

Interviews

The author chose to supplement her observations with interviews, assuming that they would provide her with insights into the team members' opinions, perceptions, and attitudes on aspects impacting the team's cohesion. The interviewees were chosen based on their length of time of being on the team. Furthermore, the information generated by the interviews helped her to dismiss or support certain impressions she gathered during the observations, thus helping her to avoid incorrect assumptions and inferences to ensure internal validity.

In accordance with Bernard (2006), the author chose to conduct semi-structured interviews with an interview guide to cover a list of topics that addressed her research questions. However, instead of following her questions in a predetermined order and always asking them in almost the same way (structured interviews), her questions were rather open-ended and were developed in such a way as to keep open the opportunity for spontaneous follow-up questions. The semi-structured interviewing gave the author the opportunity to stay flexible but also provided the interviewees with a chance to open up in a conversational manner, in case they wanted to discuss issues they felt were important.

The author developed the interview guide based on different criteria. The first questions were about personal demographic and socioeconomic data. Other questions were based on findings of former studies, for example, enquiring if the teammates lived together, since Stura and Johnston's (2011) study reported that sharing the same apartment may impact the team's cohesion. Most of the questions, however, were based on the observations the author made. In total, she designed questions for all team members as well as some additional ones for each group (players and coaches). While the players were asked about interactions between themselves and other team members as well as about their perception of the coaches' roles in team cohesion building, the coaches were asked about their perceived leadership behavior as well as about their interactions with the team players.

Questionnaire

In addition to the qualitative methods, the author used the quantitative Group Environment Questionnaire (GEQ) to measure the study participants' perception of their team cohesion and to compare these results with the qualitative research findings. This quantitative instrument had been predominantly used to measure group cohesion in sports (Widmeyer, Brawley, and Carron 1985). The GEQ consists of four aspects of team cohesion. The Individual Attraction to the Group-Task (ATG-T) measures the individual team member's feelings about their personal involvement with the group task, productivity, goals, and objectives. The Individual Attraction to the Group-Social (ATG-S) measures the individual team member's feelings about personal involvement, desire to be accepted, and social interaction with the group. The third subscale Group Integration-Task (GI-T) measures the individual team member's feelings about closeness, and bonding within the team as a whole, while the Group Integration-Social (GI-S) measures the individual team member's feelings about the similarity, closeness, and bonding with the team as a social unit.

Analysis

For the analysis of this study, the author applied both the inductive as well as the deductive coding approach. She used the deductive approach of content analysis, because factors indicating sports team's cohesion were also examined in former studies, such as in Widmeyer, Brawley, and Carron's (1985), Spink, Nickel, Wilson, and Odnokon's (2005), Carron's (1988), Laios and Tzetzis' (2005), as well as Widmeyer and William's (1991).

This deductive approach was combined with an inductive approach to explore aspects that had not emerged in former studies, but that may have influenced the team cohesion of this sample (Bernard 2006). The author read through a small sample of transcripts of her interviews and through the field notes of her observations. Based on the discovery of certain themes, she identified analytical categories, which she used for developing further codes. After setting up all codes, she coded all the texts for the presence or absence of all themes, and in a next step, collected all the data for each coding category together.

Results and Discussion

The coaches have been coaching for between two and twenty years. For this particular team, they have been coaching between two and four years. The players, aged between nineteen and twenty-one, have been on the volleyball team between one semester and four years. Currently, the team has been together since the beginning of this semester (i.e., since August 2011).

The interviewees had varied perceptions and opinions about their team performance. While some stated that they perceived themselves as performing at a very high level, others stressed that they are not where they needed to be. One coach emphasized, "But we are on our way," whereas a player complained, "I think, our performance is not good; I am not happy with it."

Perception of the Team's Cohesion

The descriptive analysis of the data of the GEQ questionnaire showed the following scores on the Likert scale from 1 (strongly disagree) to 9 (strongly agree): the volleyball team had an average of 7.69 in the ATG-T subscale, indicating a high level of individual team member's feelings about their personal involvement with the group task, productivity, goals, and objectives. The ATG-S had an average score of 7.11, implying a high level of the team members' perception of their cohesion concerning their feelings about personal involvement, desire to be accepted, and social interaction with the group. The third subscale GI-T had an average score of 7.09, indicating that the individual team member's feelings about closeness and bonding within the team as a whole was also high. The GI-S scored the lowest with 6.39. This result referred to a medium to high level of the team members' feelings about the similarity, closeness, and bonding with the team as a social unit.

The Interplay between the Behavior of the Coaches and Team Cohesion

The observations and interviews showed that the coach clarified group goals and member roles continuously, in particular in situations that might have otherwise caused tension within the group. For example, when the team had lost a game, the coach stepped in by talking to each team member individually to clarify again their specific responsibilities and the areas where they needed to improve their performance. This behavior supports several former study results, such as Widmeyer, Brawley, and Carron's (1985) as well as Carron and Chelladurai's (1981) studies. The scholars found that pursuing and clarifying shared goals were the decisive factors contributing to team cohesion. As Widmeyer and Williams (1991) found, communicating team goals related only to the task and not to the social aspects of cohesion. The continuous effort by the head coach to clarify and communicate the goals of the group and the members' roles may indicate a focus on the team's task cohesiveness. Furthermore, the aspect of clarifying responsibilities supports Bosselut, Heuze, Eys, and Bouthier's (2010) as well as Eys and Carron's (2001) findings, indicating that a greater clarity of responsibilities supports a team's task cohesiveness.

Additionally, the head coach seemed to intervene when there is conflict between team members. Should the members fail to resolve their issues with one another, the coach used her authority to decide on the course of action. This type of behavior is supported by the findings of Widmeyer and Williams' (1991) study. Here, the scholars stressed the importance of the coach in developing team cohesion when there is tension in the group.

Another finding was that of the head coach's *conscious* development of social as well as task cohesion. She did that by talking in detail about her personal observations concerning interpersonal issues on the team, and about weaknesses on the court with her assistant coaches and her captains. During team meetings, almost everyone had to talk, one person talks at a time, and everybody else listened. The coach then changed roles and became an observer, studying each person very closely and trying to engage everybody in solution finding and problem solving. A similar study result was presented by Widmeyer and Williams (1991), who stressed the importance of the coach's conscious steps to develop cohesion within the group as main factors in success.

The coach also talked with the staff, the captains, and some other players on a regular basis about their perceptions on important issues, such as certain dynamics or incidents that had happened. As one of the players stated, "She is a very good reminder on how we need to be a family" but also "Our coach, she is our rock, she would do anything for us."

The coaches, especially the head coach, also facilitated communication among the team members in order to strengthen social cohesion. To achieve this, she made different team members pair up for lunch every week, expecting that this quality time was going to increase the comfort level between people who normally can or would not spend time together. Personal preferences did not come into play here, quite the opposite: the coach joined individuals who may be very different in both character and/or performance.

The coach talked very directly or may have said something twice, using different terminology. She also stated that she listened a lot to how the players communicated and tried to decode their cultural body language. For example, she looked at whether "they like this much distance as oppose to that much distance. I really believe, strongly believe, in those types of human humantics." This aspect refers to Carron's (1988) finding which identified a coach's usage of a clear, consistent, and unambiguous communication style as a positive influence to the team's social and task cohesion.

The interviews with the coaches supported the author's observations that the head coach had a major influence on the team's cohesion. She actively worked on developing and maintaining social relationships within the group by promoting and facilitating communication among the group. These results support similar findings of Gardner, Shields, Bredemeier, and Bostrom (1996) as well as Turman (2003), who pointed out the valuable role of the coach in team cohesion building in sport teams.

The GEQ scores indicated an individual team member's perception of their team's cohesion on a medium to high level. Since cohesion building takes time to develop (Widmeyer and Williams 1991), and this team is composed as such since August 2011, this result may be interpreted as the team cohesion has developed well so far, supporting the positive influence of the coach's behavior.

The Interplay between Conflict and the Team's Cohesion

On the court, the author observed that players corrected each other concerning their play. In her interview, one of the players stated in this regard, "I try to challenge my teammates with their skills to get them outside of their comfort level. People learn to get over it; they take it and work on it." Some players seemed to accept corrections constructively, while others did not respond very well to it. As one interviewee stressed, "I don't need somebody coming to me telling me you need to do this and that. Sometimes it can cause tension on the team." She further explained that " . . . there is a lot of frustration, but because we are doing well right now, people don't worry about it, they are not sure how to handle it, or, they are afraid to say what needs to be said."

These task conflicts did not seem to be well addressed or even avoided. This observational impression was affirmed by two coaches during their interviews. One of assistant coach stated, "I don't see any arguments. I see a lot of passive aggressive frustration ... and that may influence the team's cohesion." The head coach, on the other hand, addressed conflicts. When she witnessed a task or a relational conflict, she interjected. As she stressed in the interview:

> If I see a continuing pattern, smart comments, even just eye contact, someone who won't make eye contact among that group for an extended amount of time. I step in and tell the players: Stop, that's an example of what I am talking about. You both have to communicate about whose ball this is and whose ball that is.

When a team member talked back at her, she seemed to manage these relational conflicts successfully by not taking them personally. As she stated in the interview, " . . . even as sometimes their frustration gets directed at me, I am like, it is okay, I can handle it." Moreover, the head coach seemed to encourage the team members to come in and talk to her. As a player pointed out in her interview, they talked about conflicts among themselves and when they violated certain rules, such as drinking alcohol; "We talk about everything, when we are all together without the coaches, we talk about an issue that has happened or what someone feels and we talk about ways how we could change it," one underlined in the interview. If the players failed to solve the issue or even avoided talking about it at all, the head coach put that person on the "hot seat" in the locker room. Everybody was encouraged and sometimes even required to take a stand in the matter. The person in the hot seat had to listen and accept it, and should then respond to each statement. If the issue was still not resolved after the "hot seat," the coaches stepped in.

According to some players, however, the coach may also have been the reason for some relational conflicts. They indicated that her degree of involvement may sometimes be too much; it may limit their cohesion somehow, as one player stated during her interview:

> We went way above and beyond, made things much bigger than they needed to be . . . we *caused* the trust issue. I didn't feel that we actually had a trust issue before coach said that and then it became much bigger and much more personal than it needed to and since then little things . . . as you didn't do your job became a trust issue and it's been very noticeable.

The conflict management styles that the team used were very diverse: some players used the collaborating conflict management style by taking others' mistakes on them in dealing with task conflicts, but many seemed to use the avoiding style, as was explained earlier. If the players didn't resolve their conflicts with each other by themselves, the head coach tried "to clear up" in meetings with all players. The author observed her mainly applying the confrontational conflict management style with all players, addressing issues directly:

> Some of the younger girls coming in who were probably more from a more diverse background (. . .) they were joking about things "oh, we are segregated, oh we need to break down (. . .) and some of the white girls who were more from an open community were taking offence, but none was really saying anything and I said: That is enough, stop it. Here is why, this is someone's experience, you don't know, it's not something to joke about. If you are not mature enough to sit down and discuss it, then don't mock it."

The conflict avoidance management style that the players mainly used in terms of their task conflicts, seemed to influence the team's task cohesion in a negative way, while the rules they followed when someone had violated certain group rules, such as partying, seemed to influence the social cohesion positively, as some interviewees indicated. Furthermore, the interviews and observations showed that the direct and confrontational conflict management style of the coach seemed to influence the team's social and task cohesion positively.

These findings seem to reject the traditional literature that viewed intrateam conflict as the antithesis of team cohesion (Murrell and Gaertner 1992), since the GEQ stated a medium to high level of team cohesion. Furthermore, the conflict management styles of the team members seemed to support Sullivan and Feltz's (2001) study findings. While the players usage of the avoidance management style seemed to influence the team's task cohesion rather in a negative way, the rules the players followed when someone had violated certain group standards, and the confrontational conflict management style of the head coach seemed to influence the social and task cohesion rather in a positive way.

Other Influences on Team Cohesion

This study also found other factors impacting the volleyball team's cohesion. Trust had to be named as the most important factor, because it was mentioned by all interviewees. Some of the players remarked that sometimes they think they have a false sense of trust in the team. As one of the player stated, "If we don't trust each other or doubt, that breaks the team up into groups." "Trust is the backbone of cohesiveness," one of the coaches pointed out and it seems to be especially important in volleyball. For instance, "the closer you are to someone else on the court, the more open space you are leaving for your opponent to hit to." Hence, lack of trust and "crowding one person leaves the team vulnerable in other areas." In this regard, the head coach explained that:

> The less you trust each other, the more you tend to be closer to someone on the court, because the ball is coming to you. If you are a player, and you are gonna get the ball, I am gonna come over and help you, coz I don't trust you're gonna get it done.

This finding is consistent with the literature that names trust as an important element of effective team work (Larson and LaFasto 1989).

Another important factor in team cohesion building seemed to be holding each other accountable. As one player stated, "We hold each other accountable very well. We all hold on to the same standards," as one player stressed. In a contradictory manner, two players stated in their interviews explicitly that they are willing to take the blame for others. If teammates mess up, they preferred being held accountable for someone else's mistake than "getting them all rattled inside their own heads," one player stressed.

In addition, interviewees stated that living together, sharing rooms or apartments, also influenced the team's cohesion, but their opinions on whether that is a positive or negative thing differed. While some players said that it might help to get closer to each other and that it created closer relationships, others stated that it might also create divisions and small cliques in the team. Both aspects have been mentioned before. While Stura and Johnston (2011) reported a rather negative effect, the NBA player Joakim Noah emphasized its positive effects in an interview to the Sporting News (Deveney 2006).

The team's rituals also seemed to affect their team cohesion. At the beginning of every practice, they talked about a quote that the coach or a player brought in (they rotate), the team high fived after every drill and every point they made, and they pray together and do a dance before every game in the locker room. After games, they circled up, put their arms around each other and talked. As several interviewees stated, their rituals brought them closer together and promoted a sense of togetherness, "a sense of unity." Their praying supported Turman's (2003) finding, who also reported that this type of motivational techniques promoted or deterred a team's cohesion.

Being a starter or a nonstarter on the court seemed to be another crucial aspect in the team's cohesion; "There is a common bond and a vibe between the starters," as a player stressed during the interview. Most of the time nonstarters felt that they are not always a part of the immediate action and thus did not contribute directly to the performance, as the head coach explained. This result supports Spink's (1992) as well as Granito and Rainey's (1988) findings, in which they maintained that starters tended to score higher on measures of cohesiveness than nonstarters.

Supplementary to this, all of the interviewees talked about specific incidents that had impacted their team cohesion in the past. The head coach mentioned one specific incident in her interview. After they lost a game, she encouraged them to talk about the things that were bothering them. "They did that and agreed to move on," she said and emphasized further, "and from there, I saw a transformation in how they competed. So, that has to happen for every team, I think." One of the players referred to an incident when they had lost a game and the coach took away their cell phones and laptops. They got mad at the coach, ". . . but at the same time," as the player pointed out, "it was the first time we really bonded."

The assumption that interpersonal attraction between team members influenced the team's cohesion was also supported by the findings of former studies (Bergeles and Hatziharistos 2003; Carron, Hausenblas, and Eys 2005). Whereas there seemed to be no need to make friends among the team members, as some players stated, they also stressed the importance of interpersonal likeability and emphasized the necessity to support each other. Others stressed that it is important to be good friends off court with some teammates to achieve a high level of understanding and respect for them.

Conclusion

This study found that the head coach's behavior is a decisive factor in impacting the team's social and task cohesion. The head coach's way of actively facilitating communication, addressing, and clarifying group goals and member roles by using a direct communication style seemed to be crucial in this regard. On the other hand, some players indicated that her degree of involvement limited their cohesion somehow. Moreover, the study found that the conflict avoidance management style, that the players mainly seemed to use in terms of their individual task conflicts, seemed to influence the team's task cohesion in a negative way. Conversely, the rules the players followed when someone had violated certain group rules, seemed to influence the social cohesion positively. Furthermore, the direct and confrontational conflict management style of the head coach seemed to be important in the team's social and task cohesion building.

In addition to these findings, this study also discovered other factors influencing the volleyball team's cohesion, which had not been reported in prior research. These included the use of rituals and the influence of holding each other accountable. Both aspects need to be examined in further studies.

The author encountered some limitations in the direct observations. She was not able to hear some conversations, comments, or remarks on the field or to see people's looks and/or gestures. By concentrating on their tone of voice or/and their nonverbal behavior she realized, however, that something was going on, but would have needed to hear the words in order to comprehend the full extent of the incident; in some instances, she was simply too far away. Furthermore, while the interviews took place in the coaches' offices or in the tool shed (before or during practice), sometimes team members walked in and interrupted the interviews. The author had the impression that some interviewees did not feel safe to speak openly. This would speak to the need in the future to conduct the interviews in an off-site or more neutral location.

Moreover, the author was not able to be with the team all the time. Since important interactions also may have occurred when she was not around, she may have missed out on events which might have been important to be considered in the study. Finally, it is possible that her study participants acted differently with her around. This was rather the case during practice than during meetings, since she was the only person at the gym without an interactive part, which made it hard for the team to forget about her. If the author had spent more time with the team, such as traveling with the team, it could have changed their attitude toward her, but because of her own scheduling and financial constraints, this was not possible.

In general, the study was limited by its time frame. One semester may not have been long enough. Studying the team's cohesion over a longer period of time would be necessary to examine the factors that appeared to impact the team's cohesion more profoundly.

The findings of this study provide an understanding of factors influencing the team cohesion of this volleyball team. Based on these findings, factors influencing team cohesion of a larger population of professional volleyball teams playing on the same professional level as the team in this case study needs to be examined in a next step. From a follow-up study, the author expects a much more complete understanding of the factors influencing team cohesion than this single case was able to discern.

In conclusion, the results in the "microcosm" volleyball may offer important aspects to be considered in sports programs used to build coexistence and positive peace. Furthermore, factors that build cohesion among sports teams may also be important for building cohesion in non-sport team settings, where members do not only share a common goal, but also are highly interdependent to reach it.

References

Bergeles, Nikolaos, and Dimitris Hatziharistos. 2003. "Interpersonal Attraction as a Measure of Estimation of Cohesiveness in Elite Volleyball Teams." *Perceptual & Motor Skills* 96, no. 1: 81–91.

Bernard, H. Russell. 2006. *Research Methods in Anthropology—Qualitative and Quantitative Approaches*. New York: AltaMira Press.

Bosselut, Gregoire, Colin D. McLaren, Mark A. Eys, and Jean-Philippe Heuze. 2012. "Reciprocity of the Relationship between Role Ambiguity and Group Cohesion in Youth Interdependent Sport." *Psychology of Sport and Exercise* 13: 341–48.

Bosselut, Gregoire, Jean-Philippe Heuze, Mark A. Eys, and Daniel Bouthier. 2010. "Influence of Task Cohesion and Role Ambiguity on Cognitive Anxiety during a European Rugby Union Championship." *Athletic Insight* 12, no. 2: 17–34.

Carless, Sally A., and Caroline De Paola. 2000. "The Measurement of Cohesion in Work Teams." *Small Group Research* 31, no. 1: 71–88.

Carron, Albert V. 1985. "Cohesion in Sport Teams." In *Psychological Foundations of Sport*, ed. J. M. Silba and R. S. Weinberg, 340–51. Champaign, IL: Human Kinetics.

Carron, Albert V. 1988. *Group Dynamics in Sport*. London, Ontario: Spodym.

Carron, Albert V., and Heather Hausenblas. 1998. *Group Dynamics in Sport*. Morgantown, WV: Fitness Information Technology.

Carron, Albert V., Heather Hausenblas, and Mark A. Eys. 2005. *Group Dynamics in Sport*. Champaign, IL: Human Kinetics.

Carron, Albert V., and Kevin S. Spink. 1993. "Team Building in an Exercise Setting." *The Sport Psychologist* 7, no. 1: 8–18.

Carron, Albert V., Lawrence R. Brawley, and William N. Widmeyer. 1998. "The Measurement of Cohesiveness in Sport Groups." In *Advances in Sport and Exercise Psychology Measurement*, ed. J. L. Duda, 213–26. Morgantown, WV: Fitness Information Technology.

Carron, Albert V., Mark A. Eys, and Shauna M. Burke. 2007. "Team Cohesion: Nature, Correlates, and Development." In *Social Psychology in Sport*, ed. S. Jowett and D. Lavallee, 91–102. Champaign, IL: Human Kinetics.

Carron, Albert V., Michelle M. Colman, Jennifer J. Wheeler, and Diane D. Stevens. 2002. "Cohesion and Performance in Sport: A Meta Analysis." *Journal of Sport & Exercise Psychology* 24, no. 2: 168–88.

Carron, Albert V., and Packianathan Chelladurai. 1981. "Cohesiveness as a Factor in Sport Performance." *International Review of Sport Sociology* 16, no. 2: 21–43.

Carron, Albert V., and Paul W. Dennis. 1998. "The Sport Team as an Effective Group." In *Applied Sport Psychology: Personal Growth to Peak Performance*, ed. J. M. Williams, 110–121. Mountain View, CA: Mayfield Publishing.

Chang, Artemis, and Prasant Bordia. 2001. "A Multidimensional Approach to the Group Cohesion-Group Performance Relationship." *Small Group Research* 32, no. 4: 379–405.

Chou, Huey-Wen, and Ying-Jung Yeh. 2007. "Conflict, Conflict Management, and Performance in ERP Teams." *Social Behavior and Personality* 35, no. 8: 1035–48.

Cota, Albert A., Charles R. Evans, Kenneth L. Dion, Lindy Kilik, and R. Stewart Longman. 1995. "The Structure of Group Cohesion." *Personality and Social Psychology Bulletin* 21, no. 6: 572–80.

De Dreu, Carsten K. W., and Laurie R. Weingart. 2003. "Task versus Relationship Conflict, Team Performance, and Team Member Satisfaction: A Meta-Analysis." *Journal of Applied Psychology* 88, no. 4: 741–49.

Deveney, Sean. 2006. "The Team That Lives Together Wins Together." *Sporting News* 230, no. 14: 21.

Estabrooks, Paul A., and Albert V. Carron. 1999. "Group Cohesion in Older Adult Exercises: Prediction and Intervention Effects." *Journal of Behavioral Medicine* 22: 575–88.

Eys, Mark A., and Albert V. Carron. 2001. "Role Ambiguity, Task Cohesion, and Task Self-Efficacy." *Small Group Research* 32: 356–73.

Festinger, Leon, Stanley Schachter, and Kurt Back. 1950. *Social Pressures in Informal Groups: A Study of Human Factors in Housing.* New York: Harper.

Frasier, Shawn, and Kevin S. Spink. 2002. "Examining the Role of Social Support and Group Cohesion in Exercise Compliance." *Journal of Behavioral Medicine* 25, no. 3: 233–49.

Gardner, Douglas E., David L. Shields, Brenda J. Bredemeier, and Alan Bostrom. 1996. "The Relationship between Perceived Coaching Behaviors and Team Cohesion among Baseball and Softball Players." *The Sport Psychologist* 10: 367–81.

Granito, Vincent J., and David W. Rainey. 1988. "Differences in Cohesion between High School and College Football Teams and Starters and Non-Starters." *Perceptual and Motor Skills* 66: 471–77.

Henley, Robert, and Claire Colliard. 2005. "Overcoming Trauma through Sport." Paper presented at the Second Magglingen Conference Sport and Development held in Switzerland, December 4–6, 2005.

Jehn, Karen. 1995. "A Multimethod Examination of the Benefits and Detriments of Intragroup Conflict." *Administrative Science Quarterly* 40: 256–82.

Kamphoff, C. S., D. L. Gill, and S. Huddleston. 2005. "Jealousy in Sport: Exploring Jealousy's Relationship to Cohesion." *Journal of Applied Sport Psychology* 17, no. 4: 290–305.

Laios, Athanasios, and George Tzetzis. 2005. "Styles of Managing Team Conflict in Professional Sports: The Case of Greece." *Management Research News* 28, no. 6: 36–54.

Larson, Carl E., and Frank M. J. LaFasto. 1989. *Teamwork.* Newbury Park, CA: Sage.

Maxwell, Joseph A. 2005. *Qualitative Research Design.* Thousand Oaks, CA: Sage.

Mullen, Brian, and Carolyn Copper. 1994. "The Relation between Group Cohesiveness and Performance: An Integration." *Psychological Bulletin* 115, no. 2: 210–27.

Murrell, Audrey, and Samuel Gaertner. 1992. "Cohesion and Sport Team Effectiveness: The Benefit of a Common Group Identity." *Journal of Sport and Social Issues* 16, no. 1: 162–83.

NurFarah, G. 2003. "Improving Sport Performances through Team Cohesiveness." *ICHPER-SD Journal* 39, no. 12: 37.

NurFarah, G. A., and M. S. Omar-Fauzee. 2003. "Sport: Improving Sport Performances through Team Cohesiveness." *ICHPER-SD Journal* 39, no. 1: 37–41.

Prapavessis, Harry, and Albert V. Carron. 1997. "Sacrifice, Cohesion, and Conformity to Norms in Sport Teams." *Group Dynamics: Theory, Research, and Practice* 1, no. 3: 231–40.

Simons, T. L., and R. S. Peterson. 2000. "Task Conflict and Relationship Conflict in Top Management Teams: The Pivotal Role of Intragroup Trust." *Journal of Applied Psychology* 85, no. 1: 102–11.

Spink, Kevin. 1992. "Group Cohesion and Starting Status in Successful and Less Successful Elite Volleyball Teams." *Journal of Sports Sciences* 10: 379–88.

Spink, Kevin S., Darren Nickel, Kathleen Wilson, and Pat Odnokon. 2005. "Using a Multilevel Approach to Examine the Relationship between Task Cohesion and Team Task Satisfaction in Elite Ice Hockey Players." *Small Group Research* 36, no. 5: 539–54.

Stokes, Joseph P. 1983. "Components of Group Cohesion: Inter Member Attraction, Instrumental Value, and Risk Taking." *Small Group Research* 14, no. 2: 163–73.

Stura, Claudia, and Linda M. Johnston. 2011. "Cross-Cultural Conflicts among Sport Teams." Article submitted for publication.

Sullivan, Philip J., and Deborah L. Feltz. 2001. "The Relationship between Intrateam Conflict and Cohesion within Hockey Teams." *Small Group Research* 32, no. 3: 342–55.

Tokarski, Walter. 2009. "Conflict Resolution through Sport Intervention in Mulit-Ethnic Societies." *Polish Journal of Sport and Tourism* 16, no. 4: 193–200.

Turman, Paul D. 2003. "Coaches and Cohesion: The Impact of Coaching Techniques on Team Cohesion in the Small Group Sport Setting." *Journal of Sport Behavior* 26, no. 1: 86–104.

Widmeyer, William N., and J. M. Williams. 1991. "The Cohesion-Performance Outcome Relationship in a Coacting Sport." *Journal of Sport & Exercise Psychology* 13, no. 4: 364–71.

Widmeyer, William N., Lawrence R. Brawley, and Albert V. Carron. 1985. *The Measurement of Cohesion in Sports Teams: The Group Environment Questionnaire.* London, Ontario: Sports Dynamics.

———. 1990. "The Effects of Group Size in Sport." *Journal of Sport and Exercise Psychology* 12: 177–90.

Repairing the Human Spirit through Structured and Unstructured Sports Programs: The Core Values Worth Knowing Were Learned through Athletics and Beyond

Dr. H. E. "Doc" Holliday

Tis a lesson you should heed, try, try again;
If at first you don't succeed, try, try, again;
Then your courage should appear,
For, if you will persevere,
You will conquer, never fear;
Try, try again.

—Author Unknown

Sports are second only to religion as the most powerful cultural force in American society (Katz 2002). They provide young people with several fundamentally healthy ways to develop. They provide fun and instant gratification. They fulfill a need for friendship and a sense of belonging to a particular organization. They offer an opportunity for our youth to build healthier minds and bodies through physical exercise. They encourage young people to embrace the concepts of hard work and the power to dream.

The Crisis in Masculinity and Male Loneliness

There are many things that help to shape the future success of young males (Holliday 2011). The challenges that males face, begin long before they enter school and will exist well into their adult lives. The intergenerational impact of growing up in poverty, with no father in the home is particularly damaging. These growing numbers of males are far too often disengaged and unprepared to enter young adulthood. These young men may grow up and lack the prerequisite skills to marry, raise children, and make positive contributions to the community at large.

Recently, social psychologists have generated a term called "Male Loneliness" (Anderson 1993). There is much research that concludes that women have better relational skills which help them to be more successful at making and keeping friends. Women are more likely than men to express their emotions and display empathy and compassion in response to the emotions of others (Anderson 1993). Men, on the other hand, are frequently more isolated and competitive and therefore have fewer (if any) close friends. Men in fact, may not even be conscious of their loneliness and isolation (Anderson 1993).

Important research generated by Jackson Katz (2002) in his work of "Crisis, Media, and the Crisis in Masculinity" attempts to dissect the modern twenty-first century male. He noted that they have very different attitudes and beliefs and that many of these beliefs are self-destructive and antiestablishment. There appears to be a growing generational communications gap because these new beliefs emanate from nontraditional sources.

Modern day media has bombarded young men into believing that being a man is determined by physical characteristics. Things like being *strong, independent, intimidating, athletic,* and *tough* are terms often used to determine a man's veracity (Phillips and Pope 2002). The movie industry has done an exceptional job of misguiding a generation of young men who have allowed media leaders to determine whether or not men are acceptable examples of maleness. Young boys start out early in life by avoiding the nicknames that would indicate that they were feminine, homosexual, studious, or easily scared. All of these connotations generate negative perceptions that are to be avoided at all cost by boys. What and how would the world of our aggressive young men be improved if we were to consistently introduce a more civilized, peaceful, and serene approach to growing up? Why is it that we cannot adopt the notions and attitudes displayed every four years during the International World Olympic Games? There is always intense competition but, it is the kind of competition that fosters universal brotherhood and cooperation. There is certainly an undergirding theme of trying to do your very best but not by deliberately demeaning your opponent. This approach is more centered on achieving your personal best and not solely on winning the event. This is the very same approach that people of all nationalities should adopt at the micro or local level if we are to expect individuals and countries to embrace the idea of living in a peaceful, humane world. There is no excuse for permitting individuals, teams, and countries to resort to extreme acts of negative behavior simply to gain a competitive advantage over others during any athletic activity. The idea of winning must not be attained at the cost of humiliating or degrading another human. We all must learn to win the right way! A way that promotes peace of mind whatever the outcome of that particular event may be. A more thoughtful approach to athletic competition would go a long way in reducing the number of incidents that seem to occur more often when countries compete in World Cup soccer tournaments. When comparing the Olympic Games and the World Cup matches there seems to me a very clear distinction between representing your country well and winning at any cost. I believe that there should be a very strong adherence to Olympics universal standards in how participants behave. The Olympic Games promote not only athletic competition but also an expectation of reaching out to find common ground with individuals who come from altogether different countries than the one they are most familiar with. Embracing these ideas at the local level of athletic completion will generate an avalanche of peace and good will for the remainder of an athlete's career. This movement must begin with adults modeling the types of behaviors that we expect to see in our athletes. This will help to reduce that growing uncertainty many young people struggle with when asked which is more important winning at any cost or competing with a peace of mind and a healthy respect for one's opponent.

Repairing the Human Spirit

The heart or the spirit of a man is the source of his life. It is the center of his being. If the spirit is damaged, wounded, or corrupted in any way, his ability to relate normally to others and to ourselves is hampered emotionally. A wounded spirit is one that is hurting, but one in which the hurt has generated into consistently negative attitudes and responses. A person with a wounded spirit lives in inner misery that highlights and exacerbates the injustices that consistently confront him. They may possess many of the following characteristics. They may have a negative mindset where they are preoccupied with the past. They may exhibit victim reasoning where they continuously feel that they are constantly under siege. They may display grievance mannerisms where they continuously groan and sigh to draw attention to their suffering. They may embrace blame tactics where they hold other people responsible for their life challenges.

A wounded spirit can be caused by many things, but it often results from experiencing some kind of tragedy, violation, hurt, or disappointment. Healing a wounded spirit takes resilience on the part of men and understanding that the situation does not have to be permanent. Whatever has happened to you may be the very thing that teaches you how to be strong and overcome the hurt.

I advise following these steps when addressing a man's wounded spirit. You must encourage the man to identify the hurt that caused his problem. He must then seek a trusted friend especially when the problem may be more than this individual can deal with alone. The person should take responsibility for the part he played in this problem. The individual should find something fulfilling to do that will allow him to use that same experience to understand and help others. Do not allow the pain and hurt to be bottled up and to damage your emotions.

Sports Done Right (Maine Center for Sport and Coaching 2006) identifies several basic core principles that form the basis for a sound amateur sports program from the middle and high school sports experience to the collegiate levels. The informative document seeks to clarify the role of sports in the educational process for Maine's children. The report firmly acknowledges the all-important role sports can play in the development of students, provided of course that there is proper emphasis on the rationale for offering athletics.

The Maine Center for Sport and Coaching, *Sports Done Right* (2006) insists that core elements starts with the philosophy and values that form the basis for school sports programs. Those principles through the expertise of coaches are then implemented with the expectation of modeling the desired behavior that school leadership expects. In the most basic core principles, "Philosophy, Values, and Sportsmanship are always emphasized." The report focuses on the many positives of sound athletic programs, the ability to teach the important values of respect, responsibility, fairness, and discipline. When school programs have a healthy and balanced emphasis on such values, athletes learn how to handle "success with grace" and "failure with dignity."

Sports can be used to connect lifelong values which illustrate the importance of why schools should sponsor athletic programs for students. Practicing core principles teaches children the values of hard work and discipline. Adults must always keep their sights on refocusing amateur sports toward a visionary long-term emphasis. Instead of seeing athletics as preparation for college or professional sports, schools and community members should see athletics as a preparation for life. Adults must help teach children that it is ok to be passionate about athletics as long as they keep it in perspective and understand that it is just a game and not the end of the universe if victory is not achieved.

Sports Offer Children Many Lessons

It is important to understand that sports can and should be a very prominent part of the growth process for children, provided adults keep the proper perspective. Sports provide an outlet for children, allowing a controlled and positive release of energy at the simplest level when the focus is on recreation. Recreational activities help children develop healthy minds, bodies, and spirits. In addition, loosely organized activities can provide monumental opportunity for socialization for children, that is, if adults refrain from over-structuring the activity.

Evolving to the competitive sports model provides even more lessons to teach children. The concept of teamwork, of sacrificing individual needs to work together in seeking a common goal, is one of the greatest teaching points of team sports (Hestenes 2008). The concept of working hard for a specific goal, of putting in the necessary time and commitment to be able to do a task well, is another great lesson for children. Sports can and does teach children to prepare oneself for possible success, that the willingness to prepare to excel at a task is at times far more important than actually succeeding at that task.

One of the most important lessons is the one that far too many adults go to great lengths to avoid. The ability to deal with individual failure or the loss of a game is actually at the heart of what sports can and should teach our children. Adults must continuously support and encourage young people while demanding that they maintain a healthy perspective of the real importance of athletic competition. Children develop a strong personal resiliency along with the personal ability and trait to pick themselves up even after a crushing defeat. Adults must continue to teach children that you cannot win every competition on or off the field but, you can prepare, work hard, and work smart to put yourself in a position to do your very best. Adults must help children understand the need to go to practice over and over again in order to position you to become successful. This is the essence of what sports can mean for children as they transition into adulthood.

Athletics Teaches These Ideals

There are a myriad of lifelong lessons that can be generated through participating in sports. Athletics teaches children how to perform under pressure. It teaches children how to prepare and organize a team to meet the opposition. It teaches children how to encourage their teammates. It teaches children the significance of discipline and morale. It teaches children how to set team and individual goals. It teaches children how to win with dignity and to lose gracefully. It teaches children how to make adjustments in the middle of contests. It teaches children to never give up even in the face of insurmountable odds. It teaches children how to develop clear, concise communication plans. It teaches children how to define their role and the importance to carrying out their individual assignment.

Create a Balanced Approach

One of the really tragic mistakes that children make today is to believe that sports are the only place to give their most supreme effort. Many children often summarize that an equivalent effort and commitment of doing chores at home and assignments at school is somehow less worthy. The emphasis to focus on one sport at the expense of all other activities takes the general teachings of sports to an unrealistic level. This may lead some children to believe that only one activity is the real place to demonstrate commitment and hard work. Responsible and caring adults should desire that children learn that such supreme individual effort is the proper approach to everything in life. This approach will serve them well long after their athletic playing days are over!

The movie "Coach Carter," depicts a no nonsense coach who understands that hard work transcends sports and will become an important building block as one prepares for life as an adult. Coach Carter would actually lock the players out of the gym, insisting that they get their grades together before they performed on the basketball court. He taught his players that if they put the same effort into their schoolwork they can succeed there just as they can succeed through hard work on the court. Coach Carter proved that he was a very visionary, principled man who ended up being challenged by the parents, the principal, and the school governing body who wanted to see the boys allowed to play basketball with little or no personal accountability. Sports do have a very special place in the educational process for children. They should not corrupt children and they will not as long as adults maintain the proper emphasis on the teaching points in athletics that translate into success in all aspects of life.

Hudson's (2006) study concluded that employees can learn several valuable lessons from sports. The value of working as a team: identifying and influencing what makes a good team player; the importance of commitment and dedication; the importance of collective responsibility; the importance of how talents can be developed and performance can be maximized; and the value of individual creativity. Sports can teach managers about what skill sets make a good manager. Many participants suggested that employers and employees can make better use of sports to boost morale and productivity in the workplace. Half of men and 40 percent of women suggested that employers could encourage staff to watch sports together. Being actively involved in sports was seen as a good motivator; 45 percent of male respondents and 43 percent of women suggest that encouraging staff to play sports together—such as football, volleyball, or tennis—would act as a powerful method of team bonding. Approximately, one-third (33 percent) of women and 36 percent of men believe that sponsoring staff who specialize in sports would achieve these aims. A third (34 percent) of men and 29 percent of women said that sports and competition could be used as the focus of team-building events. Men talk about sports (Hudson 2006) at work more frequently than women. More than half of men (53 percent) state that sports is a topic of conversation at work with colleagues every day or almost every day, compared to just 16 percent of women. However, almost one in four (24 percent) women use sports as a way of becoming accepted in work-related conversations, and more than half (54 percent) display keen or some interest in sports. Just under one-third (30 percent) of respondents stated that having conversations about sports at work allows them to communicate more effectively with colleagues. Talking about sports in the workplace is perceived by many employees and managers to be a great way to level the playing field, particularly in terms of crossing hierarchical boundaries. Almost one-fifth (18 percent) of men and 8 percent of women said that sporting conversations help to break down boundaries with their boss. Sport's impact goes beyond the day-to-day social environment of the workplace.

There has been much recent research that examined the social and economic implications of sporting success and failure in the workplace (*Hudson Research Study* 2006). It illustrates that sports is woven into the fabric of working life, plays a large part in creating bonds between colleagues and customers, and ultimately impacts upon productivity and the bottom line. It was noted that large-scale sporting events enable managers to generate connections that all staff can relate to. It often provides women an opportunity to tap into the traditionally male-dominated sports culture.

There is a great deal of psychological literature linking sporting success and fan self-esteem. It strongly suggests that athletics can increase self-esteem by association and affiliation. By wearing the team colors, watching every game, and knowing the players' names and positions, followers begin to feel a close connection to the team. There is a feeling of increased fan self-esteem when a team is successful or victorious. Team athletics can often generate a "feel good factor" that has a pervasive positive impact on the adult world of work. It can impact an individuals' motivation, approach to tasks, and relationships with colleagues.

The Importance of Building Strong Relationships

Many relationships are not as healthy as they should be or may even be considered dysfunctional. It takes commitment, understanding, and compromise for a good supportive relationship to blossom. Healthy relationships highlight the best qualities in both people and guide personal growth. We must sometimes make drastic changes, form healthy habits, and possibly follow the advice of a professional in order to improve relationships with family members and friends. Just about everyone has experienced or seen unhealthy relationships. Unrealistic expectations and demands tend to be placed on relationships, which can place a strain on one or both individuals in the relationship. These bad experiences and/or observations may cause one to shy away from or be fearful of ever getting close to another person. In order to establish and maintain a healthy relationship, it is important to first define why it is we may fear getting close to someone else.

Some Males Fear Getting Too Close

The "Healthy Relationships" (Torbett, Calderon, and Bell 2005), article notes that many young men believe that once they disclose too much about themselves to a significant other they will ultimately be disappointed and abandoned by that person. They are reluctant to share their most personal thoughts and dreams. Some young men fear losing their individual identity. They are very reluctant to make time in their life for someone else. Some young men do not know how to give. They are natural takers in life and find this interaction very unsettling. The act of receiving can make you feel good to see how others can care for you. Some young men fear being judged by others and falling short so they keep others at arm's length. They oftentimes feel that they are not measuring up. Many young men fear being seen as weak or vulnerable. They feel that to show any type of emotion such as caring or love is a true sign of weakness.

Healthy Relationships Are Essential

A major benefit in establishing and maintaining a healthy relationship with another person is gaining a trusted friend in your life. You will have someone listen to you and to care about you during your most difficult times. Personal relationships teach you to trust and believe in others as well as having faith in oneself (Hawke and Grayson 2005). You can gain the ability to be faithful to others which will benefit you in all aspects of your life. Healthy relationships can teach you to be better connected with your emotions (Smith, n.d.). They allow you to be comfortable in expressing oneself. Sharing yourself with someone else does involve risk but the benefits far outweigh those concerns. Research suggests that healthy relationships increase self-esteem, physical, and emotional health as well as sensitivity to one's own personal feelings. Healthy relationships increase one's own ability to be more assertive as well as becoming more cooperative with others. One learns to be more interdependent and less likely to harm one's self. There is a tendency for more employment stability and less risk for alcohol and drug abuse when one has healthy relationships (*Sports Done Right* 2006).

Adults must continue to teach lifelong lessons of respecting oneself and others, and by being empathetic and contributing to the welfare of others. These ideas are far more important than the outcome of single athletic contest. A team with a losing record would still feel like champions if they displayed compassion, a measured sense of self, and caring on and off the field.

Seek First to Understand and Always Keep the End in Mind

Societies need to decide what characteristics we want to see in young men? Is it a change in the style of clothing that has evolved so radically over the past few years? Is it their value system that unfortunately often praises the misogynistic ramblings of today's popular culture? Is it their redefining and interpretation of the twenty-first century family? What is the final product that we desire to see in young men everywhere? (Brooks and Marx 2004). Adults can no longer avoid addressing these issues in the hope that they will resolve themselves any time soon. Resolving these questions and implementing comprehensive strategies are essential if our world is to realize its mission of creating healthy, well-adjusted young men who successfully transition into strong, responsible heads of households in the years to come. Adults must make a conscientious effort to create an environment where children resist demeaning others not just because of fear of how adults will respond but, because it is the wrong thing to do. Adults must provide realistic and straightforward messages that have embedded lifelong themes that emphasize dignity and respect toward oneself and others. Adults need to neutralize and correct that false bravado and false masculinity that continuously evaluates males based upon athletic ability, sexual conquest, and economic success. Males need to understand the value and significance of community building and how we are all interconnected. Adults must resist the notion to compete and compare our personal lives at all times. Adults must teach young men how to build nurturing relationships and to find a cause worthy of devoting one's entire life toward completion. Young males must learn how to become selfless and more purposeful with their life.

Summary: The Appreciation of Sports Is a Lifelong Process

Social responsibility and leadership skills are two important reasons why sports are good for children. Sports can provide excellent educational opportunities for social development because many of the social and moral requirements for participation in sports are parallel to how individuals must function in a law-abiding society. The "Handbook of Research on Sports Psychology" (Hackfort, Duda, and Lidor 2005), strongly suggests that understanding the competitive process entails an appreciation of the social nature of competition, especially regarding the cooperative and strategic aspects of sports and an awareness of the nature of individual roles within a cooperating group. These are important lessons that impact a person for the remainder of his adult life. Adults have the responsibility of incorporating into their interactions with children and adolescents—both through our words and deeds—the message of respect for one another. The use of these messages deserves further research.

Athletics have become a very essential and prominent part of their lives by the time many young people reach their teenage years. There at times seems to be a single focus on a particular sport. There are many child development experts who feel that the emphasis on sports is hindering both the mental and physical development of children. Many adults who work with children believe that having children fixated exclusively on sports is detrimental to developing intellectual pursuits and proper lifelong work habits (*Sports Done Right* 2006).

School athletic teams provide enjoyable, supervised activities for youth. Numerous nutritionists report that student athletes develop healthier eating habits, higher levels of cardiovascular fitness, increased parental support, and decreased anxiety and depression. Participating in sports is associated with higher levels of self-esteem, motivation, and overall psychological well-being. Participation in athletics has a positive association with academic achievement. Research suggests that high school athletes have higher grades than nonathletes, lower absentee levels, a significantly smaller percentage of discipline referrals, lower percentages of dropout, and higher graduation rates (*Sports Done Right* 2006).

Sports can sometimes help to define a society. They show what people are interested in watching other people do and what they will pay to see. They show how people can make a living by being athletic and entertaining other people. They give people ways to test their athletic skill against other people. Sports can provide people something to feel passionate about, pay attention to, and follow because it provides some release from the weighty cares of everyday life. Sports bring people together and also set people apart. They are brought together in that a team, regardless of the level of play, can inspire many fans to cheer for that team.

Adult assistance and intervention is required in a profound and systematic way. Our young men must be made to feel valued and connected to a cause or to someone. We must no longer fear them or marginalize their intellectual competencies in order to celebrate their more apparent athletic prowess. Far too many adults have minimized the potential of boys to display their ability to care for others to the extent that it has permanently limited their quality of life options. We must be deliberate, strategic, and consistent when interacting with twenty-first century young men so that enhancing their compassion for others is no longer a distant dream but an important building block for all to emulate. Adults have the enormous responsibility of modeling the types of competitive behaviors we expect to see in children. Adults must accentuate the ultimate message of respect and love because it is a theme that deserves daily consideration by all who have the privilege of helping to shape our twenty-first century youth.

References

Anderson, Kerby. 1993. "Loneliness." Richardson, TX: Probe Ministries. http://wwwleadcru.com/orgs/probe/docs/lonely.html (accessed January 20, 2012).

Brooks, Robert., and Jeffrey Marx. 2004. "A Football Coach's Lessons for Life: To Nurture Respect and Dignity in Our Youth." *Parade Magazine*. http://www.drrobertbrooks.com/writing/articles/0410.html (accessed January 20, 2012).

Hackfort, Dieter, Joan Lynne Duda, and Ronnie Lidor. 2005. *Handbook of Research in Applied Sport and Exercise Psychology: International Perspectives*. Morgantown, WV: Fitness Information Technology, Inc.

Hawke, Anne, and Gisele Grayson. 2005. "Maine Aims to Ease Pressures on Student Athletes." Sports Done Right, University of Maine.

Hestenes, Roberta. 2008. "Crowded Loneliness." http://www.leaderu.com/orgs/probe/docs/lonely.html (accessed January 20, 2012).

Holliday, Henry E. 2011. *Reconnecting, Redirecting & Redefining 21st Century Males*. Lanham, Maryland: Rowman and Littlefield Publishing Group, Inc.

Hudson Research Study. 2006. Commissioned by the Social Issues Research Center (SIRC), Chandler.

Katz, Jackson M., ed. 2002. *Tough Guise: Violence, Media and the Crisis in Masculinity*. Northampton, MA: Media Education Foundation.

Phillips, Katherine, and Harrison Pope. 2002. *The Adonis Complex: How to Identify, Treat and Prevent Body Obsession in Men and Boys*. New York: Free Press.

Smith, David. "Men without Friends, Six Barriers to Friendship." http://www.leaderu.com/orgs/probe/docs/lonely/html (accessed December 5, 2011).

Sports Done Right. 2006. "Maine Center for Sport and Coaching: Making the Most of the Sport Experience." University of Maine, Maine.

Torbett, Heather, Kris S. Calderon, and Patricia Bell. 2005. "Healthy Relationships." KSC/CCAFS Health Education and Wellness Program.

Author Biographies

M. Lee Brooks has an MS in Criminal Justice from Georgia State University and is a former law enforcement senior administrator. He is the retired Deputy Chief of the Atlanta Police Department and has significant experience in both state and local law enforcement. He is a former faculty member of Mercer University and American InterContinental University. He is currently the lead investigator in the Georgia Secretary of State's Office handling a wide variety of cases including elections, professional licensing, and securities.

Kimberly Fletcher is a student in the PhD program in International Conflict Management at Kennesaw State University. She served as a Peace Corps Volunteer in The Gambia, where she taught general science and computer literacy courses at the senior secondary level. The experience prompted her current research, which focuses on the relationship between formal education and the development of individual agency in Anglophone West Africa. It also piqued her interest in disarmament, demobilization, and reintegration, particularly among former child soldiers. The interest in sports comes from more than twenty years playing and ten years coaching volleyball.

Sarah Hillyer, PhD, is the founder of Sport 4 Peace, a nonprofit organization dedicated to improving the quality and availability of sporting opportunities for girls and women around the world. Most recently, Sarah served as the Generations for Peace, HRH King Abdullah II, postdoctoral fellow at Georgetown University. Sarah received her PhD from the University of Tennessee (UT) in Sport and Exercise Science with a concentration in Sport Sociology. She is currently serving as the Director of the Center for Sport, Peace, and Society at UT.

H. E. "Doc" Holliday, PhD, is a tenured Associate Professor in the Department of Educational Leadership at Kennesaw State University. He has been a building principal for over four different decades in both Georgia and Ohio. He has experience in urban, suburban, and rural districts. He received his PhD from Ohio State University, Masters of Education from Kent State University (Ohio), and his BA from Marietta College (Ohio). He is a former Assistant Superintendent for School Improvement in the Cobb County Schools as well as the Chief of Staff in the Atlanta Public School. He just recently presented at two conferences in China. His most recent book is *Reconnecting, Redirecting and Redefining 21st Century Males*.

Linda M. Johnston, PhD, is the Executive Director of the Siegel Institute for Leadership, Ethics, and Character and a Professor at Kennesaw State University. She has received grants from the Southern Poverty Law Center and the National Endowment for the Arts, and had a Fellowship to begin a dialogue between Egyptians and Americans. She has done work in Ukraine, Republic of Georgia, Barbados, Nigeria, Zambia, Egypt, and in the United States. She is the President of the International Peace Research Association Foundation, was on the Board of Hands Along the Nile, and teaches regularly for the UN School for Peace in Costa Rica.

Marion Keim, PhD, combines her passion for peace, development, and sports as one of the two coordinators of the Western Cape Network for Community Peace and Development and as the Training Advisor for Women for Peace, Western Cape. She is associate professor at the University of the Western Cape directing the University's Interdisciplinary Center for Sports Sciences and Development. For over twenty years, her field of expertise has been in conflict, diversity, peace, leadership, and sports as a tool for peace building, social change, and development. She is also an Advocate of the High Court of South Africa.

Ji-ho Kim, PhD, is an assistant professor in the School of Sport Sciences at Wingate University. Dr. Kim's research agenda focuses on the following areas: (a) professional sport teams' social responsibility in the multicultural society, (b) the economic impact of the labor migration from Asian countries on the American professional sport leagues, (c) the sport consumer behavior observed in the multicultural contemporary sport marketplace, and (d) value of sport facilities as a nonsporting event venue.

Michael B. Shapiro is a graduate of Emory University (BA Political Science) and Emory School of Law and was admitted to the Bar in Georgia (1981) and Ohio (1991). He served as Managing Partner of multiple law firms, in-house counsel and Vice President of Operations for the Scott Group, and as the Executive Director of the Georgia Indigent Defense Council. He is a Past President of the Georgia Association of Criminal Defense Lawyers, member of the McGraw-Hill Academic Advisory Board for Weapons of Mass Destruction and Terrorism, and a Faculty Affiliate of the Siegel Institute for Leadership, Ethics, and Character. He is currently a Visiting Instructor at Georgia State University and an Adjunct Instructor at Kennesaw State University's Coles College of Business.

Kirk Smith, PhD, is an Assistant Professor of Human Resources and Leadership at Western Carolina University. He also serves as the campus leadership consultant through the Coulter Faculty Commons' Faculty Associate for Campus Engagement program. He serves as an internal leadership consultant for faculty and staff and facilitates book club discussions on topics related to leadership, ethics, and organizational culture. He received his PhD in Technology Management with a technical specialization in Human Resource Development from Indiana State University in 2010. Prior to moving into full-time academia, he served over ten years as a management consultant in leadership development, performance improvement, and project management. His research interests are in ethics and leadership, organizational culture, and measurement and evaluation of HRD initiatives.

Peter St. Pierre, PhD, is an Assistant Professor at Kennesaw State University. He received his PhD from the University of Georgia, where he was involved in several studies related to expertise in teaching and coaching. Dr. St. Pierre currently teaches Elementary Methods and Curriculum, Adapted Physical Education, and Measurement and Evaluation, and also supervises student teachers. He is the coauthor of a Biomechanics textbook and has presented over fifty sessions at local, state, district, national, and international conferences and workshops. Dr. St. Pierre has been recognized as a University Teacher of the Year at the state level.

Claudia Stura is a PhD candidate in International Conflict Management at Kennesaw State University, USA. Before going back to school, she worked as Manager Marketing and Communications at the International Council of Sport Science and Physical Education, 2008–2009; Overall Coordinator Communications, Euroschools 2008, Germany and Austria, 2007–2008; Project Manager, Freie Universität Berlin, Germany, 2006–2007; Senate Department for the Interior and Sport Berlin, Germany, FIFA World Cup 2006 Marketing/Communications Manager, 2005–2006; Project Coordinator International Relations, German Olympic Sports Confederation, 2004.

Niina Toroi has an MA in Sport Sciences from the University of Jyväskylä, Finland, and an MA in Peace Education from the UN Mandated University for Peace, Costa Rica. In Finland, she worked as a teacher for Physical Education and as a senior lecturer in a faculty of Sport and Leisure at the Rovaniemi University of Applied Sciences. In Rwanda, she worked as a volunteer yoga teacher and a researcher in a psychosocial sport for development program called Project Air which help allay some of the trauma and mental health issues left in the wake of the 1994 Rwandan Genocide. Currently, she works at the United Nations Office on Sport for Development and Peace in Geneva, Switzerland. She has a deep interest in issues related to using sport as a tool for trauma relief, education, and the empowerment of women and girls.

Olivier Urbain, PhD, is Director of the Toda Institute for Global Peace and Policy Research and Founder and Director of the Transcend: Art & Peace Network. He holds a PhD in Literature from the University of Southern California (1990) and one in Peace Studies from the University of Bradford (2009). He was formerly professor of Modern Languages and Peace Studies at Soka University, Japan, and is the founder of the Commission on Art & Peace of the International Peace Research Association (IPRA). Publications include articles about the power of the arts for peace, the book *Daisaku Ikeda's Philosophy of Peace* (2010) as well as the edition of *Music and Conflict Transformation* (2008) and the coedition of *Music and Solidarity* (2011).

CPSIA information can be obtained at www.ICGtesting.com
Printed in the USA
BVOW01s1602040214

343720BV00005B/12/P